Microsoft® SQL Server® 2012 High-Performance T-SQL Using Window Functions

Itzik Ben-Gan

Published with the authorization of Microsoft Corporation by:
O'Reilly Media, Inc.
1005 Gravenstein Highway North
Sebastopol, California 95472

ISBN: 978-0-7356-5836-3

1 2 3 4 5 6 7 8 9 LSI 7 6 5 4 3 2

Printed and bound in the United States of America.

Microsoft Press books are available through booksellers and distributors worldwide. If you need support related to this book, email Microsoft Press Book Support at mspinput@microsoft.com. Please tell us what you think of this book at *http://www.microsoft.com/learning/booksurvey*.

Microsoft and the trademarks listed at *http://www.microsoft.com/about/legal/en/us/IntellectualProperty/ Trademarks/EN-US.aspx* are trademarks of the Microsoft group of companies. All other marks are property of their respective owners.

The example companies, organizations, products, domain names, email addresses, logos, people, places, and events depicted herein are fictitious. No association with any real company, organization, product, domain name, email address, logo, person, place, or event is intended or should be inferred.

Acquisitions and Developmental Editor: Ken Jones

Production Editor: Kristen Borg

Production Services: Curtis Philips

Technical Reviewer: Adam Machanic

Copyeditor: Roger LeBlanc

Indexer: Lucie Haskins

Cover Design: Twist Creative • Seattle

Cover Composition: Karen Montgomery

Illustrators: Robert Romano and Rebecca Demarest

To the Quartet.

—Q1

Contents at a Glance

Contents

What do you think of this book? We want to hear from you!

Microsoft is interested in hearing your feedback so we can continually improve our
books and learning resources for you. To participate in a brief online survey, please visit:

microsoft.com/learning/booksurvey

Foreword

SQL is a very interesting programming language. When meeting with customers, I am constantly reminded of the language's dual nature with regard to complexity. Many people getting started with SQL see it as a simple programming language that supports four basic verbs: SELECT, INSERT, UPDATE, and DELETE. Some people never get much further than this. Maybe a few more figure out how to filter rows in a query using the WHERE clause and perhaps do the occasional JOIN. However, those who spend more time with SQL and learn about its declarative, relational, and set-based model will find a rich programming language that keeps you coming back for more.

One of the most fundamental additions to the SQL language, back in Microsoft SQL Server 2005, was the introduction of window functions with syntactic constructs such as the OVER clause and a new set of functions known as ranking functions (ROW_NUMBER, RANK, and so on). This addition enabled solving common problems in an easier, more intuitive, and often better-performing way than what was previously possible. A few years later, the single most-requested language feature was for Microsoft to extend its support for window functions—with a set of new functions and, more importantly, with the concept of frames. As a result of these requests from a wide range of customers, Microsoft decided to continue investing in window functions extensions in SQL Server 2012.

Today, when I talk to customers about new language functionality in SQL Server 2012, I always recommend they spend extra time with the new window functions and really understand the new dimension that this brings to the SQL language. I am happy that you are reading this book and thus taking what I am sure is precious time to learn how to use this rich functionality. I am confident that the combination of using SQL Server 2012 and reading this book will help you become an even more efficient SQL Server user, and help you solve both simple as well as complex problems significantly faster than before.

Enjoy!

Tobias Ternström
Lead Program Manager,
Microsoft SQL Server Engine team

Introduction

Window functions, to me, are the most profound feature supported by both standard SQL and Microsoft SQL Server's dialect—T-SQL. They allow you to perform calculations against sets of rows in a flexible, clear, and efficient manner. The design of window functions is ingenious, overcoming a number of shortcomings of the traditional alternatives. The range of problems that window functions help solve is so wide that it is well worth investing your time in learning those. SQL Server 2005 was the version in which window functions were introduced initially. SQL Server 2012 then added more complete support by enhancing some of the existing functions, as well as adding new ones. This book covers both the SQL Server–specific support for window functions, as well as standard SQL's support, including elements that were not yet implemented in SQL Server.

Who Should Read This Book

This book is intended for SQL Server developers and database administrators (DBAs); those who need to write queries and develop code using T-SQL. The book assumes that you already have at least half a year to a year of experience writing and tuning T-SQL queries.

Organization of This Book

The book covers both the logical aspects of window functions as well as their optimization and practical usage aspects. The logical aspects are covered in the first three chapters. The first chapter explains SQL windowing concepts, the second provides a breakdown of window functions, and the third covers ordered set functions. The fourth chapter covers optimization of window functions in SQL Server 2012. Finally, the fifth and last chapter covers practical uses of window functions.

Chapter 1, "SQL Windowing," covers standard SQL windowing concepts. It describes the design of window functions, the types of window functions, and the elements involved in a window specification, such as partitioning, ordering, and framing.

Chapter 2, "A Detailed Look at Window Functions," gets into the details and specifics of the different window functions. It describes window aggregate functions, window ranking functions, window offset functions, and window distribution functions.

Chapter 3, "Ordered Set Functions," describes the support standard SQL has for ordered set functions, including hypothetical set functions, inverse distribution functions, and others. The chapter also explains how to achieve similar calculations in SQL Server.

Chapter 4, "Optimization of Window Functions," covers in detail the optimization of window functions in SQL Server 2012. It provides indexing guidelines for optimal performance, explains how parallelism is handled and how to improve it, discusses the new Window Spool iterator, and more.

Chapter 5, "T-SQL Solutions Using Window Functions," covers practical uses of window functions to address common business tasks.

System Requirements

Window functions are part of the core database engine of Microsoft SQL Server 2012; hence, all editions of the product support this feature. To run the code samples in this book, you need access to an instance of the SQL Server 2012 database engine (any edition), and you need to have the sample database installed. If you don't have access to an existing instance, Microsoft provides trial versions. You can find details at: *http://www.microsoft.com/sql*. For hardware and software requirements, please consult SQL Server Books Online at: *http://msdn.microsoft.com/en-us/library/ms143506(v=sql.110).aspx*.

Code Samples

This book features a companion website that makes available to you all the code used in the book, sample data, the errata, additional resources, and more, at the following page:

http://www.insidetsql.com

In this website, go to the Books section and select the main page for the book in question. The book's page has a link to download a compressed file with the book's source code, including a file called TSQL2012.sql that creates and populates the book's sample database, TSQL2012.

Acknowledgments

A number of people contributed to making this book a reality, whether directly or indirectly, and deserve thanks and recognition.

To Lilach, for giving reason to everything I do, for tolerating me, and for helping review the text.

To my parents, Mila and Gabi, and to my siblings, Mickey and Ina, for the constant support and for accepting the fact that I'm away.

To members of the Microsoft SQL Server development team: Tobias Ternström, Lubor Kollar, Umachandar Jayachandran, Marc Friedman, Milan Stojic, and I'm sure many others. I know it wasn't a trivial effort to add support for window functions in SQL Server. Thanks for the great effort, and thanks for all the time you spent meeting with me and responding to my emails, addressing my questions, and answering my requests for clarification.

To the editorial team at O'Reilly and MSPress. Ken Jones, you spent the most Itzik hours of all, and it's a real pleasure working with you. Also thanks to Ben Ryan, Kristen Borg, Curtis Philips, and Roger LeBlanc.

To Adam Machanic. Thanks for agreeing to be the technical editor of the book. There aren't many people who understand SQL Server development as well as you do. You were the natural choice for me to fill this role for this book.

To "Q2," "Q3," and "Q4." It's great to be able to share ideas with people who understand SQL as well as you do, and are such good friends and take life lightly. I feel that I can share everything with you without worrying about any boundaries or consequences. Thanks for your early review of the text.

To SolidQ, my company for the last decade. It's gratifying to be part of such a great company that evolved to what it is today. The members of this company are much more than colleagues to me; they are partners, friends, and family. Thanks to Fernando G. Guerrero, Douglas McDowell, Herbert Albert, Dejan Sarka, Gianluca Hotz, Jeanne Reeves, Glenn McCoin, Fritz Lechnitz, Eric Van Soldt, Joelle Budd, Jan Taylor, Marilyn Templeton, Berry Walker, Alberto Martin, Lorena Jimenez, Ron Talmage, Andy Kelly, Rushabh Mehta, Eladio Rincón, Erik Veerman, Johan Richard Waymire, Carl Rabeler, Chris Randall, Åhlén, Raoul Illyés, Peter Larsson, Peter Myers, Paul Turley, and so many others.

To members of the *SQL Server Pro* editorial team: Megan Keller, Lavon Peters, Michele Crockett, Mike Otey, and I'm sure many others. I've been writing for the magazine for over a decade and am grateful for the opportunity to share my knowledge with the magazine's readers.

To SQL Server MVPs—Alejandro Mesa, Erland Sommarskog, Aaron Bertrand, Paul White, and many others—and to the MVP lead, Simon Tien. This is a great program that I'm grateful and proud to be part of. The level of expertise of this group is amazing, and I'm always excited when we all get to meet, both to share ideas and just to catch up at a personal level over beer. I believe that, in great part, Microsoft's decision to provide more complete support for window functions in SQL Server 2012 is thanks to the efforts of SQL Server MVPs and, more generally, the SQL Server community. It is great to see this synergy yielding such meaningful and important results.

Finally, to my students: teaching SQL is what drives me. It's my passion. Thanks for allowing me to fulfill my calling, and for all the great questions that make me seek more knowledge.

Errata & Book Support

We've made every effort to ensure the accuracy of this book and its companion content. Any errors that have been reported since this book was published are listed on our Microsoft Press site at oreilly.com:

http://go.microsoft.com/FWLink/?Linkid=246707

If you find an error that is not already listed, you can report it to us through the same page.

If you need additional support, email Microsoft Press Book Support at *mspinput@ microsoft.com*.

Please note that product support for Microsoft software is not offered through the addresses above.

We Want to Hear from You

At Microsoft Press, your satisfaction is our top priority, and your feedback our most valuable asset. Please tell us what you think of this book at:

http://www.microsoft.com/learning/booksurvey

The survey is short, and we read every one of your comments and ideas. Thanks in advance for your input!

If you have comments, questions, or ideas regarding the book, or questions that are not answered by visiting the sites above, please send them to me via e-mail at:

itzik@SolidQ.com

Stay in Touch

Let's keep the conversation going! We're on Twitter: *http://twitter.com/MicrosoftPress*

CHAPTER 1

SQL Windowing

Window functions are functions applied to sets of rows defined by a clause called OVER. They are used mainly for analytical purposes allowing you to calculate running totals, calculate moving averages, identify gaps and islands in your data, and perform many other computations. These functions are based on an amazingly profound concept in standard SQL (which is both an ISO and ANSI standard)—the concept of *windowing*. The idea behind this concept is to allow you to apply various calculations to a set, or *window*, of rows and return a single value. Window functions can help to solve a wide variety of querying tasks by helping you express set calculations more easily, intuitively, and efficiently than ever before.

There are two major milestones in Microsoft SQL Server support for the standard window functions: SQL Server 2005 introduced partial support for the standard functionality, and SQL Server 2012 added more. There's still some standard functionality missing, but with the enhancements added in SQL Server 2012, the support is quite extensive. In this book, I cover both the functionality SQL Server implements as well as standard functionality that is still missing. Whenever I describe a feature for the first time in the book, I also mention whether it is supported in SQL Server, and if it is, in which version of the product it was added.

From the time SQL Server 2005 first introduced support for window functions, I found myself using those functions more and more to improve my solutions. I keep replacing older solutions that rely on more classic, traditional language constructs with the newer window functions. And the results I'm getting are usually simpler and more efficient. This happens to such an extent that the majority of my querying solutions nowadays make use of window functions. Also, standard SQL and relational database management systems (RDBMSs) in general are moving toward analytical solutions, and window functions are an important part of this trend. Therefore, I feel that window functions are the future in terms of SQL querying solutions, and that the time you take to learn them is time well spent.

This book provides extensive coverage of window functions, their optimization, and querying solutions implementing them. This chapter starts by explaining the concept. It provides the background of window functions, a glimpse of solutions using them, coverage of the elements involved in window specifications, an account of the query elements supporting window functions, and a description of the standard's solution for reusing window definitions.

Background of Window Functions

Before you learn the specifics of window functions, it can be helpful to understand the context and background of those functions. This section provides such background. It explains the difference between set-based and cursor/iterative approaches to addressing querying tasks and how window functions bridge the gap between the two. Finally, this section explains the drawbacks of alternatives to window functions and why window functions are often a better choice than the alternatives. Note that although window functions can solve many problems very efficiently, there are cases where there are better alternatives. Chapter 4, "Optimization of Window Functions," goes into details about optimizing window functions, explaining when you get optimal treatment of the computations and when treatment is nonoptimal.

Window Functions Described

A window function is a function applied to a set of rows. A *window* is the term standard SQL uses to describe the context for the function to operate in. SQL uses a clause called OVER in which you provide the window specification. Consider the following query as an example:

See Also *See the book's Introduction for information about the sample database TSQL2012 and companion content.*

```
USE TSQL2012;

SELECT orderid, orderdate, val,
  RANK() OVER(ORDER BY val DESC) AS rnk
FROM Sales.OrderValues
ORDER BY rnk;
```

Here's abbreviated output for this query:

```
orderid  orderdate                  val        rnk
-------- -------------------------- ---------- ---
10865    2008-02-02 00:00:00.000 16387.50  1
10981    2008-03-27 00:00:00.000 15810.00  2
11030    2008-04-17 00:00:00.000 12615.05  3
10889    2008-02-16 00:00:00.000 11380.00  4
10417    2007-01-16 00:00:00.000 11188.40  5
10817    2008-01-06 00:00:00.000 10952.85  6
10897    2008-02-19 00:00:00.000 10835.24  7
10479    2007-03-19 00:00:00.000 10495.60  8
10540    2007-05-19 00:00:00.000 10191.70  9
10691    2007-10-03 00:00:00.000 10164.80  10
...
```

The OVER clause is where you provide the window specification that defines the exact set of rows that the current row relates to, the ordering specification, if relevant, and other elements. Absent any elements that restrict the set of rows in the window—as is the case in this example—the set of rows in the window is the final result set of the query.

Note More precisely, the window is the set of rows, or relation, given as input to the logical query processing phase where the window function appears. But this explanation probably doesn't make much sense yet. So to keep things simple, for now I'll just refer to the final result set of the query, and I'll provide the more precise explanation later.

For ranking purposes, ordering is naturally required. In this example, it is based on the column *val* ranked in descending order.

The function used in this example is RANK. This function calculates the rank of the current row with respect to a specific set of rows and a sort order. When using descending order in the ordering specification—as in this case—the rank of a given row is computed as one more than the number of rows in the relevant set that have a greater ordering value than the current row. So pick a row in the output of the sample query—say, the one that got rank 5. This rank was computed as 5 because based on the indicated ordering (by *val* descending), there are 4 rows in the final result set of the query that have a greater value in the *val* attribute than the current value (11188.40), and the rank is that number plus 1.

What's most important to note is that conceptually the OVER clause defines a window for the function with respect to the current row. And this is true for all rows in the result set of the query. In other words, with respect to each row, the OVER clause defines a window independent of the other rows. This idea is really profound and takes some getting used to. Once you get this, you get closer to a true understanding of the windowing concept, its magnitude, and its depth. If this doesn't mean much to you yet, don't worry about it for now—I wanted to throw it out there to plant the seed.

The first time standard SQL introduced support for window functions was in an extension document to SQL:1999 that covered, what they called "OLAP functions" back then. Since then, the revisions to the standard continued to enhance support for window functions. So far the revisions have been SQL:2003, SQL:2008, and SQL:2011. The latest SQL standard has very rich and extensive coverage of window functions, showing the standard committee's belief in the concept, and the trend seems to be to keep enhancing the standard's support with more window functions and more functionality.

Note You can purchase the standards documents from ISO or ANSI. For example, from the following URL, you can purchase from ANSI the foundation document of the SQL:2011 standard, which covers the language constructs: *http://webstore.ansi.org/RecordDetail.aspx? sku=ISO%2fIEC+9075-2%3a2011.*

Standard SQL supports several types of window functions: aggregate, ranking, distribution, and offset. But remember that windowing is a concept; therefore, we might see new types emerging in future revisions of the standard.

Aggregate window functions are the all-familiar aggregate functions you already know—like SUM, COUNT, MIN, MAX, and others—though traditionally, you're probably used to using them in the context of grouped queries. An aggregate function needs to operate on a set, be it a set defined by a grouped query or a window specification. SQL Server 2005 introduced partial support for window aggregate functions, and SQL Server 2012 added more functionality.

Ranking functions are RANK, DENSE_RANK, ROW_NUMBER, and NTILE. The standard actually puts the first two and the last two in different categories, and I'll explain why later. I prefer to put all four functions in the same category for simplicity, just like the official SQL Server documentation does. SQL Server 2005 introduced these four ranking functions, with already complete functionality.

Distribution functions are PERCENT_RANK, CUME_DIST, PERCENTILE_CONT, and PERCENTILE_DISC. SQL Server 2012 introduces support for these four functions.

Offset functions are LAG, LEAD, FIRST_VALUE, LAST_VALUE, and NTH_VALUE. SQL Server 2012 introduces support for the first four. There's no support for the NTH_VALUE function yet in SQL Server as of SQL Server 2012.

Chapter 2, "A Detailed Look at Window Functions," provides the meaning, the purpose, and details about the different functions.

With every new idea, device, and tool—even if the tool is better and simpler to use and implement than what you're used to—typically, there's a barrier. New stuff often seems hard. So if window functions are new to you and you're looking for motivation to justify making the investment in learning about them and making the leap to using them, here are a few things I can mention from my experience:

- Window functions help address a wide variety of querying tasks. I can't emphasize this enough. As mentioned, nowadays I use window functions in most of my query solutions. After you've had a chance to learn about the concept and the optimization of the functions, the last chapter in the book (Chapter 5) shows some practical applications of window functions. But just to give you a sense of how they are used, querying tasks that can be solved with window functions include:

  - Paging

  - De-duplicating data

  - Returning top n rows per group

  - Computing running totals

  - Performing operations on intervals such as packing intervals, and calculating the maximum number of concurrent sessions

  - Identifying gaps and islands

  - Computing percentiles

  - Computing the mode of the distribution

  - Sorting hierarchies

  - Pivoting

  - Computing recency

- I've been writing SQL queries for close to two decades and have been using window functions extensively for several years now. I can say that even though it took a bit of getting used to the concept of windowing, today I find window functions both simpler and more intuitive in many cases than alternative methods.

- Window functions lend themselves to good optimization. You'll see exactly why this is so in later chapters.

Declarative Language and Optimization

You might wonder why in a declarative language such as SQL, where you logically just declare your request as opposed to describing how to achieve it, two different forms of the same request—say, one with window functions and the other without—can get different performance? Why is it that an implementation of SQL such as SQL Server, with its T-SQL dialect, doesn't always figure out that the two forms really represent the same thing, and hence produce the same query execution plan for both?

There are several reasons for this. For one, SQL Server's optimizer is not perfect. I don't want to sound unappreciative—SQL Server's optimizer is truly a marvel when you think of what this software component can achieve. But it's a fact that it doesn't have all possible optimization rules encoded within it. Two, the optimizer has to limit the amount of time spent on optimization; otherwise, it could spend a much longer time optimizing a query than the amount of time the optimization shaves off from the run time of the query. The situation could be as absurd as producing a plan in a matter of several dozen milliseconds without going over all possible plans and getting a run time of only seconds, but producing all possible plans in hopes of shaving off a couple of seconds might take a year or even several. You can see that, for practical reasons, the optimizer needs to limit the time spent on optimization. Based on factors like the sizes of the tables involved in the query, SQL Server calculates two values: one is a cost considered *good enough* for the query, and the other is the maximum amount of time to spend on optimization before stopping. If either threshold is reached, optimization stops, and SQL Server uses the best plan found at that point.

The design of window functions, which we will get to later, often lends itself to better optimization than alternative methods of achieving the same thing.

What's important to understand from all this is that you need to make a conscious effort to make the switch to using SQL windowing because it's a new idea, and as such it takes some getting used to. But once the switch is made, SQL windowing is simple and intuitive to use; think of any gadget you can't live without today and how it seemed like a difficult thing to learn at first.

Set-Based vs. Iterative/Cursor Programming

People often characterize T-SQL solutions to querying tasks as either set-based or iterative/cursor-based solutions. The general consensus among T-SQL developers is to try and stick to the former approach, but still, there's wide use of the latter. There are several interesting questions here. Why is the set-based approach the recommended one? And if it is the recommended one, why do so many developers use the iterative approach? What are the obstacles that prevent people from adopting the recommended approach?

To get to the bottom of this, one first needs to understand the foundations of T-SQL, and what the set-based approach truly is. When you do, you realize that the set-based approach is nonintuitive for most people, whereas the iterative approach is. It's just the way our brains are programmed, and I will try to clarify this shortly. The gap between iterative and set-based thinking is quite big. The gap can be closed, though it certainly isn't easy to do so. And this is where window functions can play an important role; I find them to be a great tool that can help bridge the gap between the two approaches and allow a more gradual transition to set-based thinking.

So first, I'll explain what the set-based approach to addressing T-SQL querying tasks is. T-SQL is a dialect of standard SQL (both ISO and ANSI standards). SQL is based (or attempts to be based) on the relational model, which is a mathematical model for data management formulated and proposed initially by E. F. Codd in the late 1960s. The relational model is based on two mathematical foundations: set-theory and predicate logic. Many aspects of computing were developed based on intuition, and they keep changing very rapidly—to a degree that sometimes makes you feel that you're chasing your tail. The relational model is an island in this world of computing because it is based on much stronger foundations—mathematics. Some think of mathematics as the ultimate truth. Being based on such strong mathematical foundations, the relational model is very sound and stable. It keeps evolving, but not as fast as many other aspects of computing. For several decades now, the relational model has held strong, and it's still the basis for the leading database platforms—what we call *relational database management systems (RDBMSs)*.

SQL is an attempt to create a language based on the relational model. SQL is not perfect and actually deviates from the relational model in a number of ways, but at the same time it provides enough tools that, if you understand the relational model, you can use SQL relationally. It is doubtless the leading, de facto language used by today's RDBMSs.

However, as mentioned, thinking in a relational way is not intuitive for many. Part of what makes it hard for people to think in relational terms is the key differences between the iterative and set-based approaches. It is especially difficult for people who have a procedural programming background, where interaction with data in files is handled in an iterative way, as the following pseudocode demonstrates:

```
open file
fetch first record
while not end of file
begin
  process record
  fetch next record
end
```

Data in files (or, more precisely, in indexed sequential access method, or ISAM, files) is stored in a specific order. And you are guaranteed to fetch the records from the file in that order. Also, you fetch the records one at a time. So your mind is programmed to think of data in such terms: ordered, and manipulated one record at a time. This is similar to cursor manipulation in T-SQL; hence, for developers with a procedural programming background, using cursors or any other form of iterative processing feels like an extension to what they already know.

A relational, set-based approach to data manipulation is quite different. To try and get a sense of this, let's start with the definition of a *set* by the creator of set theory—Georg Cantor:

> *By a "set" we mean any collection M into a whole of definite, distinct objects m (which are called the "elements" of M) of our perception or of our thought.*
> —*Joseph W. Dauben,* Georg Cantor *(Princeton University Press, 1990)*

There's so much in this definition of a set that I could spend pages and pages just trying to interpret the meaning of this sentence. But for the purposes of our discussion, I'll focus on two key aspects—one that appears explicitly in this definition and one that is implied:

- **Whole** Observe the use of the term *whole*. A set should be perceived and manipulated as a whole. Your attention should focus on the set as a whole, and not on the individual elements of the set. With iterative processing, this idea is violated because records of a file or a cursor are manipulated one at a time. A table in SQL represents (albeit not completely successfully) a relation from the relational model, and a relation is a set of elements that are alike (that is, have the same attributes). When you interact with tables using set-based queries, you interact with tables as whole, as opposed to interacting with the individual rows (the tuples of the relations)—both in terms of how you phrase your declarative SQL requests and in terms of your mindset and attention. This type of thinking is what's very hard for many to truly adopt.

- **Order** Observe that nowhere in the definition of a set is there any mention of the order of the elements. That's for a good reason—there is no order to the elements of a set. That's another thing that many have a hard time getting used to. Files and cursors do have a specific order to their records, and when you fetch the records one at a time, you can rely on this order. A table has no order to its rows because a table is a set. People who don't realize this often confuse the logical layer of the data model and the language with the physical layer of the implementation. They assume that if there's a certain index on the table, you get an implied guarantee that, when querying the table, the data will always be accessed in index order. And sometimes even the correctness of the solution will rely on this assumption. Of course, SQL Server doesn't provide any such guarantees. For example, the only way to guarantee that the rows in a result will be presented in a certain order is to add a presentation ORDER BY clause to the query. And if you do add one, you need to realize that what you get back is not relational because the result has a guaranteed order.

If you need to write SQL queries and you want to understand the language you're dealing with, you need to think in set-based terms. And this is where window functions can help bridge the gap between iterative thinking (one row at a time, in a certain order) and set-based thinking (seeing the set as a whole, with no order). What can help you transition from one type of thinking to the other is the ingenious design of window functions.

For one, window functions support an ORDER BY clause when relevant, where you specify the order. But note that just because the function has an order specified doesn't mean it violates any relational concepts. The input to the query is relational with no ordering expectations, and the output of the query is relational with no ordering guarantees. It's just that there's ordering as part of the specification of the calculation, producing a result attribute in the resulting relation. There's no assurance that the result rows will be returned in the same order used by the window function; in fact, different window functions in the same query can specify different ordering. This kind of ordering has nothing to do—at least conceptually—with the query's presentation ordering. Figure 1-1 tries to illustrate the idea that both the input to a query with a window function and the output are relational, even though the window function has ordering as part of its specification. By using ovals in the illustration, and having the positions of the rows look different in the input and the output, I'm trying to express the fact that the order of the rows does not matter.

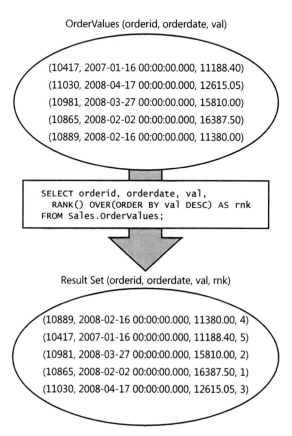

OrderValues (orderid, orderdate, val)

(10417, 2007-01-16 00:00:00.000, 11188.40)
(11030, 2008-04-17 00:00:00.000, 12615.05)
(10981, 2008-03-27 00:00:00.000, 15810.00)
(10865, 2008-02-02 00:00:00.000, 16387.50)
(10889, 2008-02-16 00:00:00.000, 11380.00)

```
SELECT orderid, orderdate, val,
  RANK() OVER(ORDER BY val DESC) AS rnk
FROM Sales.OrderValues;
```

Result Set (orderid, orderdate, val, rnk)

(10889, 2008-02-16 00:00:00.000, 11380.00, 4)
(10417, 2007-01-16 00:00:00.000, 11188.40, 5)
(10981, 2008-03-27 00:00:00.000, 15810.00, 2)
(10865, 2008-02-02 00:00:00.000, 16387.50, 1)
(11030, 2008-04-17 00:00:00.000, 12615.05, 3)

FIGURE 1-1 Input and output of a query with a window function.

There's another aspect of window functions that helps you gradually transition from thinking in iterative, ordered terms to thinking in set-based terms. When teaching a new topic, teachers sometimes have to "lie" when explaining it. Suppose that you, as a teacher, know the student's mind is not ready to comprehend a certain idea if you explain it in full depth. You can sometimes get better results if you initially explain the idea in simpler, albeit not completely correct, terms to allow the student's mind to start processing the idea. Later, when the student's mind is ready for the "truth," you can provide the deeper, more correct meaning.

Such is the case with understanding how window functions are conceptually calculated. There's a basic way to explain the idea, although it's not really conceptually correct, but it's one that leads to the correct result! The basic way uses a row-at-a-time, ordered approach. And then there's the deep, conceptually correct way to explain the idea, but one's mind needs to be in a state of maturity to comprehend it. The deep way uses a set-based approach.

To demonstrate what I mean, consider the following query:

```
SELECT orderid, orderdate, val,
  RANK() OVER(ORDER BY val DESC) AS rnk
FROM Sales.OrderValues;
```

Here's an abbreviated output of this query (note there's no guarantee of presentation ordering here):

```
orderid  orderdate               val        rnk
-------- ---------------------- ---------- ---
10865    2008-02-02 00:00:00.000 16387.50  1
10981    2008-03-27 00:00:00.000 15810.00  2
11030    2008-04-17 00:00:00.000 12615.05  3
10889    2008-02-16 00:00:00.000 11380.00  4
10417    2007-01-16 00:00:00.000 11188.40  5
...
```

The basic way to think of how the rank values are calculated conceptually is the following example (expressed as pseudocode):

```
arrange the rows sorted by val
iterate through the rows
for each row
  if the current row is the first row in the partition emit 1
  else if val is equal to previous val emit previous rank
  else emit count of rows so far
```

Figure 1-2 is a graphical depiction of this type of thinking.

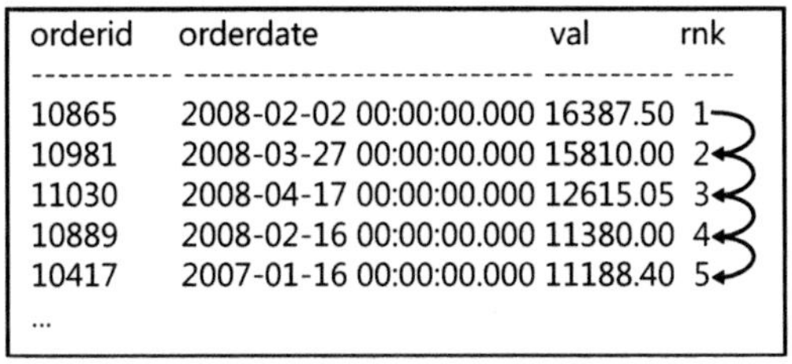

FIGURE 1-2 Basic understanding of the calculation of rank values.

Again, although this type of thinking leads to the correct result, it's not entirely correct. In fact, making my point is even more difficult because the process just described is actually very similar to how SQL Server physically handles the rank calculation. But my focus at this point is not the physical implementation, but rather the conceptual layer—the language and the logical model. What I meant by "incorrect type of thinking" is that conceptually, from a language perspective, the calculation is thought of differently, in a set-based manner—not iterative. Remember that the language is not concerned with the physical implementation in the database engine. The physical layer's responsibility is to figure out how to handle the logical request and both produce a correct result and produce it as fast as possible.

So let me attempt to explain what I mean by the deeper, more correct understanding of how the language thinks of window functions. The function logically defines—for each row in the result set of the query—a separate, independent window. Absent any restrictions in the window specification, each window consists of the set of all rows from the result set of the query as the starting point. But you can add elements to the window specification (for example, partitioning, framing, and so on, which I'll say more about later) that will further restrict the set of rows in each window. Figure 1-3 is a graphical depiction of this idea as it applies to our query with the RANK function.

```
orderid    orderdate                    val        rnk
---------  ---------------------------- ---------- ----
10865      2008-02-02 00:00:00.000 16387.50      1
10981      2008-03-27 00:00:00.000 15810.00 ......2
11030      2008-04-17 00:00:00.000 12615.05      3
10889      2008-02-16 00:00:00.000 11380.00      4
10417      2007-01-16 00:00:00.000 11188.40      5
...
```

FIGURE 1-3 Deep understanding of the calculation of rank values.

With respect to each window function and row in the result set of the query, the OVER clause conceptually creates a separate window. In our query, we have not restricted the window specification in any way; we just defined the ordering specification for the calculation. So in our case, all windows are made of all rows in the result set. And they all coexist at the same time. And in each, the rank is calculated as one more than the number of rows that have a greater value in the *val* attribute than the current value.

As you might realize, it's more intuitive for many to think in the basic terms of the data being in an order and a process iterating through the rows one at a time. And that's okay when you're starting out with window functions because you get to write your queries—or at least the simple ones— correctly. As time goes by, you can gradually transition to the deeper understanding of the window functions' conceptual design and start thinking in a set-based manner.

Drawbacks of Alternatives to Window Functions

Window functions have several advantages compared to alternative, more traditional, ways to achieve the same calculations—for example, grouped queries, subqueries, and others. Here I'll provide a couple of straightforward examples. There are several other important differences beyond the advantages I'll show here, but it's premature to discuss those now.

I'll start with traditional grouped queries. Those do give you insight into new information in the form of aggregates, but you also lose something—the detail.

Once you group data, you're forced to apply all calculations in the context of the group. But what if you need to apply calculations that involve both detail and aggregates? For example, suppose that you need to query the Sales.OrderValues view and calculate for each order the percentage of the current order value of the customer total, as well as the difference from the customer average. The current order value is a detail element, and the customer total and average are aggregates. If you group the data by customer, you don't have access to the individual order values. One way to handle this need with traditional grouped queries is to have a query that groups the data by customer, define a table expression based on this query, and then join the table expression with the base table to match the detail with the aggregates. Here's a query that implements this approach:

```
WITH Aggregates AS
(
  SELECT custid, SUM(val) AS sumval, AVG(val) AS avgval
  FROM Sales.OrderValues
  GROUP BY custid
)
SELECT O.orderid, O.custid, O.val,
  CAST(100. * O.val / A.sumval AS NUMERIC(5, 2)) AS pctcust,
  O.val - A.avgval AS diffcust
FROM Sales.OrderValues AS O
  JOIN Aggregates AS A
    ON O.custid = A.custid;
```

Here's the abbreviated output generated by this query:

```
orderid  custid  val      pctcust  diffcust
-------- ------- -------  -------- ------------
10835    1       845.80   19.79    133.633334
10643    1       814.50   19.06    102.333334
10952    1       471.20   11.03    -240.966666
10692    1       878.00   20.55    165.833334
11011    1       933.50   21.85    221.333334
10702    1       330.00   7.72     -382.166666
10625    2       479.75   34.20    129.012500
10759    2       320.00   22.81    -30.737500
10926    2       514.40   36.67    163.662500
10308    2       88.80    6.33     -261.937500
...
```

Now imagine needing to also involve the percentage from the grand total and the difference from the grand average. To do this, you need to add another table expression, like so:

```
WITH CustAggregates AS
(
  SELECT custid, SUM(val) AS sumval, AVG(val) AS avgval
  FROM Sales.OrderValues
  GROUP BY custid
),
GrandAggregates AS
(
  SELECT SUM(val) AS sumval, AVG(val) AS avgval
  FROM Sales.OrderValues
)
SELECT O.orderid, O.custid, O.val,
  CAST(100. * O.val / CA.sumval AS NUMERIC(5, 2)) AS pctcust,
  O.val - CA.avgval AS diffcust,
  CAST(100. * O.val / GA.sumval AS NUMERIC(5, 2)) AS pctall,
  O.val - GA.avgval AS diffall
FROM Sales.OrderValues AS O
  JOIN CustAggregates AS CA
    ON O.custid = CA.custid
  CROSS JOIN GrandAggregates AS GA;
```

Here's the output of this query:

```
orderid  custid  val     pctcust  diffcust      pctall  diffall
-------- ------- ------- -------- ------------- ------- -------------
10835    1       845.80  19.79    133.633334    0.07    -679.252072
10643    1       814.50  19.06    102.333334    0.06    -710.552072
10952    1       471.20  11.03    -240.966666   0.04    -1053.852072
10692    1       878.00  20.55    165.833334    0.07    -647.052072
11011    1       933.50  21.85    221.333334    0.07    -591.552072
10702    1       330.00  7.72     -382.166666   0.03    -1195.052072
10625    2       479.75  34.20    129.012500    0.04    -1045.302072
10759    2       320.00  22.81    -30.737500    0.03    -1205.052072
10926    2       514.40  36.67    163.662500    0.04    -1010.652072
10308    2       88.80   6.33     -261.937500   0.01    -1436.252072
...
```

You can see how the query gets more and more complicated, involving more table expressions and more joins.

Another way to perform similar calculations is to use a separate subquery for each calculation. Here are the alternatives, using subqueries to the last two grouped queries:

```
-- subqueries with detail and customer aggregates
SELECT orderid, custid, val,
  CAST(100. * val /
         (SELECT SUM(O2.val)
          FROM Sales.OrderValues AS O2
          WHERE O2.custid = O1.custid) AS NUMERIC(5, 2)) AS pctcust,
  val - (SELECT AVG(O2.val)
          FROM Sales.OrderValues AS O2
          WHERE O2.custid = O1.custid) AS diffcust
FROM Sales.OrderValues AS O1;
```

```
-- subqueries with detail, customer and grand aggregates
SELECT orderid, custid, val,
  CAST(100. * val /
        (SELECT SUM(O2.val)
         FROM Sales.OrderValues AS O2
         WHERE O2.custid = O1.custid) AS NUMERIC(5, 2)) AS pctcust,
  val - (SELECT AVG(O2.val)
         FROM Sales.OrderValues AS O2
         WHERE O2.custid = O1.custid) AS diffcust,
  CAST(100. * val /
        (SELECT SUM(O2.val)
         FROM Sales.OrderValues AS O2) AS NUMERIC(5, 2)) AS pctall,
  val - (SELECT AVG(O2.val)
         FROM Sales.OrderValues AS O2) AS diffall
FROM Sales.OrderValues AS O1;
```

There are two main problems with the subquery approach. One, you end up with lengthy complex code. Two, SQL Server's optimizer is not coded at the moment to identify cases where multiple subqueries need to access the exact same set of rows; hence, it will use separate visits to the data for each subquery. This means that the more subqueries you have, the more visits to the data you get. Unlike the previous problem, this one is not a problem with the language, but rather with the specific optimization you get for subqueries in SQL Server.

Remember that the idea behind a window function is to define a window, or a set, of rows for the function to operate on. Aggregate functions are supposed to be applied to a set of rows; therefore, the concept of windowing can work well with those as an alternative to using grouping or subqueries. And when calculating the aggregate window function, you don't lose the detail. You use the OVER clause to define the window for the function. For example, to calculate the sum of all values from the result set of the query, simply use the following:

```
SUM(val) OVER()
```

If you do not restrict the window (empty parentheses), your starting point is the result set of the query.

To calculate the sum of all values from the result set of the query where the customer ID is the same as in the current row, use the partitioning capabilities of window functions (which I'll say more about later), and partition the window by *custid*, as follows:

```
SUM(val) OVER(PARTITION BY custid)
```

Note that the term *partitioning* suggests filtering rather than grouping.

Using window functions, here's how you address the request involving the detail and customer aggregates, returning the percentage of the current order value of the customer total as well as the difference from the average (with window functions in bold):

```
SELECT orderid, custid, val,
  CAST(100. * val / SUM(val) OVER(PARTITION BY custid) AS NUMERIC(5, 2)) AS pctcust,
  val - AVG(val) OVER(PARTITION BY custid) AS diffcust
FROM Sales.OrderValues;
```

And here's another query where you also add the percentage of the grand total and the difference from the grand average:

```
SELECT orderid, custid, val,
  CAST(100. * val / SUM(val) OVER(PARTITION BY custid) AS NUMERIC(5, 2)) AS pctcust,
  val - AVG(val) OVER(PARTITION BY custid) AS diffcust,
  CAST(100. * val / SUM(val) OVER() AS NUMERIC(5, 2)) AS pctall,
  val - AVG(val) OVER() AS diffall
FROM Sales.OrderValues;
```

Observe how much simpler and more concise the versions with the window functions are. Also, in terms of optimization, note that SQL Server's optimizer was coded with the logic to look for multiple functions with the same window specification. If any are found, SQL Server will use the same visit (whichever kind of scan was chosen) to the data for those. For example, in the last query, SQL Server will use one visit to the data to calculate the first two functions (the sum and average that are partitioned by *custid*), and it will use one other visit to calculate the last two functions (the sum and average that are nonpartitioned). I will demonstrate this concept of optimization in Chapter 4, "Optimization of Window Functions."

Another advantage window functions have over subqueries is that the initial window prior to applying restrictions is the result set of the query. This means that it's the result set after applying table operators (for example, joins), filters, grouping, and so on. You get this result set because of the phase of logical query processing in which window functions get evaluated. (I'll say more about this later in this chapter.) Conversely, a subquery starts from scratch—not from the result set of the outer query. This means that if you want the subquery to operate on the same set as the result of the outer query, it will need to repeat all query constructs used by the outer query. As an example, suppose that you want our calculations of the percentage of the total and the difference from the average to apply only to orders placed in the year 2007. With the solution using window functions, all you need to do is add one filter to the query, like so:

```
SELECT orderid, custid, val,
  CAST(100. * val / SUM(val) OVER(PARTITION BY custid) AS NUMERIC(5, 2)) AS pctcust,
  val - AVG(val) OVER(PARTITION BY custid) AS diffcust,
  CAST(100. * val / SUM(val) OVER() AS NUMERIC(5, 2)) AS pctall,
  val - AVG(val) OVER() AS diffall
FROM Sales.OrderValues
WHERE orderdate >= '20070101'
  AND orderdate < '20080101';
```

The starting point for all window functions is the set after applying the filter. But with subqueries, you start from scratch; therefore, you need to repeat the filter in all of your subqueries, like so:

```
SELECT orderid, custid, val,
  CAST(100. * val /
        (SELECT SUM(O2.val)
         FROM Sales.OrderValues AS O2
         WHERE O2.custid = O1.custid
           AND orderdate >= '20070101'
           AND orderdate < '20080101') AS NUMERIC(5, 2)) AS pctcust,
```

```
  val - (SELECT AVG(O2.val)
         FROM Sales.OrderValues AS O2
         WHERE O2.custid = O1.custid
           AND orderdate >= '20070101'
           AND orderdate < '20080101') AS diffcust,
  CAST(100. * val /
         (SELECT SUM(O2.val)
          FROM Sales.OrderValues AS O2
          WHERE orderdate >= '20070101'
            AND orderdate < '20080101') AS NUMERIC(5, 2)) AS pctall,
  val - (SELECT AVG(O2.val)
         FROM Sales.OrderValues AS O2
         WHERE orderdate >= '20070101'
           AND orderdate < '20080101') AS diffall
FROM Sales.OrderValues AS O1
WHERE orderdate >= '20070101'
  AND orderdate < '20080101';
```

Of course, you could use workarounds, such as first defining a common table expression (CTE) based on a query that performs the filter, and then have both the outer query and the subqueries refer to the CTE. However, my point is that with window functions, you don't need any workarounds because they operate on the result of the query. I will provide more details about this aspect in the design of window functions later in the chapter, in the "Query Elements Supporting Window Functions" section.

As mentioned earlier, window functions also lend themselves to good optimization, and often, alternatives to window functions don't get optimized as well, to say the least. Of course, there are cases where the inverse is also true. I explain the optimization of window functions in Chapter 4 and provide plenty of examples for using them efficiently in Chapter 5.

A Glimpse of Solutions Using Window Functions

The first four chapters of the book describe window functions and their optimization. The material is very technical, and even though I find it fascinating, I can see how some might find it a bit boring. What's usually much more interesting for people to read about is the use of the functions to solve practical problems, which is what this book gets to in the final chapter. When you see how window functions are used in problem solving, you truly realize their value. So how can I convince you it's worth your while to go through the more technical parts and not give up reading before you get to the more interesting part later? What if I give you a glimpse of a solution using window functions right now?

The querying task I will address here involves querying a table holding a sequence of values in some column and identifying the consecutive ranges of existing values. This problem is also known as the *islands problem*. The sequence can be a numeric one, a temporal one (which is more common), or any data type that supports *total ordering*. The sequence can have unique values or allow duplicates. The interval can be any fixed interval that complies with the column's type (for example, the integer 1, the integer 7, the temporal interval 1 day, the temporal interval 2 weeks, and so on). In Chapter 5, I will get to the different variations of the problem. Here, I'll just use a simple case to give you a sense of how it works—using a numeric sequence with the integer 1 as the interval. Use the following code to generate the sample data for this task:

```
SET NOCOUNT ON;
USE TSQL2012;

IF OBJECT_ID('dbo.T1', 'U') IS NOT NULL DROP TABLE dbo.T1;
GO

CREATE TABLE dbo.T1
(
  col1 INT NOT NULL
    CONSTRAINT PK_T1 PRIMARY KEY
);

INSERT INTO dbo.T1(col1)
  VALUES(2),(3),(11),(12),(13),(27),(33),(34),(35),(42);
GO
```

As you can see, there are some gaps in the col1 sequence in T1. Your task is to identify the consecutive ranges of existing values (also known as *islands*) and return the start and end of each island. Here's what the desired result should look like:

```
start_range end_range
----------- -----------
2           3
11          13
27          27
33          35
42          42
```

If you're curious as to the practicality of this problem, there are numerous production examples. Examples include producing availability reports, identifying periods of activity (for example, sales), identifying consecutive periods in which a certain criterion is met (for example, periods where a stock value was above or below a certain threshold), identifying ranges of license plates in use, and so on. The current example is very simplistic on purpose so that we can focus on the techniques used to solve it. The technique you will use to solve a more complicated case requires minor adjustments to the one you use to address the simple case. So consider it a challenge to come up with an efficient, set-based solution to this task. Try to first come up with a solution that works. Then repopulate the table with a decent number of rows—say, 10,000,000—and try your technique again. See how it performs. Only then take a look at my solutions.

Before showing the solution using window functions, I'll show one of the many possible solutions that use more traditional language constructs. In particular, I'll show one that uses subqueries. To explain the strategy of the first solution, examine the values in the T1.col1 sequence, where I added a conceptual attribute that doesn't exist at the moment and that I think of as a group identifier:

```
col1  grp
----- ---
2     a
3     a
11    b
```

12	b
13	b
27	c
33	d
34	d
35	d
42	e

The *grp* attribute doesn't exist yet. Conceptually, it is a value that uniquely identifies an island. This means that it has to be the same for all members of the same island and different then the values generated for other islands. If you manage to calculate such a group identifier, you can then group the result by this *grp* attribute and return the minimum and maximum *col1* values in each group (island). One way to produce this group identifier using traditional language constructs is to calculate, for each current *col1* value, the minimum *col1* value that is greater than or equal to the current one, and that has no following value.

As an example, following this logic, try to identify with respect to the value 2 what the minimum *col1* value is that is greater than or equal to 2 and that appears before a missing value? It's 3. Now try to do the same with respect to 3. You also get 3. So 3 is the group identifier of the island that starts with 2 and ends with 3. For the island that starts with 11 and ends with 13, the group identifier for all members is 13. As you can see, the group identifier for all members of a given island is actually the last member of that island.

Here's the T-SQL code required to implement this concept:

```
SELECT col1,
  (SELECT MIN(B.col1)
    FROM dbo.T1 AS B
    WHERE B.col1 >= A.col1
      -- is this row the last in its group?
      AND NOT EXISTS
        (SELECT *
          FROM dbo.T1 AS C
          WHERE C.col1 = B.col1 + 1)) AS grp
FROM dbo.T1 AS A;
```

This query generates the following output:

```
col1         grp
----------- -----------
2            3
3            3
11           13
12           13
13           13
27           27
33           35
34           35
35           35
42           42
```

The next part is pretty straightforward—define a table expression based on the last query, and in the outer query, group by the group identifier and return the minimum and maximum *col1* values for each group, like so:

```
SELECT MIN(col1) AS start_range, MAX(col1) AS end_range
FROM (SELECT col1,
        (SELECT MIN(B.col1)
         FROM dbo.T1 AS B
         WHERE B.col1 >= A.col1
           AND NOT EXISTS
             (SELECT *
              FROM dbo.T1 AS C
              WHERE C.col1 = B.col1 + 1)) AS grp
      FROM dbo.T1 AS A) AS D
GROUP BY grp;
```

There are two main problems with this solution. One, it's a bit complicated to follow the logic here. Two, it's horribly slow. I don't want to start going over query execution plans yet—there will be plenty of this later in the book—but I can tell you that for each row in the table, SQL Server will perform almost two complete scans of the data. Now think of a sequence of 10,000,000 rows, and try to translate it to the amount of work involved. The total number of rows that will need to be processed is simply enormous.

The next solution is also one that calculates a group identifier, but using window functions. The first step in the solution is to use the ROW_NUMBER function to calculate row numbers based on *col1* ordering. I will provide the gory details about the ROW_NUMBER function later in the book; for now, it suffices to say that it computes unique integers within the partition starting with 1 and incrementing by 1 based on the given ordering.

With this in mind, the following query returns the *col1* values and row numbers based on *col1* ordering:

```
SELECT col1, ROW_NUMBER() OVER(ORDER BY col1) AS rownum
FROM dbo.T1;
```

```
col1        rownum
----------- --------------------
2           1
3           2
11          3
12          4
13          5
27          6
33          7
34          8
35          9
42          10
```

Now focus your attention on the two sequences. One (*col1*) is a sequence with gaps, and the other (*rownum*) is a sequence without gaps. With this in mind, try to figure out what's unique to the relationship between the two sequences in the context of an island. Within an island, both sequences keep incrementing by a fixed interval. Therefore, the difference between the two is constant. For the next island, *col1* increases by more than 1, whereas *rownum* increases just by 1, so the difference keeps growing. In other words, the difference between the two is constant and unique for each island. Run the following query to calculate this difference:

```
SELECT col1, col1 - ROW_NUMBER() OVER(ORDER BY col1) AS diff
FROM dbo.T1;
```

```
col1         diff
-----------  --------------------
2            1
3            1
11           8
12           8
13           8
27           21
33           26
34           26
35           26
42           32
```

You can see that this difference satisfies the two requirements of our group identifier; therefore, you can use it as such. The rest is the same as in the previous solution; namely, you group the rows by the group identifier and return the minimum and maximum *col1* values in each group, like so:

```
SELECT MIN(col1) AS start_range, MAX(col1) AS end_range
FROM (SELECT col1,
        -- the difference is constant and unique per island
        col1 - ROW_NUMBER() OVER(ORDER BY col1) AS grp
      FROM dbo.T1) AS D
GROUP BY grp;
```

Observe how concise and simple the solution is. Of course, it's always a good idea to add comments to help those who see the solution for the first time better understand it.

The solution is also highly efficient. The work involved in assigning the row numbers is negligible compared to the previous solution. It's just a single ordered scan of the index on *col1* and an iterator that keeps incrementing a counter. In a performance test I ran with a sequence with 10,000,000 rows, this query finished in 10 seconds. Other solutions ran for a much longer time.

I hope that this glimpse to solutions using window functions was enough to intrigue you and help you see that they contain immense power. Now we'll get back to studying the technicalities of window functions. Later in the book, you will have a chance to see many more examples.

Elements of Window Functions

The specification of a window function's behavior appears in the function's OVER clause and involves multiple elements. The three core elements are partitioning, ordering, and framing. Not all window functions support all elements. As I describe each element, I'll also indicate which functions support it.

Partitioning

The partitioning element is implemented with a PARTITION BY clause and is supported by all window functions. It restricts the window of the current calculation to only those rows from the result set of the query that have the same values in the partitioning columns as in the current row. For example, if your function uses *PARTITION BY custid* and the *custid* value in the current row is 1, the window with respect to the current row is all rows from the result set of the query that have a *custid* value of 1. If the *custid* value of the current row is 2, the window with respect to the current row is all rows with a *custid* of 2.

If a PARTITION BY clause is not specified, the window is not restricted. Another way to look at it is that inf case explicit partitioning wasn't specified, the default partitioning is to consider the entire result set of the query as one partition.

If it wasn't obvious, let me point out that different functions in the same query can have different partitioning specifications. Consider the query in Listing 1-1 as an example.

LISTING 1-1 Query with Two RANK Calculations

```
SELECT custid, orderid, val,
  RANK() OVER(ORDER BY val DESC) AS rnk_all,
  RANK() OVER(PARTITION BY custid
              ORDER BY val DESC) AS rnk_cust
FROM Sales.OrderValues;
```

Observe that the first RANK function (which generates the attribute *rnk_all*) relies on the default partitioning, and the second RANK function (which generates *rnk_cust*) uses explicit partitioning by *custid*. Figure 1-4 illustrates the partitions defined for a sample of three results of calculations in the query: one *rnk_all* value and two *rnk_cust* values.

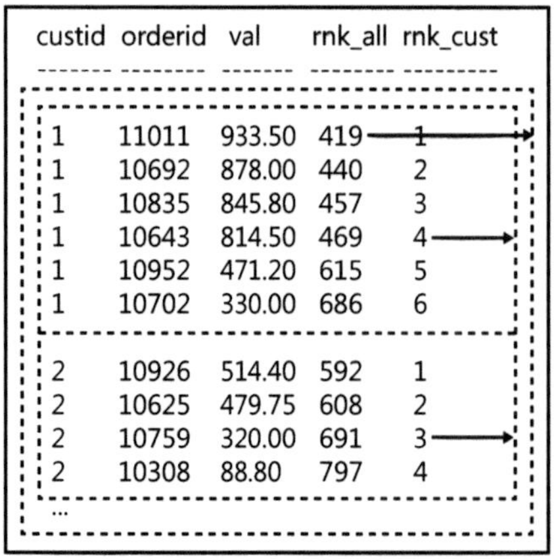

custid	orderid	val	rnk_all	rnk_cust
1	11011	933.50	419	1
1	10692	878.00	440	2
1	10835	845.80	457	3
1	10643	814.50	469	4
1	10952	471.20	615	5
1	10702	330.00	686	6
2	10926	514.40	592	1
2	10625	479.75	608	2
2	10759	320.00	691	3
2	10308	88.80	797	4
...				

FIGURE 1-4 Window partitioning.

The arrows point from the result values of the functions to the window partitions that were used to compute them.

Ordering

The ordering element defines the ordering for the calculation, if relevant, within the partition. In standard SQL, all functions support an ordering element. As for SQL Server, initially it didn't support the ordering element with aggregate functions; rather, it only supported partitioning. Support for ordering for aggregates was added in SQL Server 2012.

Interestingly, the ordering element has a slightly different meaning for different function categories. With ranking functions, ordering is intuitive. For example, when using descending ordering, the RANK function returns one more than the number of rows in your respective partition that have a greater ordering value than yours. When using ascending ordering, the function returns one more than the number of rows in the pattern with a lower ordering value than yours. Figure 1-5 illustrates the rank calculations from Listing 1-1 shown earlier—this time including the interpretation of the ordering element.

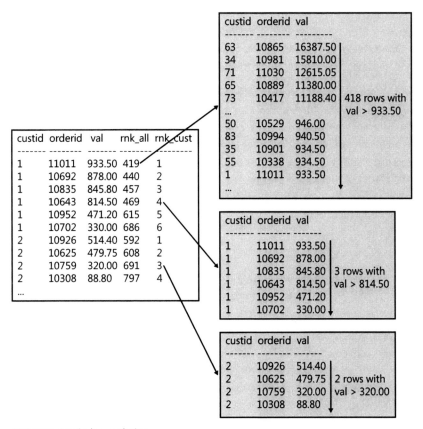

FIGURE 1-5 Window ordering.

Figure 1-5 depicts the windows of only three of the rank calculations. Of course, there are many more—1,660, to be precise. That's because there are 830 rows involved, and for each row, two rank calculations are made. What's interesting to note here is that conceptually it's as if all those windows coexist simultaneously.

Aggregate window functions have a slightly different meaning for *ordering* compared to *ranking* window functions. With aggregates, contrary to what some might think, ordering has nothing to do with the order in which the aggregate is applied; rather, the ordering element gives meaning to the framing options that I will describe next. In other words, the ordering element is an aid to define which rows to restrict in the window.

Framing

Framing is essentially another filter that further restricts the rows in the partition. It is applicable to aggregate window functions as well as to three of the offset functions: FIRST_VALUE, LAST_VALUE, and NTH_VALUE. Think of this windowing element as defining two points in the current row's partition based on the given ordering, framing the rows that the calculation will apply to.

The framing specification in the standard includes a ROWS or RANGE option that defines the starting row and ending row of the frame, as well as a window frame-exclusion option. SQL Server 2012 introduced support for framing, with full implementation of the ROWS option, partial implementation of the RANGE option, and no implementation of the window frame-exclusion option.

The ROWS option allows you to indicate the points in the frame as an offset in terms of the number of rows with respect to the current row. The RANGE option is more dynamic, defining the offsets in terms of a difference between the value of the frame point and the current row's value. The window frame-exclusion option specifies what to do with the current row and its peers in case of ties. This explanation might seem far from clear or sufficient, but I don't want to get into the details just yet. There will be plenty of that later. For now, I just want to introduce the concept and provide a simple example. Following is a query against the EmpOrders view, calculating the running total quantity for each employee and order month:

```
SELECT empid, ordermonth, qty,
  SUM(qty) OVER(PARTITION BY empid
                ORDER BY ordermonth
                ROWS BETWEEN UNBOUNDED PRECEDING
                         AND CURRENT ROW) AS runqty
FROM Sales.EmpOrders;
```

Observe that the window function applies the SUM aggregate to the *qty* attribute, partitions the window by *empid*, orders the partition rows by *ordermonth*, and frames the partition rows based on the given ordering between unbounded preceding (no low boundary point) and the current row. In other words, the result will be the sum of all prior rows in the frame, inclusive of the current row. This query generates the following output, shown here in abbreviated form:

```
empid  ordermonth              qty        run_qty
------ ----------------------  ---------  -----------
1      2006-07-01 00:00:00.000 121        121
1      2006-08-01 00:00:00.000 247        368
1      2006-09-01 00:00:00.000 255        623
1      2006-10-01 00:00:00.000 143        766
1      2006-11-01 00:00:00.000 318        1084
...
2      2006-07-01 00:00:00.000 50         50
2      2006-08-01 00:00:00.000 94         144
2      2006-09-01 00:00:00.000 137        281
2      2006-10-01 00:00:00.000 248        529
2      2006-11-01 00:00:00.000 237        766
...
```

Observe how the window specification is as easy to read as plain English. I will provide much more detail about the framing options in Chapter 2.

Query Elements Supporting Window Functions

Window functions aren't supported in all query clauses; rather, they're supported only in the SELECT and ORDER BY clauses. To help you understand the reason for this restriction, I first need to explain a concept called *logical query processing*. Then I'll get to the clauses that support window functions, and finally I'll explain how to circumvent the restriction with the other clauses.

Logical Query Processing

Logical query processing describes the conceptual way in which a SELECT query is evaluated according to the logical language design. It describes a process made of a series of steps, or phases, that proceed from the query's input tables to the query's final result set. Note that by "logical query processing," I mean the conceptual way in which the query is evaluated—not necessarily the physical way SQL Server processes the query. As part of the optimization, SQL Server can make shortcuts, rearrange the order of some steps, and pretty much do whatever it likes. But that's as long as it guarantees that it will produce the same output as the one defined by logical query processing applied to the declarative query request.

Each step in logical query processing operates on one or more tables (sets of rows) that serve as its input and returns a table as its output. The output table of one step then becomes the input table for the next step.

Figure 1-6 is a flow diagram illustrating the logical query processing flow in SQL Server 2012.

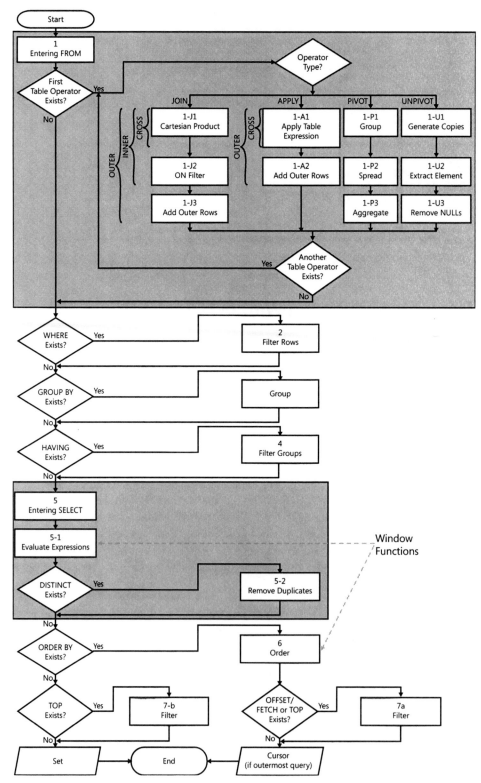

FIGURE 1-6 Logical query processing.

Note that when you write a query, the SELECT clause appears first in terms of the keyed-in order, but observe that in terms of the logical query processing order, it appears almost last—just before the ORDER BY clause is handled.

There's much more to say about logical query processing, but the details are a topic for another book. For the purposes of our discussion, what's important to note is the order in which the various clauses are evaluated. The following list shows the order (with the phases in which window functions are allowed shown in bold):

1. FROM

2. WHERE

3. GROUP BY

4. HAVING

5. SELECT

    5-1. Evaluate Expressions

    5-2. Remove Duplicates

6. **ORDER BY**

7. OFFSET-FETCH/TOP

Understanding logical query processing and the logical query processing order enables you to understand the motivation behind restricting window functions to only specific clauses.

Clauses Supporting Window Functions

As illustrated in Figure 1-6, only the query clauses SELECT and ORDER BY support window functions directly. The reason for the limitation is to avoid ambiguity by operating on (almost) the final result set of the query as the starting point for the window. If window functions are allowed in phases previous to the SELECT phase, their initial window could be different than that in the SELECT phase, and therefore, with some query forms, it could be very difficult to figure out the right result. I'll try to demonstrate the ambiguity problem through an example. First run the following code to create the table T1 and populate it with sample data:

```
SET NOCOUNT ON;
USE TSQL2012;
IF OBJECT_ID('dbo.T1', 'U') IS NOT NULL DROP TABLE dbo.T1;
GO

CREATE TABLE dbo.T1
(
  col1 VARCHAR(10) NOT NULL
    CONSTRAINT PK_T1 PRIMARY KEY
);

INSERT INTO dbo.T1(col1)
  VALUES('A'),('B'),('C'),('D'),('E'),('F');
```

Suppose that window functions were allowed in phases prior to the SELECT—for example, in the WHERE phase. Consider then the following query, and try to figure out which *col1* values should appear in the result:

```
SELECT col1
FROM dbo.T1
WHERE col1 > 'B'
  AND ROW_NUMBER() OVER(ORDER BY col1) <= 3;
```

Before you assume that the answer should obviously be the values C, D, and E, consider the all-at-once concept in SQL. The concept of *all-at-once* means that all expressions that appear in the same logical phase are conceptually evaluated at the same point in time. This means that the order in which the expressions are evaluated shouldn't matter. With this in mind, the following query should be semantically equivalent to the previous one:

```
SELECT col1
FROM dbo.T1
WHERE ROW_NUMBER() OVER(ORDER BY col1) <= 3
  AND col1 > 'B';
```

Now, can you figure out what the right answer is? Is it C, D, and E, or is it just C?

That's an example of the ambiguity I was talking about. By restricting window functions to only the SELECT and ORDER BY clauses of a query, this ambiguity is eliminated.

Looking at Figure 1-6, you might have noticed that within the SELECT phase, it's step 5-1 (Evaluate Expressions) that supports window functions, and this step is evaluated before step 5-2 (Remove Duplicates). If you wonder why it is important to know such subtleties, I'll demonstrate why.

Following is a query returning the *empid* and *country* attributes of all employees from the Employees table:

```
SELECT empid, country
FROM HR.Employees;
```

```
empid       country
----------- ---------------
1           USA
2           USA
3           USA
4           USA
5           UK
6           UK
7           UK
8           USA
9           UK
```

Next, examine the following query and see if you can guess what its output is before executing it:

```
SELECT DISTINCT country, ROW_NUMBER() OVER(ORDER BY country) AS rownum
FROM HR.Employees;
```

Some expect to get the following output:

```
country          rownum
---------------  --------------------
UK               1
USA              2
```

But in reality you get this:

```
country          rownum
---------------  --------------------
UK               1
UK               2
UK               3
UK               4
USA              5
USA              6
USA              7
USA              8
USA              9
```

Now consider that the ROW_NUMBER function in this query is evaluated in step 5-1 where the SELECT list expressions are evaluated—prior to the removal of the duplicates in step 5-2. The ROW_NUMBER function assigns nine unique row numbers to the nine employee rows, and then the DISTINCT clause has no duplicates left to remove.

When you realize this and understand that it has to do with the logical query processing order of the different elements, you can think of a solution. For example, you can have a table expression defined based on a query that just returns distinct countries and have the outer query assign the row numbers after duplicates are removed, like so:

```
WITH EmpCountries AS
(
  SELECT DISTINCT country FROM HR.Employees
)
SELECT country, ROW_NUMBER() OVER(ORDER BY country) AS rownum
FROM EmpCountries;
```

Can you think of other ways to solve the problem, perhaps even simpler ways than this one?

The fact that window functions are evaluated in the SELECT or ORDER BY phase means that the window defined for the calculation—before applying further restrictions—is the intermediate form of rows of the query after all previous phases—that is, after applying the FROM with all of its table operators (for example, joins), and after the WHERE filtering, the grouping, and the filtering of the groups. Consider the following query as an example:

```
SELECT O.empid,
  SUM(OD.qty) AS qty,
  RANK() OVER(ORDER BY SUM(OD.qty) DESC) AS rnk
FROM Sales.Orders AS O
  JOIN Sales.OrderDetails AS OD
    ON O.orderid = OD.orderid
WHERE O.orderdate >= '20070101'
```

```
      AND O.orderdate < '20080101'
GROUP BY O.empid;

empid   qty    rnk
------  -----  ---
4       5273   1
3       4436   2
1       3877   3
8       2843   4
2       2604   5
7       2292   6
6       1738   7
5       1471   8
9        955   9
```

First the FROM clause is evaluated and the join is performed. Then only the rows where the order year is 2007 are filtered. Then the remaining rows are grouped by employee ID. Only then are the expressions in the SELECT list evaluated, including the RANK function, which is calculated based on ordering by the total quantity descending. If there were other window functions in the SELECT list, they would all use the same result set as their starting point. Recall from earlier discussions about alternative options to window functions (for example, subqueries) that they start their view of the data from scratch—meaning that you have to repeat all the logic you have in the outer query in each of your subqueries, leading to much more verbose code.

Circumventing the Limitations

I explained the reasoning behind disallowing the use of window functions in logical query processing phases that are evaluated prior to the SELECT clause. But what if you need to filter by or group by a calculation based on window functions? The solution is to use a table expression such as a CTE or a derived table. Have a query invoke the window function in its SELECT list, assigning the calculation an alias. Define a table expression based on that query, and then have the outer query refer to that alias where you need it.

Here's an example showing how you can filter by the result of a window function using a CTE:

```
WITH C AS
(
  SELECT orderid, orderdate, val,
    RANK() OVER(ORDER BY val DESC) AS rnk
  FROM Sales.OrderValues
)
SELECT *
FROM C
WHERE rnk <= 5;

orderid  orderdate               val       rnk
-------  ----------------------  --------  ----
10865    2008-02-02 00:00:00.000 16387.50  1
10981    2008-03-27 00:00:00.000 15810.00  2
11030    2008-04-17 00:00:00.000 12615.05  3
10889    2008-02-16 00:00:00.000 11380.00  4
10417    2007-01-16 00:00:00.000 11188.40  5
```

With modification statements, window functions are disallowed altogether because those don't support SELECT and ORDER BY clauses. But there are cases where involving window functions in modification statements is needed. Table expressions can be used to address this need as well because T-SQL supports modifying data through table expressions. I'll demonstrate this capability with an UPDATE example. First run the following code to create a table called T1 with columns *col1* and *col2* and populate it with sample data:

```
SET NOCOUNT ON;
USE TSQL2012;
IF OBJECT_ID('dbo.T1', 'U') IS NOT NULL DROP TABLE dbo.T1;
GO

CREATE TABLE dbo.T1
(
  col1 INT NULL,
  col2 VARCHAR(10) NOT NULL
);

INSERT INTO dbo.T1(col2)
  VALUES('C'),('A'),('B'),('A'),('C'),('B');
```

Explicit values were provided in *col2*, and NULLs were used as defaults in *col1*.

Suppose this table represents a situation with data-quality problems. A key wasn't enforced in this table, and therefore it is not possible to uniquely identify rows. You want to assign unique *col1* values in all rows. You're thinking of using the ROW_NUMBER function in an UPDATE statement, like so:

```
UPDATE dbo.T1
  SET col1 = ROW_NUMBER() OVER(ORDER BY col2);
```

But remember that this is not allowed. The workaround is to write a query against T1 returning *col1* and an expression based on the ROW_NUMBER function (call it *rownum*); define a table expression based on this query; finally, have an outer UPDATE statement against the CTE assign *rownum* to *col1*, like so:

```
WITH C AS
(
  SELECT col1, col2,
    ROW_NUMBER() OVER(ORDER BY col2) AS rownum
  FROM dbo.T1
)
UPDATE C
  SET col1 = rownum;
```

Query T1, and observe that all rows got unique *col1* values:

```
SELECT col1, col2
FROM dbo.T1;

col1        col2
----------- ----------
5           C
1           A
3           B
2           A
6           C
4           B
```

Potential for Additional Filters

I provided a workaround in T-SQL that allows you to use window functions indirectly in query elements that don't support those directly. The workaround is a table expression in the form of a CTE or derived table. It's nice to have a workaround, but a table expression adds an extra layer to the query and complicates it a bit. The examples I showed are quite simple, but think about long and complex queries to begin with. Can you have a simpler solution that doesn't require this extra layer?

With window functions, SQL Server doesn't have a solution at the moment. It's interesting, though, to see how others coped with this problem. Teradata for example created a filtering clause it calls *QUALIFY* that is conceptually evaluated after the SELECT clause. This means that it can refer to window functions directly, as in the following example:

```
SELECT orderid, orderdate, val
FROM Sales.OrderValues
QUALIFY RANK() OVER(ORDER BY val DESC) <= 5;
```

Furthermore, you can refer to column aliases defined in the SELECT list, like so:

```
SELECT orderid, orderdate, val,
  RANK() OVER(ORDER BY val DESC) AS rnk
FROM Sales.OrderValues
QUALIFY rnk <= 5;
```

The QUALIFY clause isn't defined in standard SQL; rather, it's a Teradata-specific feature. However, it seems like a very interesting solution, and it would be nice to see both the standard and SQL Server providing a solution to this need.

Reuse of Window Definitions

Suppose that you need to invoke multiple window functions in the same query and part of the window specification (or all of it) is common to multiple functions. If you indicate the complete window specifications in all functions, the code can quickly get lengthy. Here's an example illustrating the problem:

```
SELECT empid, ordermonth, qty,
  SUM(qty) OVER (PARTITION BY empid
                ORDER BY ordermonth
                ROWS BETWEEN UNBOUNDED PRECEDING
                          AND CURRENT ROW) AS run_sum_qty,
  AVG(qty) OVER (PARTITION BY empid
                ORDER BY ordermonth
                ROWS BETWEEN UNBOUNDED PRECEDING
                          AND CURRENT ROW) AS run_avg_qty,
  MIN(qty) OVER (PARTITION BY empid
                ORDER BY ordermonth
                ROWS BETWEEN UNBOUNDED PRECEDING
                          AND CURRENT ROW) AS run_min_qty,
  MAX(qty) OVER (PARTITION BY empid
                ORDER BY ordermonth
                ROWS BETWEEN UNBOUNDED PRECEDING
                          AND CURRENT ROW) AS run_max_qty
FROM Sales.EmpOrders;
```

Standard SQL has an answer to this problem in the form of a clause called WINDOW that allows naming a window specification or part of it; then you can refer to that name in other window definitions—ones used by window functions or even by a definition of another window name. This clause is conceptually evaluated after the HAVING clause and before the SELECT clause.

SQL Server doesn't yet support the WINDOW clause. But according to standard SQL, you can abbreviate the preceding query using the WINDOW clause like so:

```
SELECT empid, ordermonth, qty,
  SUM(qty) OVER W1 AS run_sum_qty,
  AVG(qty) OVER W1 AS run_avg_qty,
  MIN(qty) OVER W1 AS run_min_qty,
  MAX(qty) OVER W1 AS run_max_qty
FROM Sales.EmpOrders
WINDOW W1 AS ( PARTITION BY empid
              ORDER BY ordermonth
              ROWS BETWEEN UNBOUNDED PRECEDING
                        AND CURRENT ROW );
```

That's quite a difference, as you can see. In this case, the WINDOW clause assigns the name W1 to a complete window specification with partitioning, ordering, and framing options. Then all four functions refer to W1 as their window specification. The WINDOW clause is actually quite sophisticated. As mentioned, it doesn't have to name a complete window specification; rather, it can even name only part of it. Then a window definition can include a mix of named parts plus explicit parts. As an aside, the coverage of standard SQL for the WINDOW clause is a striking length of 10 pages! And trying to decipher the details is no picnic.

It would be great to see SQL Server add such support in the future, especially now that it has extensive support for window functions and people are likely to end up with lengthy window specifications.

Summary

This chapter introduced the concept of windowing in SQL. It provided the background to window functions, explaining the motivation for their use. The chapter then provided a glimpse of solving querying tasks using window functions by addressing the task of identifying ranges of existing values in a sequence—a problem also known as *identifying islands*. The chapter then proceeded to explain the design of window functions, covering the elements involved in window specifications: partitioning, ordering, and framing. Finally, this chapter explained how standard SQL addresses the need to reuse a window specification or part of it. The next chapter provides a breakdown of window functions, getting into more detail.

A Detailed Look at Window Functions

This chapter looks at the various types of window functions, getting into the details of each. Still, the focus in this chapter is on the logical aspects of the functions. Optimization will be covered separately in Chapter 4, "Optimization of Window Functions."

The main reason for separating the discussion of the two layers into different chapters is that standard SQL deals only with the logical layer. And because Microsoft SQL Server implements the functions based on the standard, the coverage of the logical aspects of the functions in this book could be interesting for readers who use database platforms other than SQL Server as well. Chapter 4 focuses on the optimization of the functions—namely, the physical layer, which is very platform-specific—and will be of interest mainly to readers who use SQL Server.

This chapter is organized in sections based on the function categories: window aggregate functions, rank functions, distribution functions, and offset functions. With each category of functions, I first explain the windowing elements supported by the category, and then I explain the specifics of each function. If the function was introduced or enhanced in SQL Server 2012, I usually provide alternatives available prior to SQL Server 2012 or point to a later section in the book where such alternatives are discussed.

Window Aggregate Functions

This section covers window aggregate functions. I first explain how the windowing concept works with aggregate functions; then I describe the supported elements in the specification of window aggregate functions and their meaning in detail. And then I get to more specialized aspects such as further filtering ideas, handling distinct aggregates, and handling nested aggregates.

Window Aggregate Functions Described

Window aggregate functions are the same functions as grouped aggregate functions; only instead of applying them to groups in grouped queries, you apply them to windows defined by the OVER clause. An aggregate function is supposed to be applied to a set of rows, and it shouldn't matter to the function which language mechanism defines the set.

Supported Windowing Elements

In standard SQL, window aggregate functions support three elements: partitioning, ordering, and framing. The general form of a window aggregate function is as follows:

```
function_name(<arguments>) OVER(
  [ <window partition clause> ]
  [ <window order clause> [ <window frame clause> ] ] )
```

The purpose of all three elements is to filter the rows in the window. SQL Server 2005 introduced support for the partitioning element, including support for Common Language Runtime (CLR) aggregates. SQL Server 2012 added the ordering and framing options, but support for CLR aggregates has not yet been added.

When you don't apply any restrictions to the window—namely, when you use empty parentheses in the OVER clause—the window consists of all rows in the result set of the underlying query. More precisely, the initial window consists of the set of rows in the virtual table provided as input to the logical query processing phase where the window function appears. This means that if the window function appears in the query's SELECT list, it is the virtual table provided as input to phase 5-1. (See Figure 1-6 in Chapter 1, "SQL Windowing.") This phase appears after processing the FROM, WHERE, GROUP BY, and HAVING clauses, and before the removal of duplicate rows if a DISTINCT clause was specified (phase 5-2). But that's the initial window prior to applying restrictions. The next sections explain how to further restrict the window.

Partitioning

The partitioning element allows you to restrict the window to only those rows that have the same values in the partitioning attributes as the current row. Some think of the partitioning element like grouping and some think of it like correlated subqueries, but it's actually different from both. Unlike grouping, partitioning is specific to one function's window and can be different for different functions in the same query. Unlike correlated subqueries, partitioning filters rows from the virtual table provided to the SELECT phase as input, as opposed to starting with a fresh view of the data and needing to repeat all constructs that appear in the outer query.

As the first partitioning example, the following query invokes two window SUM aggregate functions—one without partitioning and another partitioned by *custid*:

```
USE TSQL2012;

SELECT orderid, custid, val,
   SUM(val) OVER() AS sumall,
   SUM(val) OVER(PARTITION BY custid) AS sumcust
FROM Sales.OrderValues AS O1;

orderid  custid  val      sumall       sumcust
-------- ------- ------- ----------- --------
10643    1       814.50  1265793.22  4273.00
10692    1       878.00  1265793.22  4273.00
10702    1       330.00  1265793.22  4273.00
10835    1       845.80  1265793.22  4273.00
```

```
10952   1      471.20  1265793.22  4273.00
11011   1      933.50  1265793.22  4273.00
10926   2      514.40  1265793.22  1402.95
10759   2      320.00  1265793.22  1402.95
10625   2      479.75  1265793.22  1402.95
10308   2      88.80   1265793.22  1402.95
. . .
```

The first window function calculates for each row the grand total *val* (the *sumall* attribute). The second function calculates the customer total *val* (the *sumcust* attribute). Figure 2-1 calls out three arbitrary sums and illustrates the windows used to calculate those.

orderid	custid	val	sumall	sumcust
10643	1	814.50	1265793.22	4273.00
10692	1	878.00	1265793.22	4273.00
10702	1	330.00	1265793.22	4273.00
10835	1	845.80	1265793.22	4273.00
10952	1	471.20	1265793.22	4273.00
11011	1	933.50	1265793.22	4273.00
10926	2	514.40	1265793.22	1402.95
10759	2	320.00	1265793.22	1402.95
10625	2	479.75	1265793.22	1402.95
10308	2	88.80	1265793.22	1402.95
...				

FIGURE 2-1 The first partitioning example.

Observe that in the case of the *sumall* attribute calculated for order 10692, the respective window consists of all rows from the result set of the underlying query, because an explicit partitioning element wasn't specified. Therefore, the grand total *val* for the row that was called out is 1,265,793.22, as is the case for all other rows. As for the *sumcust* attribute, the window function calculating it is partitioned by *custid*; therefore, rows with different *custid* values have different, disjoint, subsets of rows in their respective windows. That's the case with the two orders that were called out: 10643 and 10926. The former was placed by customer 1; hence, the respective window consists of the rows with customer ID 1, yielding 4,273.00 as the customer total. The latter was placed by customer 2; therefore, its respective window consists of the rows with customer ID 2, yielding 1,402.95 as the customer total.

As the second partitioning example, the following query mixes detail elements and window aggregate functions to calculate the percent of the current order value out of the grand total, as well as out of the customer total:

```
SELECT orderid, custid, val,
  CAST(100. * val / SUM(val) OVER() AS NUMERIC(5, 2)) AS pctall,
  CAST(100. * val / SUM(val) OVER(PARTITION BY custid) AS NUMERIC(5, 2)) AS pctcust
FROM Sales.OrderValues AS O1;

orderid  custid  val     pctall  pctcust
-------- ------- ------- ------- --------
10643    1       814.50  0.06    19.06
10692    1       878.00  0.07    20.55
```

```
10702    1        330.00   0.03    7.72
10835    1        845.80   0.07   19.79
10952    1        471.20   0.04   11.03
11011    1        933.50   0.07   21.85
10926    2        514.40   0.04   36.67
10759    2        320.00   0.03   22.81
10625    2        479.75   0.04   34.20
10308    2         88.80   0.01    6.33
...
```

Figure 2-2 illustrates the applicable window partitions used by the three calculations that were called out.

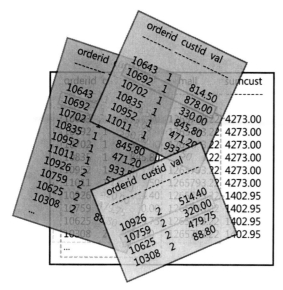

FIGURE 2-2 The second partitioning example.

The figure also attempts to visually express the idea that all windows conceptually coexist at the same time. Each rectangle calls out a window for one function for one specific underlying order. The largest rectangle at the back is an example for a window generated for one of the orders when using the OVER clause with empty parentheses. The two smaller rectangles call out the windows for two sample orders when using the OVER clause with *PARTITION BY custid*. The top rectangle is generated for an order with a *custid* value of 1, and the bottom rectangle for an order with a *custid* value of 2.

Ordering and Framing

Framing is another option that enables you to further restrict the rows in the window partition. The ordering element plays a different role for window aggregate functions than for ranking, distribution, and offset functions. With aggregate functions, ordering just gives meaning to the framing option. Once ordering is defined, framing identifies two bounds in the window partition, and only the rows between those two bounds are filtered.

Earlier, I provided the general form of a window aggregate function. Here it is again as a reminder:

```
function_name(<arguments>) OVER(
  [ <window partition clause> ]
  [ <window order clause> [ <window frame clause> ] ] )
```

The window frame clause can include three parts and takes the following form:

```
<window frame units> <window frame extent> [ <window frame exclusion> ]
```

In the *window frame units* part, you indicate ROWS or RANGE. The former means that the bounds, or endpoints, of the frame can be expressed as offsets in terms of the number of rows of difference from the current row. The latter means that the offsets are more dynamic and expressed as a logical value difference from the current row's (only) ordering attribute value. This part will become clearer in the upcoming examples.

The *window frame extent* part is where you indicate the offsets of the bounds with respect to the current row.

SQL Server 2012 implements the ROWS option with all related *window frame extent* options, and it implements the RANGE option with a partial implementation of the related *window frame extent* options.

Finally, the *window frame exclusion* part allows you to specify whether to exclude the current row, its peers, or both. The *window frame exclusion* part isn't implemented in SQL Server 2012.

The ROWS window frame extent option   I'll start with examples for using the ROWS clause. As mentioned, using ROWS as the *window frame units* part means that you indicate the frame bounds as offsets in terms of the number of rows with respect to the current row. The standard ROWS clause supports the following options, all of which are implemented in SQL Server 2012:

```
ROWS BETWEEN UNBOUNDED PRECEDING  |
             <n> PRECEDING        |
             <n> FOLLOWING        |
             CURRENT ROW
        AND
             UNBOUNDED FOLLOWING  |
             <n> PRECEDING        |
             <n> FOLLOWING        |
             CURRENT ROW
```

These options are probably straightforward, but just in case they're not, I'll provide a brief explanation. For the low bound of the frame, UNBOUNDED PRECEDING means there is no low boundary point; *<n> preceding* and *<n> following* specifies a number of rows before and after the current one, respectively; and CURRENT ROW, obviously, means that the starting row is the current row.

As for the high bound of the frame, you can see the options are quite similar, except that if you don't want a high boundary point, you indicate UNBOUNDED FOLLOWING, naturally.

As an example, consider the following frame:

```
PARTITION BY custid
ORDER BY ordermonth
ROWS BETWEEN UNBOUNDED PRECEDING
  AND CURRENT ROW
```

The window frame created for each row contains all rows from the first order month through the current row. Note that you can use ROWS UNBOUNDED PRECEDING as a shorthand way of saying "ROWS BETWEEN UNBOUNDED PRECEDING AND CURRENT ROW." But if you omit the *window frame extent* part altogether, just leaving the partitioning and ordering parts, you get something a bit different by default. I'll get to this later when discussing the RANGE option.

As the first example using the ROWS option, consider the following query against the Sales.EmpOrders view, followed by its output shown here in abbreviated form:

```
SELECT empid, ordermonth, qty,
  SUM(qty) OVER(PARTITION BY empid
               ORDER BY ordermonth
               ROWS BETWEEN UNBOUNDED PRECEDING
                     AND CURRENT ROW) AS runqty
FROM Sales.EmpOrders;
```

```
empid       ordermonth              qty          runqty
----------- ----------------------- -----------  -----------
1           2006-07-01 00:00:00.000 121          121
1           2006-08-01 00:00:00.000 247          368
1           2006-09-01 00:00:00.000 255          623
1           2006-10-01 00:00:00.000 143          766
1           2006-11-01 00:00:00.000 318          1084
...
2           2006-07-01 00:00:00.000 50           50
2           2006-08-01 00:00:00.000 94           144
2           2006-09-01 00:00:00.000 137          281
2           2006-10-01 00:00:00.000 248          529
2           2006-11-01 00:00:00.000 237          766
...
```

This query uses the aforementioned frame specification to calculate a running total quantity for each employee and order month. Recall that you can use a more concise form to indicate the frame while retaining the same meaning:

```
SELECT empid, ordermonth, qty,
  SUM(qty) OVER(PARTITION BY empid
               ORDER BY ordermonth
               ROWS UNBOUNDED PRECEDING) AS runqty
FROM Sales.EmpOrders;
```

Figure 2-3 provides an illustration that depicts the applicable frame with respect to each row using arrows.

FIGURE 2-3 Frame example: ROWS UNBOUNDED PRECEDING.

As a second example for using the ROWS option, the following query invokes three window functions with three different frame specifications:

```
SELECT empid, ordermonth,
  MAX(qty) OVER(PARTITION BY empid
                ORDER BY ordermonth
                ROWS BETWEEN 1 PRECEDING
                         AND 1 PRECEDING) AS prvqty,
  qty AS curqty,
  MAX(qty) OVER(PARTITION BY empid
                ORDER BY ordermonth
                ROWS BETWEEN 1 FOLLOWING
                         AND 1 FOLLOWING) AS nxtqty,
  AVG(qty) OVER(PARTITION BY empid
                ORDER BY ordermonth
                ROWS BETWEEN 1 PRECEDING
                         AND 1 FOLLOWING) AS avgqty
FROM Sales.EmpOrders;
```

```
empid  ordermonth               prvqty  curqty  nxtqty  avgqty
------ ------------------------  ------- ------- ------- -------
1      2006-07-01 00:00:00.000  NULL     121     247     184
1      2006-08-01 00:00:00.000  121      247     255     207
1      2006-09-01 00:00:00.000  247      255     143     215
1      2006-10-01 00:00:00.000  255      143     318     238
1      2006-11-01 00:00:00.000  143      318     536     332
...
1      2008-01-01 00:00:00.000  583      397     566     515
1      2008-02-01 00:00:00.000  397      566     467     476
1      2008-03-01 00:00:00.000  566      467     586     539
1      2008-04-01 00:00:00.000  467      586     299     450
1      2008-05-01 00:00:00.000  586      299     NULL    442
...
```

The calculation that generates the attribute *prvqty* defines a frame in terms of rows between 1 preceding and 1 preceding. This means that the frame includes just the previous row in the partition. The MAX aggregate applied to the *qty* attribute is artificial here because, at most, there will be just one row in the frame. The maximum *qty* value is the *qty* value from that row or NULL if there are no rows in the frame (if the current row is the first one in the partition). Figure 2-4 illustrates the applicable frame with respect to each row, containing at most just one row.

```
empid   ordermonth                    prvqty curqty nxtqty avgqty
--------  -----------------------------  -------  ------- --------- -------
1        2006-07-01 00:00:00.000 NULL   121     247     184
1        2006-08-01 00:00:00.000 121    247     255     207
1        2006-09-01 00:00:00.000 247    255     143     215
1        2006-10-01 00:00:00.000 255    143     318     238
1        2006-11-01 00:00:00.000 143    318     536     332
...
1        2008-01-01 00:00:00.000 583    397     566     515
1        2008-02-01 00:00:00.000 397    566     467     476
1        2008-03-01 00:00:00.000 566    467     586     539
1        2008-04-01 00:00:00.000 467    586     299     450
1        2008-05-01 00:00:00.000 586    299     NULL    442
...
```

FIGURE 2-4 Frame example: ROWS BETWEEN 1 PRECEDING AND 1 PRECEDING.

Note that there's no previous row with respect to the first one in the partition; therefore, the *prvqty* value in the first row in the partition is NULL.

Similarly, the calculation that generates the attribute *nxtqty* defines a frame in terms of rows between 1 following and 1 following, meaning that the frame includes just the next row. Then the *MAX(qty)* aggregate returns the *qty* value from the next row. Figure 2-5 illustrates the applicable frame with respect to each row.

```
empid   ordermonth                    prvqty curqty nxtqty avgqty
--------  -----------------------------  -------  ------- --------- -------
1        2006-07-01 00:00:00.000 NULL   121     247     184
1        2006-08-01 00:00:00.000 121    247     255     207
1        2006-09-01 00:00:00.000 247    255     143     215
1        2006-10-01 00:00:00.000 255    143     318     238
1        2006-11-01 00:00:00.000 143    318     536     332
...
1        2008-01-01 00:00:00.000 583    397     566     515
1        2008-02-01 00:00:00.000 397    566     467     476
1        2008-03-01 00:00:00.000 566    467     586     539
1        2008-04-01 00:00:00.000 467    586     299     450
1        2008-05-01 00:00:00.000 586    299     NULL    442
...
```

FIGURE 2-5 Frame example: ROWS BETWEEN 1 FOLLOWING AND 1 FOLLOWING.

Just like there's no previous row with respect to the first one in the partition, there's no next row with respect to the last one in the partition; therefore, the *nxtqty* value in the last row in the partition is NULL.

The calculation that generates the result attribute *avgqty* defines a frame of rows between 1 preceding and 1 following, meaning that the frame consists of up to three rows. Figure 2-6 illustrates the applicable frame with respect to two arbitrary rows just as an example.

```
empid   ordermonth                  prvqty curqty nxtqty  avgqty
-------- --------------------------- ------- ------ --------- -------
1       2006-07-01 00:00:00.000 NULL  121    247      184
1       2006-08-01 00:00:00.000 121   247    255      207
1       2006-09-01 00:00:00.000 247   255    143      215
1       2006-10-01 00:00:00.000 255   143    318      238
1       2006-11-01 00:00:00.000 143   318    536      332
...
1       2008-01-01 00:00:00.000 583   397    566      515
1       2008-02-01 00:00:00.000 397   566    467      476
1       2008-03-01 00:00:00.000 566   467    586      539
1       2008-04-01 00:00:00.000 467   586    299      450
1       2008-05-01 00:00:00.000 586   299    NULL     442
...
```

FIGURE 2-6 Frame example: ROWS BETWEEN 1 PRECEDING AND 1 FOLLOWING.

As with the other calculations, there's no row preceding the first one in the partition and no row following the last one; hence, the frame in this case can consist of fewer than, but no more than, three rows. The AVG correctly divides the sum by the actual count of rows in the frame.

Combined, the partitioning and ordering elements in the EmpOrders view are unique. This means that the same combination of *empid* and *ordermonth* values cannot repeat itself in the view. And this, in turn, means that the three calculations used in our query are deterministic—in other words, the query has only one possible correct result for a given state of the input.

Things are different, though, when the combination of partitioning and ordering elements isn't unique. Then calculations using the ROWS option might be nondeterministic. I'll demonstrate this with an example. Run the code in Listing 2-1 to create and populate a table called T1.

LISTING 2-1 DDL and Sample Data for Table T1

```
SET NOCOUNT ON;
USE TSQL2012;
IF OBJECT_ID('dbo.T1', 'U') IS NOT NULL DROP TABLE dbo.T1;
GO
CREATE TABLE dbo.T1
(
  keycol INT        NOT NULL CONSTRAINT PK_T1 PRIMARY KEY,
  col1   VARCHAR(10) NOT NULL
);
```

```
INSERT INTO dbo.T1 VALUES
  (2, 'A'),(3, 'A'),
  (5, 'B'),(7, 'B'),(11, 'B'),
  (13, 'C'),(17, 'C'),(19, 'C'),(23, 'C');
```

Consider the following query, which is followed by its output:

```
SELECT keycol, col1,
  COUNT(*) OVER(ORDER BY col1
                ROWS BETWEEN UNBOUNDED PRECEDING
                     AND CURRENT ROW) AS cnt
FROM dbo.T1;
```

```
keycol       col1        cnt
-----------  ----------  -----------
2            A           1
3            A           2
5            B           3
7            B           4
11           B           5
13           C           6
17           C           7
19           C           8
23           C           9
```

Observe that different rows that share the same partitioning (inapplicable, in our case) and ordering values get different counts. That's because ordering among peers (rows that share the same partitioning and explicit ordering) is arbitrary—in other words, left to the implementation. In SQL Server, this simply depends on optimization. For example, I created the following index:

```
CREATE UNIQUE INDEX idx_col1D_keycol ON dbo.T1(col1 DESC, keycol);
```

Then I ran the query again, and the second time I got the following output:

```
keycol       col1        cnt
-----------  ----------  -----------
3            A           1
2            A           2
5            B           3
11           B           4
7            B           5
23           C           6
19           C           7
17           C           8
13           C           9
```

Technically, as far as the standard is concerned, this output is just as correct as the previous output.

If you need to guarantee a deterministic result, you should make sure that the combination of partitioning and ordering elements is unique. You can achieve this by adding a tiebreaker to the ordering specification—in our case, by adding the primary key column, like so:

```
SELECT keycol, col1,
  COUNT(*) OVER(ORDER BY col1, keycol
                  ROWS BETWEEN UNBOUNDED PRECEDING
                          AND CURRENT ROW) AS cnt
FROM dbo.T1;

keycol      col1       cnt
----------- ---------- -----------
2           A          1
3           A          2
5           B          3
7           B          4
11          B          5
13          C          6
17          C          7
19          C          8
23          C          9
```

Now the query is deterministic, meaning that there's only one correct result.

The RANGE window frame extent option   Standard SQL also supports specifying the *window frame extent* using the RANGE option. Here are the possibilities for the low and high bounds, or end-points, of the frame:

```
RANGE BETWEEN UNBOUNDED PRECEDING  |
              <val> PRECEDING      |
              <val> FOLLOWING      |
              CURRENT ROW
          AND
              UNBOUNDED FOLLOWING  |
              <val> PRECEDING      |
              <val> FOLLOWING      |
              CURRENT ROW
```

This option is supposed to enable you to specify the low and high bounds of the frame more dynamically—as a logical difference between the current row's ordering value and the bound's value. Think about the difference between saying "Give me the total quantities for the last three periods of activity," versus saying "Give me the total quantities for the period starting two months before the current period and until the current period." The former concept is what ROWS was designed to provide, and the latter concept is what RANGE was designed to provide. (I'll say more about this example shortly.)

As of SQL Server 2012, RANGE is not implemented fully. It is currently supported only with UNBOUNDED and CURRENT ROW window-frame delimiters. What's also still missing is support for a temporal INTERVAL type that, combined with full support for the RANGE option, would provide a lot of flexibility in the frame definition. As an example, the following query defines a frame based on a range between two months before the current month and the current month (and this query doesn't run in SQL Server 2012).

```
SELECT empid, ordermonth, qty,
  SUM(qty) OVER(PARTITION BY empid
               ORDER BY ordermonth
               RANGE BETWEEN INTERVAL '2' MONTH PRECEDING
                         AND CURRENT ROW) AS sum3month
FROM Sales.EmpOrders;
```

This is different than using ROWS BETWEEN 2 PRECEDING AND CURRENT ROW even when the order month is unique for each employee. Consider the possibility that an employee can be inactive in certain months. With the ROWS option, the frame simply starts two rows before the current one, which might be more than two months before the current one. With RANGE, the frame is more dynamic, starting two months before the current one—whatever number of rows this translates to. Figure 2-7 illustrates the applicable frame of rows for some of the rows in the underlying query.

```
empid  ordermonth  qty          sum3month
------ ----------- ----------- ---------------
...
9      2006-07-01  294 ↓         294
9      2006-10-01  256 ↓         256
9      2006-12-01  25            281
9      2007-01-01  74            99
9      2007-03-01  137           211
9      2007-04-01  52            189
9      2007-05-01  8             197
9      2007-06-01  161           221
9      2007-07-01  4             173
9      2007-08-01  98            263
...
```

FIGURE 2-7 Frame example: RANGE INTERVAL '2' MONTH PRECEDING.

Observe that the number of rows in the different frames varies between 1, 2, and 3. This happens because, in some cases, there aren't three consecutive months of activity for the same employee.

Just like with the ROWS option, the RANGE option also supports more concise ways to express what you want. If you don't specify an upper bound, CURRENT ROW is assumed. So, in our example, instead of using RANGE BETWEEN INTERVAL '2' MONTH PRECEDING AND CURRENT ROW, you can use just RANGE INTERVAL '2' MONTH PRECEDING. But as mentioned, this query won't run in SQL Server 2012 because of the incomplete support for the RANGE option and the lack of support for the INTERVAL type. For now, you need to use alternative methods. It's still possible to handle the task with the existing support for window functions, but the solutions are quite convoluted. Another option is to rely on more traditional constructs such as subqueries, as the following example shows:

```
SELECT empid, ordermonth, qty,
  (SELECT SUM(qty)
   FROM Sales.EmpOrders AS O2
   WHERE O2.empid = O1.empid
     AND O2.ordermonth BETWEEN DATEADD(month, -2, O1.ordermonth)
                           AND O1.ordermonth) AS sum3month
FROM Sales.EmpOrders AS O1;
```

As mentioned, SQL Server 2012 does support the RANGE option with UNBOUNDED and CURRENT ROW as delimiters. For example, the window function in the following query calculates the running total quantity from the beginning of the employee activity until the current month:

```
SELECT empid, ordermonth, qty,
  SUM(qty) OVER(PARTITION BY empid
              ORDER BY ordermonth
              RANGE BETWEEN UNBOUNDED PRECEDING
                          AND CURRENT ROW) AS runqty
FROM Sales.EmpOrders;
```

```
empid       ordermonth                qty         runqty
----------- ------------------------- ----------- -----------
1           2006-07-01 00:00:00.000   121         121
1           2006-08-01 00:00:00.000   247         368
1           2006-09-01 00:00:00.000   255         623
1           2006-10-01 00:00:00.000   143         766
1           2006-11-01 00:00:00.000   318         1084
...
2           2006-07-01 00:00:00.000   50          50
2           2006-08-01 00:00:00.000   94          144
2           2006-09-01 00:00:00.000   137         281
2           2006-10-01 00:00:00.000   248         529
2           2006-11-01 00:00:00.000   237         766
...
```

Figure 2-8 illustrates the applicable frame with respect to each row in the underlying query.

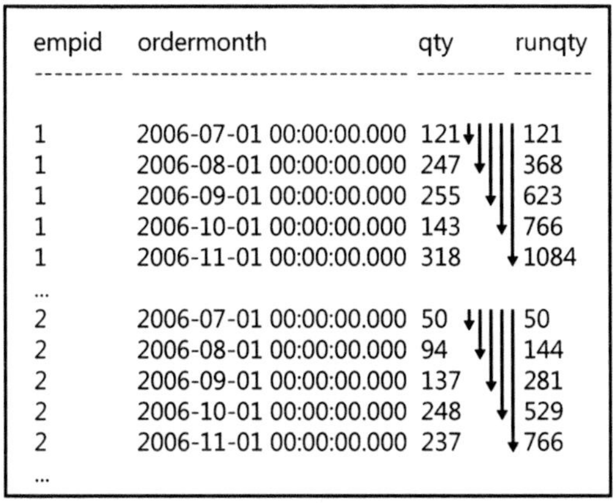

FIGURE 2-8 Frame example: RANGE UNBOUNDED PRECEDING.

As mentioned, if you don't indicate the upper bound, the default is CURRENT ROW. So instead of using RANGE BETWEEN UNBOUNDED PRECEDING AND CURRENT ROW, you can use the shorter form of RANGE UNBOUNDED PRECEDING, like so:

```
SELECT empid, ordermonth, qty,
  SUM(qty) OVER(PARTITION BY empid
              ORDER BY ordermonth
              RANGE UNBOUNDED PRECEDING) AS runqty
FROM Sales.EmpOrders;
```

This window frame extent, as it turns out, is also the default when you indicate window ordering without an explicit *window frame extent* specification. So the following query is logically equivalent to the last two:

```
SELECT empid, ordermonth, qty,
  SUM(qty) OVER(PARTITION BY empid
               ORDER BY ordermonth) AS runqty
FROM Sales.EmpOrders;
```

That's quite a significant savings in the amount of code.

If you carefully followed the examples with both the ROWS and RANGE options, at this point you might wonder whether there's any difference between the two when using only UNBOUNDED and CURRENT ROW as delimiters. For example, when comparing Figure 2-3 (which shows the frames defined with ROWS UNBOUNDED PRECEDING) and Figure 2-8 (which shows the frames defined with RANGE UNBOUNDED PRECEDING), they seem identical. Indeed, the two frame extent specifications have the same logical meaning when the combination of partitioning plus ordering elements is unique. Querying the EmpOrders view, with *empid* as the partitioning element and *ordermonth* as the ordering element, you do get a unique combination. So, in this case, both options are logically equivalent. There is a difference between the meanings of the two when the combination of partitioning and ordering elements isn't unique, meaning that there is potential for ties.

To demonstrate the difference, I'll use the table T1 you created and populated earlier by running the code in Listing 2-1. As a reminder, the option ROWS BETWEEN UNBOUNDED PRECEDING AND CURRENT ROW (or the equivalent ROWS UNBOUNDED PRECEDING) ends the frame at the current row and doesn't include any further peers:

```
SELECT keycol, col1,
  COUNT(*) OVER(ORDER BY col1
               ROWS BETWEEN UNBOUNDED PRECEDING
                            AND CURRENT ROW) AS cnt
FROM dbo.T1;
```

```
keycol        col1       cnt
-----------   ---------- -----------
2             A          1
3             A          2
5             B          3
7             B          4
11            B          5
13            C          6
17            C          7
19            C          8
23            C          9
```

Here's a similar query, only this one uses RANGE instead of ROWS:

```
SELECT keycol, col1,
  COUNT(*) OVER(ORDER BY col1
                RANGE BETWEEN UNBOUNDED PRECEDING
                          AND CURRENT ROW) AS cnt
FROM dbo.T1;

keycol      col1       cnt
----------- ---------- -----------
2           A          2
3           A          2
5           B          5
7           B          5
11          B          5
13          C          9
17          C          9
19          C          9
23          C          9
```

With RANGE, when the upper bound is CURRENT_ROW, by default peers are included. Even though the terminology is CURRENT ROW, it actually means *current ordering value*. Conceptually, expressed as a predicate, it means *<window_row>.ordermonth <= <current_row>.ordermonth*.

Window Frame Exclusion Window functions in standard SQL support an option called *window frame exclusion* that is part of the framing specification. This option controls whether to include the current row and its peers in case of ties in the ordering element's values. SQL Server 2012 doesn't support this option.

The standard supports four window frame exclusion possibilities, listed here with a short description:

- **EXCLUDE CURRENT ROW** Exclude the current row.

- **EXCLUDE GROUP** Exclude the current row as well as its peers.

- **EXCLUDE TIES** Keep the current row, but exclude its peers.

- **EXCLUDE NO OTHERS (default)** Don't exclude any further rows.

Note that the window frame exclusion option can only further remove rows from the frame; it won't return a row if the previous framing options (window frame unit and window frame extent) removed it.

I'll use the table T1 created and populated with the code provided earlier in Listing 2-1 to demonstrate the concept of window frame exclusion through examples. Following are four queries with the different window frame exclusion possibilities, each followed by what would be its desired output (according to my interpretation of the standard, because this code is not supported by SQL Server 2012 or any other platform that I know of):

```
-- EXCLUDE NO OTHERS (don't exclude rows)
SELECT keycol, col1,
  COUNT(*) OVER(ORDER BY col1
                ROWS BETWEEN UNBOUNDED PRECEDING
                        AND CURRENT ROW
                EXCLUDE NO OTHERS) AS cnt
FROM dbo.T1;

keycol      col1       cnt
----------- ---------- -----------
2           A          1
3           A          2
5           B          3
7           B          4
11          B          5
13          C          6
17          C          7
19          C          8
23          C          9


-- EXCLUDE CURRENT ROW (exclude cur row)
SELECT keycol, col1,
  COUNT(*) OVER(ORDER BY col1
                ROWS BETWEEN UNBOUNDED PRECEDING
                        AND CURRENT ROW
                EXCLUDE CURRENT ROW) AS cnt
FROM dbo.T1;

keycol      col1       cnt
----------- ---------- -----------
2           A          0
3           A          1
5           B          2
7           B          3
11          B          4
13          C          5
17          C          6
19          C          7
23          C          8


-- EXCLUDE GROUP (exclude cur row, exclude peers)
SELECT keycol, col1,
  COUNT(*) OVER(ORDER BY col1
                ROWS BETWEEN UNBOUNDED PRECEDING
                        AND CURRENT ROW
                EXCLUDE GROUP) AS cnt
FROM dbo.T1;
```

```
keycol      col1       cnt
----------- ---------- -----------
2           A          0
3           A          0
5           B          2
7           B          2
11          B          2
13          C          5
17          C          5
19          C          5
23          C          5


-- EXCLUDE TIES (keep cur row, exclude peers)
SELECT keycol, col1,
  COUNT(*) OVER(ORDER BY col1
                ROWS BETWEEN UNBOUNDED PRECEDING
                         AND CURRENT ROW
                EXCLUDE TIES) AS cnt
FROM dbo.T1;

keycol      col1       cnt
----------- ---------- -----------
2           A          1
3           A          1
5           B          3
7           B          3
11          B          3
13          C          6
17          C          6
19          C          6
23          C          6
```

Further Filtering Ideas

Recall that the various elements in the window specification (partitioning, ordering, and framing) are essentially different filtering options. There are additional filtering needs that the aforementioned options don't address. Some of those needs are addressed by the standard with a clause called FILTER that wasn't implemented in SQL Server 2012. There are also attempts to address other filtering needs with proposals to the standard that I hope will find their way, in some form, to both the standard and SQL Server.

I'll start with the FILTER clause. This is a clause that the standard defines for aggregate functions as a way to filter the set of rows that the aggregate applies to using a predicate. The form of this clause is as follows:

```
<aggregate_function>(<input_expression>) FILTER (WHERE <search_condition>)
```

As an example, the following query calculates the difference between the current quantity and the employee monthly average up to three months before the present date (not the current row's month):

```
SELECT empid, ordermonth, qty,
  qty - AVG(qty)
        FILTER (WHERE ordermonth <= DATEADD(month, -3, CURRENT_TIMESTAMP))
        OVER(PARTITION BY empid) AS diff
FROM Sales.EmpOrders;
```

SQL Server 2012 doesn't support the FILTER clause. In fact, I don't know of any database platform that implements it. If you need such capability, there's a pretty simple workaround—using a CASE expression as input to the aggregate function, like so:

```
<aggregate_function>(CASE WHEN <search_condition> THEN <input_expression> END)
```

Here's the complete query that addresses the last example:

```
SELECT empid, ordermonth, qty,
  qty - AVG(CASE WHEN ordermonth <= DATEADD(month, -3, CURRENT_TIMESTAMP) THEN qty END)
        OVER(PARTITION BY empid) AS diff
FROM Sales.EmpOrders;
```

What is still missing in both the standard (as of SQL:2008) and SQL Server 2012 is the ability to refer to elements from the current row for filtering purposes. This could be applicable to the FILTER clause, to the workaround with the CASE expression, as well as to other filtering concepts.

To demonstrate this need, suppose for a moment that you could refer to an element from the current row by prefixing it with *$current_row*. Then, say you needed to write a query against the Sales.OrderValues view and calculate for each order the difference between the current order value and the employee average for customers other than the current one. You use the following query to achieve this task with the FILTER clause:

```
SELECT orderid, orderdate, empid, custid, val,
  val - AVG(val)
        FILTER (WHERE custid <> $current_row.custid)
        OVER(PARTITION BY empid) AS diff
FROM Sales.OrderValues;
```

And you can use the following query with the CASE expression as an alternative:

```
SELECT orderid, orderdate, empid, custid, val,
  val - AVG(CASE WHEN custid <> $current_row.custid THEN val END)
        OVER(PARTITION BY empid) AS diff
FROM Sales.OrderValues;
```

Again, I'm just inventing stuff now to illustrate what's missing at the moment in the language, so don't try this at home.

Proposals for Enhancements

There are very interesting proposals for additions to the standard to address this need and more. One example is a proposal for a feature the authors refer to as *comparative window functions*. You can find a blog entry by Tom Kyte about this proposal here:

http://tkyte.blogspot.com/2009/11/comparative-window-functions.html

And you can find the actual proposal document here:

*http://asktom.oracle.com/pls/asktom/z?p_url=ASKTOM%2Edownload_file%3Fp_*
file%3D7575682831744048130&p_cat=comparative_window_fns_proposal.pdf

The concept of comparative window functions looks interesting. It's pretty straightforward and solves the need to refer to elements from the current row. But what's really going to get your brain working is an insanely cool proposal to the standard called *row pattern recognition*, which addresses the need to refer to elements from the current row, and so much more.

The concept allows for identifying patterns in sequences of rows using semantics based on regular expressions. The idea can be applied to define a table expression, as well as to filter rows in a window specification. It can be used for streaming technologies that work with a stream of moving data, such as SQL Server's StreamInsight, but also with queries that work with nonmoving data, or data at rest. Here is a link to a publicly available document:

http://www.softwareworkshop.com/h2/SQL-RPR-review-paper.pdf

Before you read this document, I suggest you make sure you have a clear mind and, say, a gallon thermos full of coffee (caffeinated). It's not an easy read, but it's a very, very interesting idea that I sure hope will find its way into the standard and into SQL Server, with support also for data at rest and not just moving data.

Distinct Aggregates

SQL Server 2012 doesn't support using the DISTINCT option with window aggregate functions. For example, suppose that you need to query the Sales.OrderValues view and return with each order the number of distinct customers that were handled by the current employee up to, and including, the current date. What you want to run is the following query:

```
SELECT empid, orderdate, orderid, val,
  COUNT(DISTINCT custid) OVER(PARTITION BY empid
                              ORDER BY orderdate) AS numcusts
FROM Sales.OrderValues;
```

But because this query is not supported, you need a workaround. One way to address this need is with the help of the ROW_NUMBER function. I will describe this function in more detail later in this chapter. For now, it suffices to say that it returns a unique integer for each row in the partition, starting with 1 and incrementing by 1 based on the window ordering specification. Using the ROW_NUMBER function, you can assign row numbers partitioned by *empid* and *custid*, and ordered by *orderdate*. This means that the rows marked with row number 1 represent the first occurrence of a customer for each employee based on order-date ordering. Using a CASE expression, you can return the *custid* value only when the row number is equal to 1 and use NULL otherwise. Here's a query implementing the logic described so far, followed by an abbreviated form of its output:

```
SELECT empid, orderdate, orderid, custid, val,
  CASE
    WHEN ROW_NUMBER() OVER(PARTITION BY empid, custid
                           ORDER BY orderdate) = 1
      THEN custid
  END AS distinct_custid
FROM Sales.OrderValues;
```

empid	orderdate	orderid	custid	val	distinct_custid
1	2006-07-17 00:00:00.000	10258	20	1614.88	20
1	2006-08-01 00:00:00.000	10270	87	1376.00	87
1	2006-08-07 00:00:00.000	10275	49	291.84	49
1	2006-08-20 00:00:00.000	10285	63	1743.36	63
1	2006-08-28 00:00:00.000	10292	81	1296.00	81
1	2006-08-29 00:00:00.000	10293	80	848.70	80
1	2006-09-12 00:00:00.000	10304	80	954.40	NULL
1	2006-09-16 00:00:00.000	10306	69	498.50	69
1	2006-09-20 00:00:00.000	10311	18	268.80	18
1	2006-09-25 00:00:00.000	10314	65	2094.30	65
1	2006-09-27 00:00:00.000	10316	65	2835.00	NULL
1	2006-10-09 00:00:00.000	10325	39	1497.00	39
1	2006-10-29 00:00:00.000	10340	9	2436.18	9
1	2006-11-11 00:00:00.000	10351	20	5398.73	NULL
1	2006-11-19 00:00:00.000	10357	46	1167.68	46
1	2006-11-22 00:00:00.000	10361	63	2046.24	NULL
1	2006-11-26 00:00:00.000	10364	19	950.00	19
1	2006-12-03 00:00:00.000	10371	41	72.96	41
1	2006-12-05 00:00:00.000	10374	91	459.00	91
1	2006-12-09 00:00:00.000	10377	72	863.60	72
1	2006-12-09 00:00:00.000	10376	51	399.00	51
1	2006-12-17 00:00:00.000	10385	75	691.20	75
1	2006-12-18 00:00:00.000	10387	70	1058.40	70
1	2006-12-25 00:00:00.000	10393	71	2556.95	71
1	2006-12-25 00:00:00.000	10394	36	442.00	36
1	2006-12-27 00:00:00.000	10396	25	1903.80	25
1	2007-01-01 00:00:00.000	10400	19	3063.00	NULL
1	2007-01-01 00:00:00.000	10401	65	3868.60	NULL

. . .

Observe that only the first occurrence of each *custid* value for each employee based on order-date ordering is returned, and NULLs are returned instead of the subsequent occurrences. The next step is to define a CTE based on the previous query, and then apply a running count aggregate to the result of the CASE expression, like so:

```
WITH C AS
(
  SELECT empid, orderdate, orderid, custid, val,
    CASE
      WHEN ROW_NUMBER() OVER(PARTITION BY empid, custid
                             ORDER BY orderdate) = 1
        THEN custid
    END AS distinct_custid
  FROM Sales.OrderValues
)
SELECT empid, orderdate, orderid, val,
  COUNT(distinct_custid) OVER(PARTITION BY empid
                              ORDER BY orderdate) AS numcusts
FROM C;
```

```
empid  orderdate                orderid   val       numcusts
------ ----------------------   --------  --------  ---------
1      2006-07-17 00:00:00.000  10258     1614.88   1
1      2006-08-01 00:00:00.000  10270     1376.00   2
1      2006-08-07 00:00:00.000  10275     291.84    3
1      2006-08-20 00:00:00.000  10285     1743.36   4
1      2006-08-28 00:00:00.000  10292     1296.00   5
1      2006-08-29 00:00:00.000  10293     848.70    6
1      2006-09-12 00:00:00.000  10304     954.40    6
1      2006-09-16 00:00:00.000  10306     498.50    7
1      2006-09-20 00:00:00.000  10311     268.80    8
1      2006-09-25 00:00:00.000  10314     2094.30   9
1      2006-09-27 00:00:00.000  10316     2835.00   9
1      2006-10-09 00:00:00.000  10325     1497.00   10
1      2006-10-29 00:00:00.000  10340     2436.18   11
1      2006-11-11 00:00:00.000  10351     5398.73   11
1      2006-11-19 00:00:00.000  10357     1167.68   12
1      2006-11-22 00:00:00.000  10361     2046.24   12
1      2006-11-26 00:00:00.000  10364     950.00    13
1      2006-12-03 00:00:00.000  10371     72.96     14
1      2006-12-05 00:00:00.000  10374     459.00    15
1      2006-12-09 00:00:00.000  10377     863.60    17
1      2006-12-09 00:00:00.000  10376     399.00    17
1      2006-12-17 00:00:00.000  10385     691.20    18
1      2006-12-18 00:00:00.000  10387     1058.40   19
1      2006-12-25 00:00:00.000  10393     2556.95   21
1      2006-12-25 00:00:00.000  10394     442.00    21
1      2006-12-27 00:00:00.000  10396     1903.80   22
1      2007-01-01 00:00:00.000  10400     3063.00   22
1      2007-01-01 00:00:00.000  10401     3868.60   22
...
```

Nested Aggregates

By now, you know that there are grouped aggregates and window aggregates. As mentioned, the functions themselves are the same, but the context is different. Grouped aggregates operate on groups of rows defined by the GROUP BY clause and return one value per group. Window aggregates operate on windows of rows and return one value for each row in the underlying query. Recall the discussion about logical query processing from Chapter 1. As a reminder, here's the order in which the various query clauses are conceptually evaluated:

1. FROM

2. WHERE

3. GROUP BY

4. HAVING

5. SELECT

6. ORDER BY

Grouped aggregates are used when the query is a grouped query, and they are allowed in phases that are evaluated after the groups have been defined—namely, from phase 4 and on. Keep in mind that each group is represented by only one row in the result. Window aggregates are allowed from phase 5 and on because they are supposed to operate on rows from the underlying query—after the HAVING phase.

The two types of aggregates—even though they share the same function names and calculation logic—operate in different contexts. And to the point I want to make in this section: What if you want to sum a value grouped by employee ID and, at the same time, aggregate those sums across all employees?

It's perfectly valid, albeit strange at first sight, to apply a window aggregate to a window that contains rows with attributes produced by grouped aggregates. I say strange because at first sight an expression like *SUM(SUM(val))* in a query usually doesn't seem right. But it could very well be. Consider the following query, which addresses the task at hand, followed by its output:

```
SELECT empid,
  SUM(val) AS emptotal,
  SUM(val) / SUM(SUM(val)) OVER() * 100. AS pct
FROM Sales.OrderValues
GROUP BY empid;

empid   emptotal    pct
------  ----------  -----------
3       202812.88   16.022500
6       73913.15    5.839200
9       77308.08    6.107400
7       124568.24   9.841100
1       192107.65   15.176800
4       232890.87   18.398800
2       166537.76   13.156700
5       68792.30    5.434700
8       126862.29   10.022300
```

To distinguish between the two types of aggregates, the grouped SUM aggregate is italicized, and the window SUM aggregate is bolded. The grouped aggregate *SUM(val)* calculates the total values of all orders for each employee. This means that the result of the underlying query has a row for each employee, with that total. Then the window aggregate calculates the total of all employee totals—in other words, the grand total—and divides the grouped aggregate by the window aggregate to calculate the percentage of the employee total out of the grand total.

It can be easier to see the logic behind the nested aggregates if you think of the query in two steps. The first step calculates the grouped aggregate, like so:

```
SELECT empid,
  SUM(val) AS emptotal
FROM Sales.OrderValues
GROUP BY empid;
```

```
empid  emptotal
------ -----------
3      202812.88
6      73913.15
9      77308.08
7      124568.24
1      192107.65
4      232890.87
2      166537.76
5      68792.30
8      126862.29
```

You can think of this result as being the starting point for further window aggregation. So you can apply a window SUM aggregate to the expression that the alias *emptotal* represents. Unfortunately, you cannot apply it directly to the alias for reasons discussed in Chapter 1. (Remember the all-at-once concept?) But you can apply it to the underlying expression, as in *SUM(SUM(val)) OVER(...)*, and in your mind think of it as *SUM(emptotal) OVER(...)*. And thus, you get the following:

```
SELECT empid,
  SUM(val) AS emptotal,
  SUM(val) / SUM(SUM(val)) OVER() * 100. AS pct
FROM Sales.OrderValues
GROUP BY empid;
```

Note that you can avoid the complexity of direct nesting of aggregates by using table expressions such as CTEs. You can define a CTE based on the query that computes the grouped aggregate and have the outer query compute the windowed aggregate, like so:

```
WITH C AS
(
  SELECT empid,
    SUM(val) AS emptotal
  FROM Sales.OrderValues
  GROUP BY empid
)
SELECT empid, emptotal,
  emptotal / SUM(emptotal) OVER() * 100. AS pct
FROM C;
```

Consider another example for complexities related to windowed and grouped functions. You get a request that is a variation of an earlier request in this chapter. Query the Sales.Orders table, and return for each employee the distinct order dates, along with the count of distinct customers handled by the current employee up to, and including, the current date. You make the following attempt:

```
WITH C AS
(
  SELECT empid, orderdate,
    CASE
      WHEN ROW_NUMBER() OVER(PARTITION BY empid, custid
                             ORDER BY orderdate) = 1
        THEN custid
    END AS distinct_custid
  FROM Sales.Orders
)
SELECT empid, orderdate,
  COUNT(distinct_custid) OVER(PARTITION BY empid
                              ORDER BY orderdate) AS numcusts
FROM C
GROUP BY empid, orderdate;
```

But when you run this query, you get the following error:

```
Msg 8120, Level 16, State 1, Line 12
Column 'C.distinct_custid' is invalid in the select list because it is not contained in either
an aggregate function or the GROUP BY clause.
```

The outer COUNT isn't a grouped aggregate; rather, it's a window aggregate. As such, it can operate only on elements that would have been valid if they were specified alone—namely, not as input to the window aggregate. Now ask yourself, absent the window aggregate, is the following a valid query (with the CTE definition removed for brevity)?

```
SELECT empid, orderdate, distinct_custid
FROM C
GROUP BY empid, orderdate;
```

It's clear that the answer is no. The attribute *distinct_custid* is invalid in the select list because it is not contained in either an aggregate function or the GROUP BY clause, which is pretty much what the error message says. What you need to do is apply a window SUM aggregate with a frame implementing a running total concept to a grouped COUNT aggregate that counts distinct occurrences, like so:

```
WITH C AS
(
  SELECT empid, orderdate,
    CASE
      WHEN ROW_NUMBER() OVER(PARTITION BY empid, custid
                             ORDER BY orderdate) = 1
        THEN custid
    END AS distinct_custid
  FROM Sales.Orders
)
SELECT empid, orderdate,
  SUM(COUNT(distinct_custid)) OVER(PARTITION BY empid
                                   ORDER BY orderdate) AS numcusts
FROM C
GROUP BY empid, orderdate;
```

```
empid       orderdate                numcusts
----------- ------------------------ -----------
1           2006-07-17 00:00:00.000  1
1           2006-08-01 00:00:00.000  2
1           2006-08-07 00:00:00.000  3
1           2006-08-20 00:00:00.000  4
1           2006-08-28 00:00:00.000  5
1           2006-08-29 00:00:00.000  6
1           2006-09-12 00:00:00.000  6
1           2006-09-16 00:00:00.000  7
1           2006-09-20 00:00:00.000  8
1           2006-09-25 00:00:00.000  9
1           2006-09-27 00:00:00.000  9
1           2006-10-09 00:00:00.000  10
1           2006-10-29 00:00:00.000  11
1           2006-11-11 00:00:00.000  11
1           2006-11-19 00:00:00.000  12
1           2006-11-22 00:00:00.000  12
1           2006-11-26 00:00:00.000  13
1           2006-12-03 00:00:00.000  14
1           2006-12-05 00:00:00.000  15
1           2006-12-09 00:00:00.000  17
1           2006-12-17 00:00:00.000  18
1           2006-12-18 00:00:00.000  19
1           2006-12-25 00:00:00.000  21
1           2006-12-27 00:00:00.000  22
1           2007-01-01 00:00:00.000  22
...
```

Of course, this is not the only way to achieve this desired result, but the point was to illustrate examples for the concept of nesting a grouped aggregate within a window aggregate. Remember that according to logical query processing, window functions are evaluated in the SELECT or ORDER BY phase—after the GROUP BY phase. For this reason, grouped aggregates are visible as input expressions to window aggregates. Also recall that if the code becomes complex to follow, you can always use table expressions to avoid nesting the functions directly, and in this way make the code more readable.

Ranking Functions

The standard supports four window functions that deal with ranking calculations. Those are ROW_NUMBER, NTILE, RANK, and DENSE_RANK. The standard covers the first two as one category and the last two as another, probably due to determinism-related differences. I will provide more details shortly when describing the functions.

SQL Server 2005 already introduced full support for ranking functions. Still, I will show alternative standard, set-based methods to achieve the same result for two reasons: one, because it can be an interesting exercise; two, I believe that it can help you understand the functions and their subtleties better. Note, though, that in practice it is strongly recommended that you stick to using the window functions because they are both much simpler and more efficient than the alternatives. I will get to the optimization details in Chapter 4.

Supported Windowing Elements

All four ranking functions support an optional window partition clause and a mandatory window order clause. If a window partition clause is not specified, the entire result set of the underlying query (recall the input to the SELECT phase) is considered one partition. As for the window ordering clause, it provides the ordering meaning for the calculation. As you can imagine, ranking rows without defining ordering has little meaning. For ranking window functions, ordering serves a different purpose than it does for functions that support framing, such as aggregate window functions. With the former, ordering is what gives logical meaning to the calculation itself. With the latter, ordering is tied to framing—namely, it serves a filtering purpose.

ROW_NUMBER

The ROW_NUMBER function computes a sequential row number starting with 1 within the respective window partition, based on the specified window ordering. Consider as an example the query in Listing 2-2.

LISTING 2-2 Query with ROW_NUMBER Function

```
SELECT orderid, val,
  ROW_NUMBER() OVER(ORDER BY orderid) AS rownum
FROM Sales.OrderValues;
```

Here's an abbreviated form of the output of this query:

```
orderid   val       rownum
--------  --------  -------
10248     440.00    1
10249     1863.40   2
10250     1552.60   3
10251     654.06    4
10252     3597.90   5
10253     1444.80   6
10254     556.62    7
10255     2490.50   8
10256     517.80    9
10257     1119.90   10
...
```

This calculation probably seems like a trivial thing, but there are a few important things to note here.

Because this query doesn't have a presentation ORDER BY clause, presentation ordering is not guaranteed. Therefore, you should consider presentation ordering here as arbitrary. In practice, SQL Server optimizes the query with the knowledge that absent a presentation ORDER BY clause, it can return the rows in any order. If you need to guarantee presentation ordering, make sure you add a presentation ORDER BY clause. If you want presentation ordering to be based on the calculated row number, you can specify the alias you assigned to the calculation in the presentation ORDER BY clause, like so:

```
SELECT orderid, val,
  ROW_NUMBER() OVER(ORDER BY orderid) AS rownum
FROM Sales.OrderValues
ORDER BY rownum;
```

But think of the row number calculation as simply generating another attribute in the result set of the query. Of course, if you like, you can have presentation ordering that is different than the window ordering, as in the following query:

```
SELECT orderid, val,
  ROW_NUMBER() OVER(ORDER BY orderid) AS rownum
FROM Sales.OrderValues
ORDER BY val DESC;
```

```
orderid  val        rownum
-------- ---------- -------
10865    16387.50   618
10981    15810.00   734
11030    12615.05   783
10889    11380.00   642
10417    11188.40   170
10817    10952.85   570
10897    10835.24   650
10479    10495.60   232
10540    10191.70   293
10691    10164.80   444
...
```

You can use the COUNT window aggregate to produce a calculation that is logically equivalent to the ROW_NUMBER function. Let *WPO* be the window partitioning and ordering specification used by a ROW_NUMBER function. Then ROW_NUMBER OVER WPO is equivalent to COUNT(*) OVER(WPO ROWS UNBOUNDED PRECEDING). As an example, following is a logical equivalent to the query presented earlier in Listing 2-2:

```
SELECT orderid, val,
  COUNT(*) OVER(ORDER BY orderid
               ROWS UNBOUNDED PRECEDING) AS rownum
FROM Sales.OrderValues;
```

As mentioned, it could be a good exercise to try and come up with alternatives to the use of window functions, never mind that the alternatives will tend to be more complicated and less efficient. With the ROW_NUMBER function being the focus at the moment, here's a set-based, standard alternative to the query in Listing 2-2 that doesn't use window functions:

```
SELECT orderid, val,
  (SELECT COUNT(*)
   FROM Sales.OrderValues AS O2
   WHERE O2.orderid <= O1.orderid) AS rownum
FROM Sales.OrderValues AS O1;
```

This alternative uses a COUNT aggregate in a subquery to count how many rows have an ordering value (*orderid* in our case) that is less than or equal to the current one. It's fairly simple when you have unique ordering that is based on a single attribute. Things can get tricky, though, when the ordering isn't unique, as I will demonstrate shortly when discussing determinism.

Determinism

When the window ordering is unique, as in the query in Listing 2-2, the ROW_NUMBER calculation is deterministic. This means that the query has only one correct result; hence, if you run it again without changing the input, you're guaranteed to get repeatable results. But if the window ordering isn't unique, the calculation is nondeterministic. The ROW_NUMBER function generates unique row numbers within the partition, even for rows with the same values in the window ordering attributes. Consider the following query as an example, which is followed by an abbreviated form of its output:

```
SELECT orderid, orderdate, val,
  ROW_NUMBER() OVER(ORDER BY orderdate DESC) AS rownum
FROM Sales.OrderValues;
```

```
orderid  orderdate               val       rownum
-------- ----------------------- --------  -------
11074    2008-05-06 00:00:00.000 232.09    1
11075    2008-05-06 00:00:00.000 498.10    2
11076    2008-05-06 00:00:00.000 792.75    3
11077    2008-05-06 00:00:00.000 1255.72   4
11070    2008-05-05 00:00:00.000 1629.98   5
11071    2008-05-05 00:00:00.000 484.50    6
11072    2008-05-05 00:00:00.000 5218.00   7
11073    2008-05-05 00:00:00.000 300.00    8
11067    2008-05-04 00:00:00.000 86.85     9
11068    2008-05-04 00:00:00.000 2027.08   10
...
```

Because the *orderdate* attribute isn't unique, the ordering among rows with the same *orderdate* value should be considered arbitrary. Technically, there's more than one correct result for this query. Take the four rows with the order date 2008-05-06 as an example. Any arrangement of the row numbers 1 through 4 in those rows is considered valid. So if you run the query again, technically you can get a different arrangement than the current one—never mind the likelihood for this to happen due to implementation-specific aspects in SQL Server (optimization).

If you need to guarantee repeatable results, you need to make the query deterministic. This can be achieved by adding a tiebreaker to the window ordering specification, making it unique within the partition. As an example, the following query achieves unique window ordering by adding *orderid* *DESC* to the list, like so:

```
SELECT orderid, orderdate, val,
  ROW_NUMBER() OVER(ORDER BY orderdate DESC, orderid DESC) AS rownum
FROM Sales.OrderValues;
```

```
orderid  orderdate               val      rownum
-------- ----------------------- -------- -------
11077    2008-05-06 00:00:00.000 1255.72  1
11076    2008-05-06 00:00:00.000 792.75   2
11075    2008-05-06 00:00:00.000 498.10   3
11074    2008-05-06 00:00:00.000 232.09   4
11073    2008-05-05 00:00:00.000 300.00   5
11072    2008-05-05 00:00:00.000 5218.00  6
11071    2008-05-05 00:00:00.000 484.50   7
11070    2008-05-05 00:00:00.000 1629.98  8
11069    2008-05-04 00:00:00.000 360.00   9
11068    2008-05-04 00:00:00.000 2027.08  10
...
```

With window functions, calculating row numbers in a deterministic way is a simple thing. Trying to achieve the equivalent without window functions is trickier but doable:

```
SELECT orderdate, orderid, val,
  (SELECT COUNT(*)
   FROM Sales.OrderValues AS O2
   WHERE O2.orderdate >= O1.orderdate
     AND (O2.orderdate > O1.orderdate
          OR O2.orderid >= O1.orderid)) AS rownum
FROM Sales.OrderValues AS O1;
```

Back to the ROW_NUMBER function: you saw that it can be used to create nondeterministic calculations when using nonunique ordering. So nondeterminism is allowed, but what's strange is that it's not allowed entirely. What I mean by this is that the ORDER BY clause is mandatory. But what if you just want to produce unique row numbers within the partition, in no particular order? You want to issue a query such as this:

```
SELECT orderid, orderdate, val,
  ROW_NUMBER() OVER() AS rownum
FROM Sales.OrderValues;
```

But as mentioned, the ORDER BY clause is mandatory in ranking functions, and SQL Server will produce an error:

```
Msg 4112, Level 15, State 1, Line 2
The function 'ROW_NUMBER' must have an OVER clause with ORDER BY.
```

You can try to be smart and specify a constant in the ORDER BY list, like so:

```
SELECT orderid, orderdate, val,
  ROW_NUMBER() OVER(ORDER BY NULL) AS rownum
FROM Sales.OrderValues;
```

But then SQL Server will complain and generate the following error:

```
Msg 5309, Level 16, State 1, Line 2
Windowed functions and NEXT VALUE FOR functions do not support constants as ORDER BY clause
expressions.
```

A solution exists, though, and I will present it shortly (after the "OVER Clause and Sequences" sidebar).

OVER Clause and Sequences

You might wonder what the relevance is of the NEXT VALUE FOR function in the error message you get when attempting to use a constant in the OVER clause. It's related to SQL Server 2012's extended support for sequences compared to standard SQL. A sequence is an object in the database used to autogenerate numbers, often to be used as keys. Here's an example for code creating a sequence object called dbo.Seq1:

```
CREATE SEQUENCE dbo.Seq1 AS INT START WITH 1 INCREMENT BY 1;
```

You use the NEXT VALUE FOR function to obtain new values from the sequence. Here's an example:

```
SELECT NEXT VALUE FOR dbo.Seq1;
```

You can invoke this function as part of a query that returns multiple rows, like so:

```
SELECT orderid, orderdate, val,
  NEXT VALUE FOR dbo.Seq1 AS seqval
FROM Sales.OrderValues;
```

This code is standard. SQL Server 2012 extends the capabilities of the NEXT VALUE FOR function, thereby allowing you to provide ordering specification in an OVER clause similar to the one used by window functions. This way, you can provide a guarantee that the sequence values reflect the desired ordering. Here's an example using the extended NEXT VALUE FOR function:

```
SELECT orderid, orderdate, val,
  NEXT VALUE FOR dbo.Seq1 OVER(ORDER BY orderdate, orderid) AS seqval
FROM Sales.OrderValues;
```

The same aspects of determinism apply to the OVER clause of the NEXT VALUE FOR function as they do to window functions.

So there's no direct way to get row numbers without ordering, but apparently SQL Server seems to be happy when given a subquery returning a constant as a window ordering element. Here's an example:

```
SELECT orderid, orderdate, val,
  ROW_NUMBER() OVER(ORDER BY (SELECT NULL)) AS rownum
FROM Sales.OrderValues;

orderid  orderdate                val       rownum
-------- ----------------------- --------- -------
10248    2006-07-04 00:00:00.000 440.00    1
10249    2006-07-05 00:00:00.000 1863.40   2
10250    2006-07-08 00:00:00.000 1552.60   3
10251    2006-07-08 00:00:00.000 654.06    4
```

```
10252   2006-07-09 00:00:00.000 3597.90  5
10253   2006-07-10 00:00:00.000 1444.80  6
10254   2006-07-11 00:00:00.000 556.62   7
10255   2006-07-12 00:00:00.000 2490.50  8
10256   2006-07-15 00:00:00.000 517.80   9
10257   2006-07-16 00:00:00.000 1119.90  10
...
```

I'll provide more detail about this form in Chapter 4 when discussing the optimization of window functions.

NTILE

The NTILE function allows you to arrange the rows within the window partition in roughly equally sized tiles, based on the input number of tiles and specified window ordering. For example, suppose that you want to arrange the rows from the OrderValues view in 10 equally sized tiles based on *val* ordering. There are 830 rows in the view; hence, with 10 requested tiles, the tile size is 83 (that's 830 divided by 10). So the first 83 rows (the first tenth) based on *val* ordering will be assigned with tile number 1, the next 83 with tile number 2, and so on. Here's a query calculating both row numbers and tile numbers, followed by an abbreviated form of its output:

```
SELECT orderid, val,
  ROW_NUMBER() OVER(ORDER BY val) AS rownum,
  NTILE(10) OVER(ORDER BY val) AS tile
FROM Sales.OrderValues;
```

```
orderid  val       rownum  tile
-------- --------- ------- -----
10782    12.50     1       1
10807    18.40     2       1
10586    23.80     3       1
10767    28.00     4       1
10898    30.00     5       1
...
...
10708    180.40    78      1
10476    180.48    79      1
10313    182.40    80      1
10810    187.00    81      1
11065    189.42    82      1
10496    190.00    83      1
10793    191.10    84      2
10428    192.00    85      2
10520    200.00    86      2
11040    200.00    87      2
11043    210.00    88      2
...
...
10417    11188.40  826     10
10889    11380.00  827     10
11030    12615.05  828     10
10981    15810.00  829     10
10865    16387.50  830     10
```

In case you're thinking that tiling is similar to paging, let me warn you not to confuse the two. With paging, the page size is a constant and the number of pages is dynamic—it's a result of the count of rows in the query result set divided by the page size. With tiling, the number of tiles is a constant, and the tile size is dynamic—it's a result of the count of rows divided by the requested number of tiles. It's obvious what the uses for paging are. Tiling is usually used for analytical purposes—ones that involve the need to distribute data to a predetermined, equally sized number of buckets based on some measure ordering.

Back to the result of the query that calculates both row numbers and tile numbers: as you can see, the two are closely related. In fact, you could think of a tile number as a calculation that is based on a row number. Recall from the previous section that if the window ordering is not unique, the ROW_NUMBER function is nondeterministic. If tiling is a calculation that is conceptually based on row numbers, this means that the NTILE calculation is also nondeterministic if the window ordering is nonunique. This means that there can be multiple correct results for a given query. Another way to look at it is that two rows with the same ordering values can end up with different tile numbers. If you need to guarantee determinism, you can follow the same recommendation I gave to produce deterministic row numbers—namely, add a tiebreaker to the window ordering, like so:

```
SELECT orderid, val,
  ROW_NUMBER() OVER(ORDER BY val, orderid) AS rownum,
  NTILE(10) OVER(ORDER BY val, orderid) AS tile
FROM Sales.OrderValues;
```

Now the query has only one correct result.

Earlier when describing the NTILE function, I explained that it allows you to arrange the rows within the window partition in *roughly* equally sized tiles. The reason I used the term *roughly* is because the count of rows in the underlying query might not be evenly divisible by the requested number of tiles. For example, suppose that you wanted to arrange the rows from the OrderValues view in 100 tiles. When you divide 830 by 100, you get a quotient of 8 and a remainder of 30. This means that the base tile cardinality is 8, but a subset of the tiles will get an extra row. The NTILE function doesn't attempt to evenly distribute the extra rows across the tiles with even spacing; rather, it adds one row to the first set of tiles until the remainder is gone. With a remainder of 30, the cardinality of the first 30 tiles will be one greater than the base tile cardinality. So the first 30 tiles will have 9 rows and the last 70 tiles will have 8 rows, as the following query shows:

```
SELECT orderid, val,
  ROW_NUMBER() OVER(ORDER BY val, orderid) AS rownum,
  NTILE(100) OVER(ORDER BY val, orderid) AS tile
FROM Sales.OrderValues;
```

```
orderid  val        rownum  tile
-------- ---------- ------- -----
10782    12.50      1       1
10807    18.40      2       1
10586    23.80      3       1
10767    28.00      4       1
10898    30.00      5       1
10900    33.75      6       1
10883    36.00      7       1
```

11051	36.00	8	1
10815	40.00	9	1
10674	45.00	10	2
11057	45.00	11	2
10271	48.00	12	2
10602	48.75	13	2
10422	49.80	14	2
10738	52.35	15	2
10754	55.20	16	2
10631	55.80	17	2
10620	57.50	18	2
10963	57.80	19	3
...			
10816	8446.45	814	98
10353	8593.28	815	99
10514	8623.45	816	99
11032	8902.50	817	99
10424	9194.56	818	99
10372	9210.90	819	99
10515	9921.30	820	99
10691	10164.80	821	99
10540	10191.70	822	99
10479	10495.60	823	100
10897	10835.24	824	100
10817	10952.85	825	100
10417	11188.40	826	100
10889	11380.00	827	100
11030	12615.05	828	100
10981	15810.00	829	100
10865	16387.50	830	100

Continuing our custom, try to come up with an alternative to the NTILE function without using window functions.

I'll show one way to achieve the task. First, here's code that calculates the tile number when given the cardinality, number of tiles, and row number as inputs:

```
DECLARE @cnt AS INT = 830, @numtiles AS INT = 100, @rownum AS INT = 42;

WITH C1 AS
(
  SELECT
    @cnt / @numtiles     AS basetilesize,
    @cnt / @numtiles + 1 AS extendedtilesize,
    @cnt % @numtiles     AS remainder
),
C2 AS
(
  SELECT *, extendedtilesize * remainder AS cutoffrow
  FROM C1
)
SELECT
  CASE WHEN @rownum <= cutoffrow
    THEN (@rownum - 1) / extendedtilesize + 1
    ELSE remainder + ((@rownum - cutoffrow) - 1) / basetilesize + 1
  END AS tile
FROM C2;
```

The calculation is pretty much self-explanatory. For the given inputs, this code returns 5 as the tile number.

Next apply this calculation to the rows from the OrderValues view. Use the COUNT aggregate to get the result set's cardinality instead of the *@cnt* input, and use the logic presented earlier to calculate row numbers without window functions instead of the *@rownum* input, like so:

```
DECLARE @numtiles AS INT = 100;

WITH C1 AS
(
  SELECT
    COUNT(*) / @numtiles AS basetilesize,
    COUNT(*) / @numtiles + 1 AS extendedtilesize,
    COUNT(*) % @numtiles AS remainder
  FROM Sales.OrderValues
),
C2 AS
(
  SELECT *, extendedtilesize * remainder AS cutoffrow
  FROM C1
),
C3 AS
(
  SELECT O1.orderid, O1.val,
    (SELECT COUNT(*)
     FROM Sales.OrderValues AS O2
     WHERE O2.val <= O1.val
       AND (O2.val < O1.val
            OR O2.orderid <= O1.orderid)) AS rownum
  FROM Sales.OrderValues AS O1
)
SELECT C3.*,
  CASE WHEN C3.rownum <= C2.cutoffrow
    THEN (C3.rownum - 1) / C2.extendedtilesize + 1
    ELSE C2.remainder + ((C3.rownum - C2.cutoffrow) - 1) / C2.basetilesize + 1
  END AS tile
FROM C3 CROSS JOIN C2;
```

As usual, don't do this at home! This exercise is a teaching aid; the performance of this technique in SQL Server is horrible compared with that of the NTILE function.

RANK and DENSE_RANK

The RANK and DENSE_RANK functions are calculations similar to the ROW_NUMBER function, only unlike the ROW_NUMBER function they don't have to produce unique values within the window partition. When the window ordering direction is ascending, RANK calculates one more than the number of rows with an ordering value less than the current one in the partition. DENSE_RANK calculates one more than the number of distinct ordering values that are less than the current one in the partition. When the window ordering direction is descending, RANK calculates one more than the number of rows with an ordering value greater than the current one in the partition. DENSE_RANK calculates one more than the number of distinct ordering values greater than the current one in the partition. As an example, here's a query calculating row numbers, rank, and dense rank values, all using the default window partitioning and *orderdate DESC* ordering:

```
SELECT orderid, orderdate, val,
  ROW_NUMBER() OVER(ORDER BY orderdate DESC) AS rownum,
  RANK()       OVER(ORDER BY orderdate DESC) AS rnk,
  DENSE_RANK() OVER(ORDER BY orderdate DESC) AS drnk
FROM Sales.OrderValues;
```

```
orderid  orderdate                val      rownum  rnk  drnk
-------- ------------------------ -------- ------- ---- ----
11077    2008-05-06 00:00:00.000  232.09   1       1    1
11076    2008-05-06 00:00:00.000  498.10   2       1    1
11075    2008-05-06 00:00:00.000  792.75   3       1    1
11074    2008-05-06 00:00:00.000  1255.72  4       1    1
11073    2008-05-05 00:00:00.000  1629.98  5       5    2
11072    2008-05-05 00:00:00.000  484.50   6       5    2
11071    2008-05-05 00:00:00.000  5218.00  7       5    2
11070    2008-05-05 00:00:00.000  300.00   8       5    2
11069    2008-05-04 00:00:00.000  86.85    9       9    3
11068    2008-05-04 00:00:00.000  2027.08  10      9    3
. . .
```

The *orderdate* attribute is not unique. Still, observe that row numbers are unique. The rank and dense rank values aren't unique. All rows with the same order date—for example, 2008-05-05—got the same rank 5 and dense rank 2. *Rank 5* means that there are four rows with greater order dates (notice the ordering direction is descending), and *dense rank 2* means that there's one greater distinct order date.

The alternative to the RANK and DENSE_RANK functions that doesn't use window functions is pretty straightforward:

```
SELECT orderid, orderdate, val,
  (SELECT COUNT(*)
   FROM Sales.OrderValues AS O2
   WHERE O2.orderdate > O1.orderdate) + 1 AS rnk,
  (SELECT COUNT(DISTINCT orderdate)
   FROM Sales.OrderValues AS O2
   WHERE O2.orderdate > O1.orderdate) + 1 AS drnk
FROM Sales.OrderValues AS O1;
```

To calculate rank, you count the number of rows with a greater ordering value (remember, our example uses descending ordering) and add one. To calculate dense rank, you count the distinct greater ordering values and add one.

Determinism

As you might have figured out yourself, both the RANK and DENSE_RANK functions are deterministic by definition. Given the same ordering value—never mind whether they are nonunique—they produce the same ranking value. In fact, the two functions are usually interesting when the ordering is nonunique. When the ordering is unique, both produce the same results as the ROW_NUMBER function.

Distribution Functions

Window distribution functions provide information about the distribution of data and are used mostly for statistical analysis. SQL Server 2012 introduces support for two kinds of window distribution functions: rank distribution and inverse distribution. There are two rank distribution functions: PERCENT_RANK and CUME_DIST. And there are two inverse distribution functions: PERCENTILE_CONT and PERCENTILE_DISC.

In my examples, I will use a table called Scores that holds student test scores. Run the following code to present the contents of the Scores table:

```
SELECT * FROM Stats.Scores;

testid       studentid   score
----------   ----------  -----
Test ABC     Student A   95
Test ABC     Student B   80
Test ABC     Student C   55
Test ABC     Student D   55
Test ABC     Student E   50
Test ABC     Student F   80
Test ABC     Student G   95
Test ABC     Student H   65
Test ABC     Student I   75
Test XYZ     Student A   95
Test XYZ     Student B   80
Test XYZ     Student C   55
Test XYZ     Student D   55
Test XYZ     Student E   50
Test XYZ     Student F   80
Test XYZ     Student G   95
Test XYZ     Student H   65
Test XYZ     Student I   75
Test XYZ     Student J   95
```

Supported Windowing Elements

Window rank distribution functions support an optional window partition clause and a mandatory window order clause. Window inverse distribution functions support an optional window partition clause. There is also ordering relevance to inverse distribution functions, but it's not part of the window specification. Rather, it's in a separate clause called WITHIN GROUP, which I'll describe when I get to the details of the functions.

Rank Distribution Functions

According to standard SQL, distribution functions compute the relative rank of a row in the window partition, expressed as a ratio between 0 and 1—what most of us think of as a percentage. The two variants—PERCENT_RANK and CUME_DIST—perform the computation slightly differently.

Let *rk* be the RANK of the row using the same window specification as the distribution function's window specification.

Let *nr* be the count of rows in the window partition.

Let *np* be the number of rows that precede or are peers of the current one (the same as the minimum *rk* that is greater than the current *rk* minus 1, or *nr* if the current *rk* is the maximum).

Then PERCENT_RANK is calculated as follows: *(rk – 1) / (nr – 1)*. And CUME_DIST is calculated as follows: *np / nr*. The query in Listing 2-3 computes both the percentile rank and cumulative distribution of student test scores, partitioned by *testid* and ordered by *score*.

LISTING 2-3 Query Computing PERCENT_RANK and CUME_DIST

```
SELECT testid, studentid, score,
  PERCENT_RANK() OVER(PARTITION BY testid ORDER BY score) AS percentrank,
  CUME_DIST()    OVER(PARTITION BY testid ORDER BY score) AS cumedist
FROM Stats.Scores;
```

Here is the tabular output resulting from this query:

```
testid      studentid  score percentrank  cumedist
----------  ---------- ----- ------------ ---------
Test ABC    Student E  50    0.000        0.111
Test ABC    Student C  55    0.125        0.333
Test ABC    Student D  55    0.125        0.333
Test ABC    Student H  65    0.375        0.444
Test ABC    Student I  75    0.500        0.556
Test ABC    Student F  80    0.625        0.778
Test ABC    Student B  80    0.625        0.778
Test ABC    Student A  95    0.875        1.000
Test ABC    Student G  95    0.875        1.000
Test XYZ    Student E  50    0.000        0.100
Test XYZ    Student C  55    0.111        0.300
Test XYZ    Student D  55    0.111        0.300
Test XYZ    Student H  65    0.333        0.400
Test XYZ    Student I  75    0.444        0.500
Test XYZ    Student B  80    0.556        0.700
Test XYZ    Student F  80    0.556        0.700
Test XYZ    Student G  95    0.778        1.000
Test XYZ    Student J  95    0.778        1.000
Test XYZ    Student A  95    0.778        1.000
```

The output of this query was formatted for clarity.

Unless you have a statistical background, it's probably hard to make sense of the computations. Loosely speaking, try to think of the percentile rank in our example as indicating the percent of students who have a lower test score than the current score, and think of cumulative distribution as indicating the percentage of students who have a lower score or the same test score as the current score. Just remember that when calculating the two, the divisor in the former case is *(nr – 1)* and in the latter case it's *nr*.

Calculating the percentile rank prior to SQL Server 2012 is pretty straightforward because *rk* can be computed with the RANK window function and *nr* can be calculated with the COUNT window aggregate function—both are available starting with SQL Server 2005. Computing cumulative distribution is a bit trickier because the computation for the current row requires the *rk* value associated with a different row. The computation is supposed to return the minimum *rk* that is greater than the current *rk*, or *nr* if the current *rk* is the maximum one. You can use a correlated subquery to achieve this task.

Here's a query that's compatible with SQL Server 2005 or later, computing both percentile rank and cumulative distribution:

```
WITH C AS
(
  SELECT testid, studentid, score,
    RANK() OVER(PARTITION BY testid ORDER BY score) AS rk,
    COUNT(*) OVER(PARTITION BY testid) AS nr
  FROM Stats.Scores
)
SELECT testid, studentid, score,
  1.0 * (rk - 1) / (nr - 1) AS percentrank,
  1.0 * (SELECT COALESCE(MIN(C2.rk) - 1, C1.nr)
         FROM C AS C2
         WHERE C2.rk > C1.rk) / nr AS cumedist
FROM C AS C1;
```

The reason for multiplying the numeric value 1.0 by the rest of the computation is to force implicit conversion of the integer operands to numeric ones; otherwise, you will get integer division.

As another example, the following query computes the percentile rank and cumulative distribution of employee order counts:

```
SELECT empid, COUNT(*) AS numorders,
  PERCENT_RANK() OVER(ORDER BY COUNT(*)) AS percentrank,
  CUME_DIST() OVER(ORDER BY COUNT(*)) AS cumedist
FROM Sales.Orders
GROUP BY empid;
```

empid	numorders	percentrank	cumedist
5	42	0.000	0.111
9	43	0.125	0.222
6	67	0.250	0.333
7	72	0.375	0.444
2	96	0.500	0.556
8	104	0.625	0.667
1	123	0.750	0.778
3	127	0.875	0.889
4	156	1.000	1.000

Note the mixed use of grouped aggregate functions and window rank distribution functions—that's very similar to the previously discussed mixed use of grouped aggregate functions and window aggregate functions.

Inverse Distribution Functions

Inverse distribution functions, more commonly known as *percentiles*, perform a computation you can think of as the inverse of rank distribution functions. Recall that rank distribution functions compute the relative rank of the current row in the window partition and are expressed as a ratio between 0 and 1 (percent). Inverse distribution functions accept a percentage as input and return the value from the group (or an interpolated value) that this percentage represents. Loosely speaking, given a percentage *p* as input and ordering in the group based on *ordcol*, the returned percentile is the *ordcol* value with respect to which *p* percent of the *ordcol* values are less than it. Perhaps the most known percentile is 0.5 (the fiftieth percentile), more commonly known as the median. As an example, given a group of values 2, 3, 7, 1759, 43112609, the percentile 0.5 is 7.

Recall that rank distribution functions are window functions, and it makes a lot of sense for them to be designed as such. Each row can get a different percentile rank than the others in the same partition. But inverse distribution functions are supposed to accept one input percentage, as well as ordering specification in the group, and compute a single result value per group. So you can see that, in terms of design, it makes more sense for them to be used like grouped functions—that is, apply them to groups in the context of grouped queries. You can do something like this:

```
SELECT groupcol, PERCENTILE_FUNCTION(0.5) WITHIN GROUP(ORDER BY ordcol) AS median
FROM T1
GROUP BY groupcol;
```

Observe the WITHIN GROUP clause, where you define the ordering specification within the group because this is not a window function.

Sure enough, standard SQL defines inverse distribution functions as a type of what they call *an ordered set function*, which is a type of an aggregate function and can be used as grouped aggregate functions. Alas, in SQL Server 2012, inverse distribution functions are actually implemented only as window functions that compute the same result value for all rows in the same partition. The grouped version wasn't implemented.

In this section, I will describe the supported inverse distribution functions and provide a couple of examples for using them as window functions. However, because the more common need is to calculate those per group, I will postpone part of the coverage of the topic, including alternative methods, to Chapter 3, "Ordered Set Functions."

There are two variants of inverse distribution functions: PERCENTILE_DISC and PERCENTILE_CONT.

The PERCENTILE_DISC function (DISC for *discrete distribution model*) returns the first value in the group whose cumulative distribution (see the CUME_DIST function discussed earlier) is greater than or equal to the input, assuming you treat the group as a window partition with the same ordering as that defined within the group. Consider, for example, the query in Listing 2-3 from the previous section calculating the percentile rank and cumulative distribution of student test scores, and its output. Then the function PERCENTILE_DISC(0.5) WITHIN GROUP(ORDER BY score) OVER(PARTITION BY testid) will return the score 75 for test Test ABC because that's the score associated with the cumulative distribution 0.556, which is the first cumulative distribution that is greater than or equal to the input 0.5. Here's the previous output with the relevant row bolded:

```
testid      studentid  score percentrank  cumedist
----------  ---------- ----- ------------ ---------
Test ABC    Student E   50   0.000        0.111
Test ABC    Student C   55   0.125        0.333
Test ABC    Student D   55   0.125        0.333
Test ABC    Student H   65   0.375        0.444
Test ABC    Student I   75   0.500        0.556
Test ABC    Student F   80   0.625        0.778
Test ABC    Student B   80   0.625        0.778
Test ABC    Student A   95   0.875        1.000
Test ABC    Student G   95   0.875        1.000
Test XYZ    Student E   50   0.000        0.100
Test XYZ    Student C   55   0.111        0.300
Test XYZ    Student D   55   0.111        0.300
Test XYZ    Student H   65   0.333        0.400
Test XYZ    Student I   75   0.444        0.500
Test XYZ    Student B   80   0.556        0.700
Test XYZ    Student F   80   0.556        0.700
Test XYZ    Student G   95   0.778        1.000
Test XYZ    Student J   95   0.778        1.000
Test XYZ    Student A   95   0.778        1.000
```

The PERCENTILE_CONT function (CONT for *continuous distribution model*) is a bit trickier to explain. Consider the function PERCENTILE_CONT(@pct) WITHIN GROUP(ORDER BY score).

Let *n* be the count of rows in the group.

Let *a* be *@pct*(n – 1)*, let *i* be the integer part of *a*, and let *f* be the fraction part of *a*.

Let *row0* and *row1* be the rows whose zero-based row numbers are in FLOOR(a), CEILING(a). Here I'm assuming the row numbers are calculated using the same window partitioning and ordering as the group and order of the PERCENTILE_CONT function.

Then PERCENTILE_CONT is computed as *row0.score + f * (row1.score – row0.score)*. This is an interpolation of the values in the two rows assuming continuous distribution (based on the fraction part of *a*).

As a simple, plain-English example, think of a median calculation when there is an even number of rows. You interpolate the values assuming continuous distribution. The interpolated value falls right in the middle between the two middle points, meaning that it's the average of the two middle points.

Here's an example computing the median test scores using both inverse distribution functions as window functions:

```
DECLARE @pct AS FLOAT = 0.5;

SELECT testid, score,
  PERCENTILE_DISC(@pct) WITHIN GROUP(ORDER BY score) OVER(PARTITION BY testid) AS
percentiledisc,
  PERCENTILE_CONT(@pct) WITHIN GROUP(ORDER BY score) OVER(PARTITION BY testid) AS percentilecont
FROM Stats.Scores;
```

```
testid       score percentiledisc percentilecont
----------   ----- -------------- ----------------------
Test ABC     50    75             75
Test ABC     55    75             75
Test ABC     55    75             75
Test ABC     65    75             75
Test ABC     75    75             75
Test ABC     80    75             75
Test ABC     80    75             75
Test ABC     95    75             75
Test ABC     95    75             75
Test XYZ     50    75             77.5
Test XYZ     55    75             77.5
Test XYZ     55    75             77.5
Test XYZ     65    75             77.5
Test XYZ     75    75             77.5
Test XYZ     80    75             77.5
Test XYZ     80    75             77.5
Test XYZ     95    75             77.5
Test XYZ     95    75             77.5
Test XYZ     95    75             77.5
```

Here's another example computing the tenth percentile (0.1):

```
DECLARE @pct AS FLOAT = 0.1;

SELECT testid, score,
  PERCENTILE_DISC(@pct) WITHIN GROUP(ORDER BY score) OVER(PARTITION BY testid) AS
percentiledisc,
  PERCENTILE_CONT(@pct) WITHIN GROUP(ORDER BY score) OVER(PARTITION BY testid) AS percentilecont
FROM Stats.Scores;
```

```
testid       score percentiledisc percentilecont
----------   ----- -------------- ----------------------
Test ABC     50    50             54
Test ABC     55    50             54
Test ABC     55    50             54
Test ABC     65    50             54
Test ABC     75    50             54
Test ABC     80    50             54
Test ABC     80    50             54
Test ABC     95    50             54
Test ABC     95    50             54
Test XYZ     50    50             54.5
Test XYZ     55    50             54.5
Test XYZ     55    50             54.5
Test XYZ     65    50             54.5
Test XYZ     75    50             54.5
Test XYZ     80    50             54.5
Test XYZ     80    50             54.5
Test XYZ     95    50             54.5
Test XYZ     95    50             54.5
Test XYZ     95    50             54.5
```

As mentioned, I will provide more details in Chapter 3 about inverse distribution functions, including alternative methods to calculate those, as part of the discussion about ordered set functions.

Offset Functions

Window offset functions include two categories of functions. One category is functions whose offset is relative to the current row; this category includes the LAG and LEAD functions. Another category is functions whose offset is relative to the start or end of the window frame; this category includes the functions FIRST_VALUE, LAST_VALUE, and NTH_VALUE. SQL Server 2012 supports LAG, LEAD, FIRST_VALUE, and LAST_VALUE, but not NTH_VALUE.

Supported Windowing Elements

The functions in the first category (LAG and LEAD) support a window partition clause as well as a window order clause. The latter is the one that gives meaning to the offset, of course. The functions in the second category (FIRST_VALUE, LAST_VALUE, and NTH_VALUE) also support a window frame clause in addition to the window partition and window order clauses.

LAG and LEAD

The LAG and LEAD functions allow you to return a value expression from a row in the window partition that is in a given offset before (LAG) or after (LEAD) the current row. The default offset if one is not specified is 1.

As an example, the following query returns the current order value for each customer order, as well as the values of the previous and next orders by the same customer:

```
SELECT custid, orderdate, orderid, val,
  LAG(val)  OVER(PARTITION BY custid
                ORDER BY orderdate, orderid) AS prevval,
  LEAD(val) OVER(PARTITION BY custid
                ORDER BY orderdate, orderid) AS nextval
FROM Sales.OrderValues;

custid  orderdate   orderid  val       prevval   nextval
------- ----------- -------- --------- --------- --------
1       2007-08-25  10643    814.50    NULL      878.00
1       2007-10-03  10692    878.00    814.50    330.00
1       2007-10-13  10702    330.00    878.00    845.80
1       2008-01-15  10835    845.80    330.00    471.20
1       2008-03-16  10952    471.20    845.80    933.50
1       2008-04-09  11011    933.50    471.20    NULL
2       2006-09-18  10308    88.80     NULL      479.75
2       2007-08-08  10625    479.75    88.80     320.00
2       2007-11-28  10759    320.00    479.75    514.40
2       2008-03-04  10926    514.40    320.00    NULL
3       2006-11-27  10365    403.20    NULL      749.06
3       2007-04-15  10507    749.06    403.20    1940.85
3       2007-05-13  10535    1940.85   749.06    2082.00
3       2007-06-19  10573    2082.00   1940.85   813.37
3       2007-09-22  10677    813.37    2082.00   375.50
3       2007-09-25  10682    375.50    813.37    660.00
3       2008-01-28  10856    660.00    375.50    NULL
...
```

The output is shown here abbreviated and formatted for clarity.

Because explicit offsets weren't indicated here, the query assumes an offset of 1 by default. Because the functions partition the data by *custid*, the calculations look for relative rows only within the same customer partition. As for the window ordering, what "previous" and "next" mean is determined by *orderdate* ordering, and by *orderid* as a tiebreaker. Observe in the query output that LAG returns NULL for the first row in the window partition because there's no row before the first one and, similarly, LEAD returns NULL for the last row.

If you want to use an offset other than 1, you need to specify it after the input value expression, as in the following query:

```
SELECT custid, orderdate, orderid,
  LAG(val, 3) OVER(PARTITION BY custid
                   ORDER BY orderdate, orderid) AS prev3val
FROM Sales.OrderValues;
```

```
custid  orderdate    orderid  prev3val
-------  -----------  -------  ---------
1        2007-08-25   10643    NULL
1        2007-10-03   10692    NULL
1        2007-10-13   10702    NULL
1        2008-01-15   10835    814.50
1        2008-03-16   10952    878.00
1        2008-04-09   11011    330.00
2        2006-09-18   10308    NULL
2        2007-08-08   10625    NULL
2        2007-11-28   10759    NULL
2        2008-03-04   10926    88.80
3        2006-11-27   10365    NULL
3        2007-04-15   10507    NULL
3        2007-05-13   10535    NULL
3        2007-06-19   10573    403.20
3        2007-09-22   10677    749.06
3        2007-09-25   10682    1940.85
3        2008-01-28   10856    2082.00
...
```

As mentioned, LAG and LEAD return a NULL by default when there's no row in the specified offset. If you want to return something else instead, you can indicate what you want to return as the third argument to the function. For example, *LAG(val, 3, 0.00)* returns the value 0.00 if the row in offset 3 before the current one doesn't exist.

To implement similar calculations with LAG and LEAD prior to SQL Server 2012, you can use the following strategy:

- Write a query that produces row numbers based on the same partitioning and ordering as needed for your calculations, and define a table expression based on this query.

- Join multiple instances of the table expression as needed, representing the current, previous, and next rows.

- In the join predicate, match the partitioning columns of the different instances (current with previous/next). Also in the join predicate, compute the difference between the row numbers of the current and previous/next instances, and filter based on the offset value that you need in your calculations.

Here's a query implementing this approach, returning for each order the current, previous, and next customers' order values:

```
WITH OrdersRN AS
(
  SELECT custid, orderdate, orderid, val,
    ROW_NUMBER() OVER(ORDER BY custid, orderdate, orderid) AS rn
  FROM Sales.OrderValues
)
SELECT C.custid, C.orderdate, C.orderid, C.val,
  P.val AS prevval,
  N.val AS nextval
FROM OrdersRN AS C
  LEFT OUTER JOIN OrdersRN AS P
    ON C.custid = P.custid
    AND C.rn = P.rn + 1
  LEFT OUTER JOIN OrdersRN AS N
    ON C.custid = N.custid
    AND C.rn = N.rn - 1;
```

Of course, you could address this task using simple subqueries as well.

FIRST_VALUE, LAST_VALUE, and NTH_VALUE

In the previous section, I discussed the offset functions LAG and LEAD, which allow you to specify the offset relative to the current row. This section focuses on functions that allow you to indicate the offset relative to the beginning or end of the window frame. These functions are FIRST_VALUE, LAST_VALUE, and NTH_VALUE, the last of which wasn't implemented in SQL Server 2012.

Recall that LAG and LEAD support window partition and window order clauses but not a window frame clause. This makes sense when the offset is relative to the current row. But with functions that specify the offset with respect to the beginning or end of the window, framing also becomes relevant. The FIRST_VALUE and LAST_VALUE functions return the requested value expression from the first and last rows in the frame, respectively. Here's a query demonstrating how to return, along with each customer's order, the current order value as well as the order values from the customer's first and last orders:

```
SELECT custid, orderdate, orderid, val,
  FIRST_VALUE(val) OVER(PARTITION BY custid
                        ORDER BY orderdate, orderid) AS val_firstorder,
  LAST_VALUE(val)  OVER(PARTITION BY custid
                        ORDER BY orderdate, orderid
                        ROWS BETWEEN CURRENT ROW
                             AND UNBOUNDED FOLLOWING) AS val_lastorder
FROM Sales.OrderValues;
```

custid	orderdate	orderid	val	val_firstorder	val_lastorder
1	2007-08-25	10643	814.50	814.50	933.50
1	2007-10-03	10692	878.00	814.50	933.50
1	2007-10-13	10702	330.00	814.50	933.50
1	2008-01-15	10835	845.80	814.50	933.50
1	2008-03-16	10952	471.20	814.50	933.50
1	2008-04-09	11011	933.50	814.50	933.50
2	2006-09-18	10308	88.80	88.80	514.40
2	2007-08-08	10625	479.75	88.80	514.40
2	2007-11-28	10759	320.00	88.80	514.40
2	2008-03-04	10926	514.40	88.80	514.40
3	2006-11-27	10365	403.20	403.20	660.00
3	2007-04-15	10507	749.06	403.20	660.00
3	2007-05-13	10535	1940.85	403.20	660.00
3	2007-06-19	10573	2082.00	403.20	660.00
3	2007-09-22	10677	813.37	403.20	660.00
3	2007-09-25	10682	375.50	403.20	660.00
3	2008-01-28	10856	660.00	403.20	660.00

...

Technically, you're after values from the first and last rows in the partition. With FIRST_VALUE, it's easy because you can simply rely on the default framing. Recall that if framing is applicable and you don't indicate a window frame clause, the default is RANGE BETWEEN UNBOUNDED PRECEDING AND CURRENT ROW. But with LAST_VALUE, you realize that relying on the default framing is pointless because the last row is the current row. Hence, this example uses an explicit frame specification with UNBOUNDED FOLLOWING as the upper boundary point in the frame.

Typically, you would not just return the first or last value along with all detail rows like in the last example; rather, you would apply some calculation involving a detail element and the value returned by the window function. As a simple example, the following query returns, along with each customer's order, the current order value as well as the difference between the current value and the values of the customer's first and last orders:

```
SELECT custid, orderdate, orderid, val,
  val - FIRST_VALUE(val) OVER(PARTITION BY custid
                              ORDER BY orderdate, orderid) AS difffirst,
  val - LAST_VALUE(val)  OVER(PARTITION BY custid
                              ORDER BY orderdate, orderid
                              ROWS BETWEEN CURRENT ROW
                                  AND UNBOUNDED FOLLOWING) AS difflast
FROM Sales.OrderValues;
```

custid	orderdate	orderid	val	difffirst	difflast
1	2007-08-25	10643	814.50	0.00	-119.00
1	2007-10-03	10692	878.00	63.50	-55.50
1	2007-10-13	10702	330.00	-484.50	-603.50
1	2008-01-15	10835	845.80	31.30	-87.70
1	2008-03-16	10952	471.20	-343.30	-462.30
1	2008-04-09	11011	933.50	119.00	0.00
2	2006-09-18	10308	88.80	0.00	-425.60
2	2007-08-08	10625	479.75	390.95	-34.65
2	2007-11-28	10759	320.00	231.20	-194.40

2	2008-03-04	10926	514.40	425.60	0.00
3	2006-11-27	10365	403.20	0.00	-256.80
3	2007-04-15	10507	749.06	345.86	89.06
3	2007-05-13	10535	1940.8	1537.65	1280.85
3	2007-06-19	10573	2082.0	1678.80	1422.00
3	2007-09-22	10677	813.37	410.17	153.37
3	2007-09-25	10682	375.50	-27.70	-284.50
3	2008-01-28	10856	660.00	256.80	0.00
...					

As mentioned, the standard NTH_VALUE function wasn't implemented in SQL Server 2012. What this function allows you to do is ask for a value expression that is in a given offset in terms of a number of rows from the first or last row in the window frame. You specify the offset as a second input in addition to the value expression and FROM FIRST or FROM LAST, depending on whether you need the offset to be relative to the first row or last row in the frame, respectively. For example, the following expression returns the value from the third row from the last in the partition:

```
NTH_VALUE(val, 3) FROM LAST OVER(ROWS BETWEEN CURRENT ROW
                                 AND UNBOUNDED FOLLOWING)
```

Suppose you want to create calculations similar to the FIRST_VALUE, LAST_VALUE, and NTH_VALUE prior to SQL Server 2012. You can achieve this by using constructs such as CTEs, the ROW_NUMBER function, a CASE expression, grouping, and joining, like so:

```
WITH OrdersRN AS
(
  SELECT custid, val,
    ROW_NUMBER() OVER(PARTITION BY custid
                      ORDER BY orderdate, orderid) AS rna,
    ROW_NUMBER() OVER(PARTITION BY custid
                      ORDER BY orderdate DESC, orderid DESC) AS rnd
  FROM Sales.OrderValues
),
Agg AS
(
  SELECT custid,
    MAX(CASE WHEN rna = 1 THEN val END) AS firstorderval,
    MAX(CASE WHEN rnd = 1 THEN val END) AS lastorderval,
    MAX(CASE WHEN rna = 3 THEN val END) AS thirdorderval
  FROM OrdersRN
  GROUP BY custid
)
SELECT O.custid, O.orderdate, O.orderid, O.val,
  A.firstorderval, A.lastorderval, A.thirdorderval
FROM Sales.OrderValues AS O
  JOIN Agg AS A
    ON O.custid = A.custid
ORDER BY custid, orderdate, orderid;
```

custid	orderdate	orderid	val	firstorderval	lastorderval	thirdorderval
1	2007-08-25	10643	814.50	814.50	933.50	330.00
1	2007-10-03	10692	878.00	814.50	933.50	330.00
1	2007-10-13	10702	330.00	814.50	933.50	330.00

1	2008-01-15	10835	845.80	814.50	933.50	330.00
1	2008-03-16	10952	471.20	814.50	933.50	330.00
1	2008-04-09	11011	933.50	814.50	933.50	330.00
2	2006-09-18	10308	88.80	88.80	514.40	320.00
2	2007-08-08	10625	479.75	88.80	514.40	320.00
2	2007-11-28	10759	320.00	88.80	514.40	320.00
2	2008-03-04	10926	514.40	88.80	514.40	320.00
3	2006-11-27	10365	403.20	403.20	660.00	1940.85
3	2007-04-15	10507	749.06	403.20	660.00	1940.85
3	2007-05-13	10535	1940.85	403.20	660.00	1940.85
3	2007-06-19	10573	2082.00	403.20	660.00	1940.85
3	2007-09-22	10677	813.37	403.20	660.00	1940.85
3	2007-09-25	10682	375.50	403.20	660.00	1940.85
3	2008-01-28	10856	660.00	403.20	660.00	1940.85

. . .

In the first CTE, called *OrdersRN*, you define row numbers in both ascending and descending order to mark the positions of the rows with respect to the first and last rows in the partition. In the second CTE, called *Agg*, you use a CASE expression, filter only the interesting row numbers, group the data by the partitioning element (*custid*), and apply an aggregate to the result of the CASE expression to return the requested value for each group. Finally, in the outer query, you join the result of the grouped query with the original table to match the detail with the aggregates.

Summary

This chapter delved into the details of the various window functions, focusing on their logical aspects. I showed both the functionality defined by standard SQL and indicated what SQL Server 2012 supports. In cases where SQL Server 2012 doesn't support certain functionality, I provided supported alternatives.

CHAPTER 3

Ordered Set Functions

Have you ever needed to concatenate elements of a group into one string based on some order? That's a scenario that an ordered set function could help address. An *ordered set function* is a type of aggregate function. What distinguishes it from a general set function (like SUM, MIN, MAX, and so on) is that there's ordering relevance to the calculation, such as the order in which you want to concatenate the elements.

In this chapter, I will discuss ordered set functions and then describe the kinds of solutions they help with. Because they're not yet supported in Microsoft SQL Server, I will show how to simulate them using what's provided in SQL Server 2012.

You use ordered set functions in grouped queries much like you do general set functions. As for syntax, standard SQL defines a special clause called WITHIN GROUP where you indicate the ordering, like so:

```
<ordered set function> WITHIN GROUP ( ORDER BY <sort specification list> )
```

Standard SQL defines two types of ordered set functions with very fancy, yet appropriate, names: hypothetical set functions and inverse distribution functions. When providing the specifics of each type, I will explain why they are called the way they are. Before I get to the details, I want to note that the concept of an ordered set function isn't limited to the two types of functions defined by the standard—rather, it can be extended to any aggregate function that has ordering relevance to the calculation.

As an example, a *string-concatenation* aggregate can let users specify alphabetical ordering as ascending or descending, or it can let them specify some ordering based on an external key. Also, it would be great if SQL Server supported the concept with Common Language Runtime (CLR) user-defined aggregates (UDAs) in the future. If the UDA has ordering relevance to the calculation, naturally Microsoft should follow the standard syntax using the WITHIN GROUP clause.

I'll start the chapter by describing the standard ordered set functions and the alternatives available in SQL Server. Then I'll describe additional calculations that fit the concept but aren't defined by the standard, and, finally, I'll provide information about supported solutions in SQL Server.

Hypothetical Set Functions

Hypothetical set functions include ranking and rank-distribution functions that you're already familiar with as window functions, but they are applied to groups for an input value in a hypothetical manner. I'm sure that this description doesn't make any sense yet, but soon it will.

There are two ranking ordered set functions: RANK and DENSE_RANK. There are also two rank-distribution ordered set functions: PERCENT_RANK and CUME_DIST. There's a difference in the ordering relevance between a window function and an ordered set function. With the former, the ordering is within the window partition, and with the latter, the ordering is within the group. When used as a window function, the current row's ordering value is evaluated with respect to the ordering values in the window partition. When used as an ordered set function, the input value is evaluated with respect to the ordering values in the group. When an ordered set function is given an input value, you're asking "What would be the result of the function for this input value if I added it as another element to the set?" Note that the use of "would be" indicates that this is hypothetical.

This is one of those topics that is best explained through examples, and this chapter provides plenty. I'll start with the RANK function.

RANK

Consider the following query, which uses the RANK window function, and its output, which is shown here in abbreviated form:

```
USE TSQL2012;

SELECT custid, val,
  RANK() OVER(PARTITION BY custid ORDER BY val) AS rnk
FROM Sales.OrderValues;

custid  val       rnk
------- --------  ----
1       330.00    1
1       471.20    2
1       814.50    3
1       845.80    4
1       878.00    5
1       933.50    6
2       88.80     1
2       320.00    2
2       479.75    3
2       514.40    4
3       375.50    1
3       403.20    2
3       660.00    3
3       749.06    4
3       813.37    5
3       1940.85   6
```

```
3    2082.00    7
4     191.10    1
4     228.00    2
4     282.00    3
4     319.20    4
4     390.00    5
4     407.70    6
4     480.00    7
4     491.50    8
4     899.00    9
4    1477.00   10
4    1641.00   11
4    2142.90   12
4    4441.25   13
. . .
```

The function ranks each customer's orders based on the order values. Can you rationalize why the rows that got rank 5, say, got that rank? If you recall from Chapter 2, "A Detailed Look at Window Functions," RANK, when using ascending ordering, calculates one more than the number of rows in the window partition with an ordering value that is less than the current one. Take, for example, customer 3. The row that got rank 5 for customer 3 has the ordering value 813.37. The rank was computed as 5 because there are 4 rows in the same partition with ordering values that are less than 813.37 (375.50, 403.20, 660.00, and 749.06).

Now suppose you want to do a kind of "what if" analysis and ask "How would an input value @val rank in each customer group with respect to the other values in the *val* column?" It's as if you did the following:

1. Considered each customer group as a window partition, with window ordering based on the *val* column.

2. Added a row to each partition with the input value @val.

3. Calculated the RANK window function for that row in each partition.

4. Returned just that row for each partition.

For example, suppose that the input value @val is equal to 1000.00. How would this value rank in each customer group with respect to the other values in the *val* column using ascending ordering? The result would be one more than the number of rows in each customer group that have a value that is less than 1000.00. For example, for customer 3 you should get the rank 6, because there are five rows with values in the *val* column that are less than 1000.00 (375.50, 403.20, 660.00, 749.06, and 813.37).

The standard defines the following form for the RANK ordered set function:

```
RANK(<input>) WITHIN GROUP ( ORDER BY <sort specification list> )
```

And here's how you use it as a grouped aggregate function to address the request at hand (remember this syntax is not supported by SQL Server 2012):

```
DECLARE @val AS NUMERIC(12, 2) = 1000.00;

SELECT custid,
  RANK(@val) WITHIN GROUP(ORDER BY val) AS rnk
FROM Sales.OrderValues
GROUP BY custid;
```

```
custid      rnk
----------- -----------
1           7
2           5
3           6
4           10
5           7
6           8
7           6
8           3
9           9
10          7
...
```

At this point, the concept of an ordered set function should make much more sense to you.

The last example I showed demonstrates the use of the standard RANK ordered set function, but as mentioned, SQL Server doesn't support this syntax. It is quite simple, though, to implement the calculation without a built-in function. Use a CASE expression that returns some constant when the ordering value is less than the input value, and use NULL otherwise (which is the default when an ELSE clause isn't specified). Apply a COUNT aggregate to the result of the CASE expression, and add 1. Here's the complete query:

```
DECLARE @val AS NUMERIC(12, 2) = 1000.00;

SELECT custid,
  COUNT(CASE WHEN val < @val THEN 1 END) + 1 AS rnk
FROM Sales.OrderValues
GROUP BY custid;
```

DENSE_RANK

Recall that DENSE_RANK, as a window function, is similar to RANK, only it returns one more than the number of distinct ordering values (as opposed to number of rows) in the partition that are less than the current one. Similarly, as an ordered set function, given an input value @val, DENSE_RANK returns one more than the number of distinct ordering values in the group that are less than @val. Here's what the code should look like according to the standard (again, this is not supported by SQL Server 2012):

```
DECLARE @val AS NUMERIC(12, 2) = 1000.00;

SELECT custid,
  DENSE_RANK(@val) WITHIN GROUP(ORDER BY val) AS densernk
FROM Sales.OrderValues
GROUP BY custid;

custid      densernk
----------- --------------
1           7
2           5
3           6
4           10
5           7
6           8
7           6
8           3
9           8
10          7
...
```

The alternative that is supported in SQL Server is similar to the technique used to implement RANK. Only instead of returning a constant when the ordering value is less than *@val*, you return *val* and apply a DISTINCT clause to the aggregated expression, like so:

```
DECLARE @val AS NUMERIC(12, 2) = 1000.00;

SELECT custid,
  COUNT(DISTINCT CASE WHEN val < @val THEN val END) + 1 AS densernk
FROM Sales.OrderValues
GROUP BY custid;
```

PERCENT_RANK

Very similar to ranking functions, rank distribution functions, specifically PERCENT_RANK and CUME_DIST, are also supported by the standard as hypothetical set functions. I'll start with PERCENT_RANK in this section and describe CUME_DIST in the next section.

As a reminder, PERCENT_RANK as a window function computes the relative rank of a row in the window partition and expresses it as a ratio between 0 and 1 (a percent). The rank is calculated as follows:

- Let *rk* be the RANK of the row using the same window specification as the distribution function's window specification.

- Let *nr* be the count of rows in the window partition.

- Then PERCENT_RANK is calculated as follows: $(rk - 1) / (nr - 1)$.

Now think in terms of hypothetical set functions. Suppose you want to know for a given input value what its percentile rank would be in each group if it's added to all groups. For example, consider the Scores table, which holds test scores. Given an input test score (call it *@score*), you want to know what the percentile rank of the input score would be in each test if it's added as another score to all tests. According to standard SQL, you use the PERCENT_RANK ordered set function as an aggregate function, like so:

```
DECLARE @score AS TINYINT = 80;

SELECT testid,
  PERCENT_RANK(@score) WITHIN GROUP(ORDER BY score) AS pctrank
FROM Stats.Scores
GROUP BY testid;

testid      pctrank
---------- ---------------
Test ABC   0.556
Test XYZ   0.500
```

To produce a percentile rank as a hypothetical set function in SQL Server, you need your own solution. One option is to generate *rk* and *nr* with COUNT aggregates and then compute the percentile rank as follows: *(rk – 1) / (nr – 1)*. For *rk*, you need to count the number of rows with a lower score than the input. For *nr*, simply count the number of rows and add one (for the input to be taken into consideration as part of the group). Here's the complete solution:

```
DECLARE @score AS TINYINT = 80;

WITH C AS
(
  SELECT testid,
    COUNT(CASE WHEN score < @score THEN 1 END) + 1 AS rk,
    COUNT(*) + 1 AS nr
  FROM Stats.Scores
  GROUP BY testid
)
SELECT testid, 1.0 * (rk - 1) / (nr - 1) AS pctrank
FROM C;
```

CUME_DIST

The CUME_DIST calculation is similar to PERCENT_RANK, only it's calculated slightly differently. As a window function, it is calculated as follows:

- Let *nr* be the count of rows in the window partition.

- Let *np* be the number of rows that precede or are peers of the current one.

- Then CUME_DIST is calculated as follows: *np / nr*.

As a hypothetical set function, CUME_DIST tells you what cumulative distribution an input value would get in each group if it's added to all groups. The standard version of the CUME_DIST function as an ordered set function applied to our Scores scenario looks like this:

```
DECLARE @score AS TINYINT = 80;

SELECT testid,
  CUME_DIST(@score) WITHIN GROUP(ORDER BY score) AS cumedist
FROM Stats.Scores
GROUP BY testid;

testid      cumedist
----------  ------------
Test ABC    0.800
Test XYZ    0.727
```

As for the version supported by SQL Server, it's quite similar to the alternative you used for the PERCENT_RANK function. You compute *np* as the count of rows in the group that have a score that is lower than the input, plus one to account for the input. You compute *nr* as a count of rows in the group, plus one—again, to account for the input. Finally, you compute the cumulative distribution as follows: *np / nr*. Here's the complete solution:

```
DECLARE @score AS TINYINT = 80;

WITH C AS
(
  SELECT testid,
    COUNT(CASE WHEN score <= @score THEN 1 END) + 1 AS np,
    COUNT(*) + 1 AS nr
  FROM Stats.Scores
  GROUP BY testid
)
SELECT testid, 1.0 * np / nr AS cumedist
FROM C;
```

General Solution

Because SQL Server 2012 doesn't support the standard hypothetical set functions, I provided alternative methods to achieve the same calculations. The methods I provided for the different calculations were quite different from one another. In this section, I will present a more generalized solution.

All four unsupported hypothetical set functions have supported window-function counterparts. That is, SQL Server 2012 does support RANK, DENSE_RANK, PERCENT_RANK, and CUME_DIST as window functions. Remember that a hypothetical set function is supposed to return for a given input the result that the corresponding window function would return if the input value was added to the set. With this in mind, you can create a solution that works the same for all calculations. The generalized solution might not be as optimized as the specialized ones, but it is still interesting to see. The steps involved in the solution are as follows:

1. Unify the existing set with the input value.

2. Apply the window function.

3. Filter the row representing the input value to return the result.

Here's the code form of the solution:

```
SELECT <partition_col>, wf AS osf
FROM <partitions_table> AS P
  CROSS APPLY (SELECT <window_function>() OVER(ORDER BY <ord_col>) AS wf, return_flag
               FROM (SELECT <ord_col>, 0 AS return_flag
                     FROM <details_table> AS D
                     WHERE D.<partition_col> = P.<partition_col>

                     UNION ALL

                     SELECT @input_val, 1) AS D) AS A
WHERE return_flag = 1;
```

The outer query is issued against the table holding the distinct partition values. Then with a CROSS APPLY operator, the code handles each partition separately. The innermost-derived table *U* handles the unification of the current partition's rows, which are marked with *return_flag 0*, with a row made of the input value, marked with *return_flag 1*. Then the query against *U* computes the window function, generating the derived table *A*. Finally, the outer query filters only the rows with *return_flag 1*. Those are the rows that have the computation for the input value in each partition; in other words, the hypothetical set calculation.

If this general form isn't clear yet, see if you can follow the logic through specific examples. The following code queries the table Customers (partitions) and the view Sales.OrderValues (details). It calculates both RANK and DENSE_RANK as hypothetical set calculations for an input value *@val*, with *custid* being the partitioning element and *val* being the ordering element:

```
DECLARE @val AS NUMERIC(12, 2) = 1000.00;

SELECT custid, rnk, densernk
FROM Sales.Customers AS P
  CROSS APPLY (SELECT
                  RANK() OVER(ORDER BY val) AS rnk,
                  DENSE_RANK() OVER(ORDER BY val) AS densernk,
                  return_flag
               FROM (SELECT val, 0 AS return_flag
                     FROM Sales.OrderValues AS D
                     WHERE D.custid = P.custid

                     UNION ALL

                     SELECT @val, 1) AS U) AS A
WHERE return_flag = 1;
```

custid	rnk	densernk
1	7	7
2	5	5
3	6	6
4	10	10
5	7	7
6	8	8
7	6	6

```
8            3            3
9            9            8
11           9            9
...
```

Similarly, the following code is issued against the tables Tests (partitions) and Scores (details). It calculates PERCENT_RANK and CUME_DIST as hypothetical set calculations for the input value *@score*, with *testid* being the partitioning element and *score* being the ordering element:

```
DECLARE @score AS TINYINT = 80;

SELECT testid, pctrank, cumedist
FROM Stats.Tests AS P
  CROSS APPLY (SELECT
                 PERCENT_RANK() OVER(ORDER BY score) AS pctrank,
                 CUME_DIST() OVER(ORDER BY score) AS cumedist,
                 return_flag
               FROM (SELECT score, 0 AS return_flag
                     FROM Stats.Scores AS D
                     WHERE D.testid = P.testid

                     UNION ALL

                     SELECT @score, 1) AS U) AS A
WHERE return_flag = 1;
```

```
testid      pctrank                   cumedist
----------  ------------------------  ----------------------
Test ABC    0.555555555555556         0.8
Test XYZ    0.5                       0.727272727272727
```

Of course, there are other ways to generalize a solution for hypothetical set calculations. Here I showed just one method.

I should note that this method returns rows that appear in the partitions table even if there are no related rows in the details table. If you are not interested in those, you need to add logic to exclude them—for example, by including a NOT EXISTS predicate. As an example, to exclude customers with no related orders from the query that calculates the RANK and DENSE_RANK hypothetical set calculations, you use the following code:

```
DECLARE @val AS NUMERIC(12, 2) = 1000.00;

SELECT custid, rnk, densernk
FROM Sales.Customers AS P
  CROSS APPLY (SELECT
                 RANK() OVER(ORDER BY val) AS rnk,
                 DENSE_RANK() OVER(ORDER BY val) AS densernk,
                 return_flag
               FROM (SELECT val, 0 AS return_flag
                     FROM Sales.OrderValues AS D
                     WHERE D.custid = P.custid

                     UNION ALL

                     SELECT @val, 1) AS U) AS A
```

```
WHERE return_flag = 1
  AND EXISTS
    (SELECT * FROM Sales.OrderValues AS D
     WHERE D.custid = P.custid);
```

This query returns 89 rows and not 91, because only 89 out of the 91 existing customers placed orders.

Inverse Distribution Functions

Inverse distribution functions perform calculations that you can think of as the inverse of the rank distribution functions PERCENT_RANK and CUME_DIST. Rank distribution functions compute a rank of a value with respect to others in a partition or a group, expressed as a ratio in the range of 0 through 1 (a percent). Inverse distribution functions pretty much do the inverse. Given a certain percent, *@pct*, they return a value from the partition or group that the *@pct* represents. That is, in loose terms, they return a calculated value with respect to which *@pct* percent of the values are less than. Chances are that this sentence doesn't make much sense yet, but it should be clearer after you see some examples. Inverse distribution functions are more commonly known as *percentiles*.

The standard defines two variants of inverse distribution functions: PERCENTILE_DISC, which returns an existing value from the population using a discrete distribution model, and PERCENTILE_CONT, which returns an interpolated value assuming a continuous distribution model. I explained the specifics of the two calculations in Chapter 2. As a quick reminder, PERCENTILE_DISC returns the first value in the group whose cumulative distribution is greater than or equal to the input. The PERCENTILE_CONT function identifies two rows in between which the input percent falls, and it computes an interpolation of the two ordering values assuming a continuous distribution model.

SQL Server 2012 supports only a windowed version of the functions, which I described in detail in Chapter 2. It doesn't support the more natural ordered set function versions that can be used in grouped queries. But I will provide alternatives to the ordered set function versions both in SQL Server 2012 and in prior versions of SQL Server.

First, as a reminder, here's a query against the Scores table calculating the fiftieth percentile (median) of test scores, using both function variants as well as window functions:

```
DECLARE @pct AS FLOAT = 0.5;

SELECT testid, score,
  PERCENTILE_DISC(@pct) WITHIN GROUP(ORDER BY score)
    OVER(PARTITION BY testid) AS percentiledisc,
  PERCENTILE_CONT(@pct) WITHIN GROUP(ORDER BY score)
    OVER(PARTITION BY testid) AS percentilecont
FROM Stats.Scores;
```

```
testid      score percentiledisc percentilecont
----------  ----- -------------- ----------------------
Test ABC    50    75             75
Test ABC    55    75             75
Test ABC    55    75             75
Test ABC    65    75             75
Test ABC    75    75             75
Test ABC    80    75             75
Test ABC    80    75             75
Test ABC    95    75             75
Test ABC    95    75             75
Test XYZ    50    75             77.5
Test XYZ    55    75             77.5
Test XYZ    55    75             77.5
Test XYZ    65    75             77.5
Test XYZ    75    75             77.5
Test XYZ    80    75             77.5
Test XYZ    80    75             77.5
Test XYZ    95    75             77.5
Test XYZ    95    75             77.5
Test XYZ    95    75             77.5
```

Observe that the same result percentiles are simply repeated for all members of the same partition (*test*, in our case), which is completely redundant for our purposes. You need to return the percentiles only once per group. According to the standard, you are supposed to achieve this using the ordered set versions of the functions in a grouped query, like so:

```
DECLARE @pct AS FLOAT = 0.5;

SELECT testid,
  PERCENTILE_DISC(@pct) WITHIN GROUP(ORDER BY score) AS percentiledisc,
  PERCENTILE_CONT(@pct) WITHIN GROUP(ORDER BY score) AS percentilecont
FROM Stats.Scores
GROUP BY testid;
```

But these versions weren't implemented in SQL Server 2012, so you need to figure out alternative methods to achieve this.

Because the windowed versions of the functions were implemented, one simple approach to handling the task is to use the DISTINCT option, like so:

```
DECLARE @pct AS FLOAT = 0.5;

SELECT DISTINCT testid,
  PERCENTILE_DISC(@pct) WITHIN GROUP(ORDER BY score)
    OVER(PARTITION BY testid) AS percentiledisc,
  PERCENTILE_CONT(@pct) WITHIN GROUP(ORDER BY score)
    OVER(PARTITION BY testid) AS percentilecont
FROM Stats.Scores;
```

```
testid      percentiledisc percentilecont
----------  -------------- ----------------------
Test ABC    75             75
Test XYZ    75             77.5
```

Another option is to assign unique row numbers to the rows in each partition, and then filter just the rows with row number 1, like so:

```
DECLARE @pct AS FLOAT = 0.5;

WITH C AS
(
  SELECT testid,
    PERCENTILE_DISC(@pct) WITHIN GROUP(ORDER BY score)
      OVER(PARTITION BY testid) AS percentiledisc,
    PERCENTILE_CONT(@pct) WITHIN GROUP(ORDER BY score)
      OVER(PARTITION BY testid) AS percentilecont,
    ROW_NUMBER() OVER(PARTITION BY testid ORDER BY (SELECT NULL)) AS rownum
  FROM Stats.Scores
)
SELECT testid, percentiledisc, percentilecont
FROM C
WHERE rownum = 1;
```

Another option is to use TOP (1) WITH TIES, with ordering based on similar row numbers, which also results in returning only rows with row number 1, like so:

```
DECLARE @pct AS FLOAT = 0.5;

SELECT TOP (1) WITH TIES testid,
  PERCENTILE_DISC(@pct) WITHIN GROUP(ORDER BY score)
    OVER(PARTITION BY testid) AS percentiledisc,
  PERCENTILE_CONT(@pct) WITHIN GROUP(ORDER BY score)
    OVER(PARTITION BY testid) AS percentilecont
FROM Stats.Scores
ORDER BY ROW_NUMBER() OVER(PARTITION BY testid ORDER BY (SELECT NULL));
```

Note that even though the last technique might be creative and intellectually intriguing, it is not as efficient as the previous one.

If you need to calculate percentiles in versions prior to SQL Server 2012, you need to implement the logic of the computation yourself. With PERCENTILE_DISC, you are supposed to return the first value in the group whose cumulative distribution is greater than or equal to the input percent. To calculate the cumulative distribution of each value, you need to know how many rows precede or are peers of that value (np) and how many rows there are in the group (nr). Then the cumulative distribution is np / nr.

Normally, to calculate np, you need to return one less than the minimum rank that is greater than the current one. This could involve expensive use of subqueries and the RANK function. Courtesy of Adam Machanic, you can achieve what you need with less effort. When peers cannot exist (that is, the ordering is unique), the ROW_NUMBER function returns a number that is equal to np for all rows. When peers can exist (the ordering isn't unique) the function returns a number that is equal to np for one of the peers and less than np for all others. Because we are talking about peers, by definition, in cases where the row number is less than np, the sort value is the same as the one where the row number is equal to *np*. This fact makes the ROW_NUMBER function sufficient for our very specific need of representing *np*. As for calculating *nr*, you can use a simple COUNT window function. Here's the code that implements this logic, followed by its output:

```
DECLARE @pct AS FLOAT = 0.5;

WITH C AS
(
  SELECT testid, score,
    ROW_NUMBER() OVER(PARTITION BY testid ORDER BY score) AS np,
    COUNT(*) OVER(PARTITION BY testid) AS nr
  FROM Stats.Scores
)
SELECT testid, MIN(score) AS percentiledisc
FROM C
WHERE 1.0 * np / nr >= @pct
GROUP BY testid;

testid      percentiledisc
----------  --------------
Test ABC    75
Test XYZ    75
```

As for a pre–SQL Server 2012 alternative to PERCENTILE_CONT, here's a reminder from Chapter 2 for the logic behind the computation:

- Consider the function *PERCENTILE_CONT(@pct) WITHIN GROUP(ORDER BY score)*.

- Let *n* be the count of rows in the group.

- Let *a* be *@pct*(n – 1)*, let *i* be the integer part of *a*, and let *f* be the fraction part of *a*.

- Let *row0* and *row1* be the rows whose zero-based row numbers are in *FLOOR(a), CEILING(a)*. Here I'm assuming the row numbers are calculated using the same window partitioning and ordering as the group and order of the PERCENTILE_CONT function.

Then PERCENTILE_CONT is computed as *row0.score + f * (row1.score – row0.score)*. This is an interpolation of the values in the two rows assuming continuous distribution (based on the fraction part of *a*).

The following code implements this logic:

```
DECLARE @pct AS FLOAT = 0.5;

WITH C1 AS
(
  SELECT testid, score,
    ROW_NUMBER() OVER(PARTITION BY testid ORDER BY score) - 1 AS rownum,
    @pct * (COUNT(*) OVER(PARTITION BY testid) - 1) AS a
  FROM Stats.Scores
),
```

```
C2 AS
(
  SELECT testid, score, a-FLOOR(a) AS factor
  FROM C1
  WHERE rownum IN (FLOOR(a), CEILING(a))
)
SELECT testid, MIN(score) + factor * (MAX(score) - MIN(score)) AS percentilecont
FROM C2
GROUP BY testid, factor;
```

```
testid      percentilecont
----------  ---------------------
Test ABC    75
Test XYZ    77.5
```

Offset Functions

Standard SQL doesn't define ordered set function versions of the functions FIRST_VALUE, LAST_VALUE, and NTH_VALUE; rather, it defines only windowed versions, and that's also the implementation in SQL Server 2012. As an example, the following query returns with each order the current order value, as well as the values of the first and last orders by the same customer:

```
SELECT custid, orderdate, orderid, val,
  FIRST_VALUE(val) OVER(PARTITION BY custid
                     ORDER BY orderdate, orderid) AS val_firstorder,
  LAST_VALUE(val)  OVER(PARTITION BY custid
                     ORDER BY orderdate, orderid
                     ROWS BETWEEN CURRENT ROW
                         AND UNBOUNDED FOLLOWING) AS val_lastorder
FROM Sales.OrderValues;
```

```
custid  orderdate   orderid  val      val_firstorder  val_lastorder
-------  ----------  --------  -------  ---------------  --------------
1        2007-08-25  10643    814.50   814.50           933.50
1        2007-10-03  10692    878.00   814.50           933.50
1        2007-10-13  10702    330.00   814.50           933.50
1        2008-01-15  10835    845.80   814.50           933.50
1        2008-03-16  10952    471.20   814.50           933.50
1        2008-04-09  11011    933.50   814.50           933.50
2        2006-09-18  10308    88.80    88.80            514.40
2        2007-08-08  10625    479.75   88.80            514.40
2        2007-11-28  10759    320.00   88.80            514.40
2        2008-03-04  10926    514.40   88.80            514.40
3        2006-11-27  10365    403.20   403.20           660.00
3        2007-04-15  10507    749.06   403.20           660.00
3        2007-05-13  10535    1940.85  403.20           660.00
3        2007-06-19  10573    2082.00  403.20           660.00
3        2007-09-22  10677    813.37   403.20           660.00
3        2007-09-25  10682    375.50   403.20           660.00
3        2008-01-28  10856    660.00   403.20           660.00
...
```

Observe the duplication of the information in all rows by the same customer. Often that's what you want if you need to involve in the same expression both detail elements and the first, last, and *n*th values from the partition. But what if you don't? What if you need the first, last, and *n*th values only once per group?

If you think about it, there's no reason not to support grouped-aggregate, ordered-set function versions of the functions. After all, in a given group of rows, each of those functions is supposed to return only one value. It's true that in the windowed version these functions support a window frame clause so that, for each row in the partition, there can be a different applicable frame and, therefore, a different result. But often you just want the calculation applied to the entire partition or group.

You can think of ordered-set-function forms of the FIRST_VALUE and LAST_VALUE functions as being more flexible versions of the MIN and MAX functions, respectively. They're more flexible in the sense that the MIN and MAX functions treat the input as both the ordering element and the value expression to return, plus they don't support multiple ordering elements. The FIRST_VALUE and LAST_VALUE functions allow you to return one element as the value expression based on the ordering of another element, or elements. So why not support those as grouped-aggregate, ordered-set functions?

I hope this will happen in the future. In the meanwhile, you need to use alternative methods. One method, similar to what I showed with inverse distribution functions, is to invoke the windowed version of the functions, along with calculating unique row numbers within each partition. And then filter only the rows where the row number is equal to 1, like so:

```
WITH C AS
(
  SELECT custid,
    FIRST_VALUE(val) OVER(PARTITION BY custid
                          ORDER BY orderdate, orderid) AS val_firstorder,
    LAST_VALUE(val)  OVER(PARTITION BY custid
                          ORDER BY orderdate, orderid
                          ROWS BETWEEN CURRENT ROW
                                   AND UNBOUNDED FOLLOWING) AS val_lastorder,
    ROW_NUMBER() OVER(PARTITION BY custid ORDER BY (SELECT NULL)) AS rownum
  FROM Sales.OrderValues
)
SELECT custid, val_firstorder, val_lastorder
FROM C
WHERE rownum = 1;

custid  val_firstorder  val_lastorder
-------  ---------------  --------------
1        814.50           933.50
2        88.80            514.40
3        403.20           660.00
4        480.00           491.50
5        1488.80          1835.70
6        149.00           858.00
7        1176.00          730.00
8        982.00           224.00
9        88.50            792.75
10       1832.80          525.00
...
```

But the functions FIRST_VALUE and LAST_VALUE (the windowed version) are available only in SQL Server 2012. In addition, the NTH_VALUE function is not available in any form in SQL Server 2012. There are a number of ways to handle these calculations in previous versions of SQL Server, relying on the ROW_NUMBER function alone. By calculating an ascending row number and filtering only the rows with row number 1, you get the equivalent of FIRST_VALUE. Filtering the rows with row number *n*, you get the equivalent of NTH_VALUE FROM FIRST. Similarly, using a row number with descending order, you produce the equivalents of LAST_VALUE and NTH_VALUE FROM LAST. Here's an example implementing this logic, returning the first, last, and third order values per customer, with ordering based on *orderdate, orderid*:

```
WITH OrdersRN AS
(
  SELECT custid, val,
    ROW_NUMBER() OVER(PARTITION BY custid
                      ORDER BY orderdate, orderid) AS rna,
    ROW_NUMBER() OVER(PARTITION BY custid
                      ORDER BY orderdate DESC, orderid DESC) AS rnd
  FROM Sales.OrderValues
)
SELECT custid,
  MAX(CASE WHEN rna = 1 THEN val END) AS firstorderval,
  MAX(CASE WHEN rnd = 1 THEN val END) AS lastorderval,
  MAX(CASE WHEN rna = 3 THEN val END) AS thirdorderval
FROM OrdersRN
GROUP BY custid;
```

custid	firstorderval	lastorderval	thirdorderval
1	814.50	933.50	330.00
2	88.80	514.40	320.00
3	403.20	660.00	1940.85
4	480.00	491.50	407.70
5	1488.80	1835.70	2222.40
6	149.00	858.00	330.00
7	1176.00	730.00	7390.20
8	982.00	224.00	224.00
9	88.50	792.75	1549.60
10	1832.80	525.00	966.80
...			

There's another technique to handle the first-value and last-value calculations based on a carry-along-sort concept. The idea is to generate one string that concatenates first the ordering elements (*orderdate* and *orderid*, in our case), and then whichever elements you need to return. Then, by applying MIN or MAX aggregates, you get back the string holding within it the first or last value, respectively. The trick is to make sure that when you convert the original values to strings, you format them in such a way that preserves the original ordering behavior. In our case, this means converting the *orderdate* values to a CHAR(8) string using style 112, which produces the form *YYYYMMDD*. As for the *orderid* values, which are positive integers, you want to convert them to a fixed-sized form with leading spaces or zeros.

The following query shows the first step of the solution, where you just generate the concatenated strings:

```
SELECT custid,
  CONVERT(CHAR(8), orderdate, 112)
    + STR(orderid, 10)
    + STR(val, 14, 2)
    COLLATE Latin1_General_BIN2 AS s
FROM Sales.OrderValues;
```

```
custid      s
----------- -------------------------------
85          20060704    10248        440.00
79          20060705    10249       1863.40
34          20060708    10250       1552.60
84          20060708    10251        654.06
76          20060709    10252       3597.90
34          20060710    10253       1444.80
14          20060711    10254        556.62
68          20060712    10255       2490.50
88          20060715    10256        517.80
35          20060716    10257       1119.90
...
```

Observe the use of the binary collation, which helps speed up the comparisons a bit. As for the second step, you define a CTE based on the previous query. Then, in the outer query, you apply the MIN and MAX aggregates to the string, extract the part representing the value from the result, and convert it to the original type. Here's the complete solution, followed by an abbreviated form of its output:

```
WITH C AS
(
  SELECT custid,
    CONVERT(CHAR(8), orderdate, 112)
      + STR(orderid, 10)
      + STR(val, 14, 2)
      COLLATE Latin1_General_BIN2 AS s
  FROM Sales.OrderValues
)
SELECT custid,
  CAST(SUBSTRING(MIN(s), 19, 14) AS NUMERIC(12, 2)) AS firstorderval,
  CAST(SUBSTRING(MAX(s), 19, 14) AS NUMERIC(12, 2)) AS lastorderval
FROM C
GROUP BY custid;
```

```
custid  firstorderval  lastorderval
------- -------------- -------------
1       814.50         933.50
2       88.80          514.40
3       403.20         660.00
4       480.00         491.50
5       1488.80        1835.70
6       149.00         858.00
7       1176.00        730.00
8       982.00         224.00
9       88.50          792.75
10      1832.80        525.00
...
```

Note that I relied on the fact that the integer *orderid* values are non-negative. If you have a numeric ordering element that supports negative values, you need to add logic to make it sort correctly. This is tricky yet doable. For example, suppose that *orderid* values can be negative. To ensure that negative values sort before positive ones, you could add the letter *0* in the string before a negative value and the letter *1* before a non-negative value. Then, to ensure that negative values sort correctly (for example, –2 before –1), you could add 2147483648 (the absolute of the minimum possible negative integer of –2147483648) to the value before converting it to a character string. Here's what the complete query would look like:

```
WITH C AS
(
  SELECT custid,
    CONVERT(CHAR(8), orderdate, 112)
      + CASE SIGN(orderid) WHEN -1 THEN '0' ELSE '1' END -- negative sorts before nonnegative
      + STR(CASE SIGN(orderid)
              WHEN -1 THEN 2147483648 -- if negative add abs(minnegative)
              ELSE 0
            END + orderid, 10)
      + STR(val, 14, 2)
      COLLATE Latin1_General_BIN2 AS s
  FROM Sales.OrderValues
)
SELECT custid,
  CAST(SUBSTRING(MIN(s), 20, 14) AS NUMERIC(12, 2)) AS firstorderval,
  CAST(SUBSTRING(MAX(s), 20, 14) AS NUMERIC(12, 2)) AS lastorderval
FROM C
GROUP BY custid;
```

When using this technique in production code, make sure you thoroughly comment the code because it isn't trivial.

String Concatenation

As mentioned, the standard defines only two kinds of ordered set functions: hypothetical set functions (RANK, DENSE_RANK, PERCENT_RANK, and CUME_DIST) and inverse distribution functions (PERCENTILE_DISC, and PERCENTILE_CONT). As I already demonstrated with offset functions, there's no reason why the concept wouldn't work for other functions as well. The basic idea is that if it's an aggregate function that has ordering relevance to the computation, it's a potential candidate for an ordered set function. Take a classic example such as string concatenation. At the moment, unfortunately, there's no built-in aggregate string concatenation function that concatenates strings in a group. But say there was one. Of course, you might need to concatenate the strings in the group in some order; therefore, it would make perfect sense to implement the function as an ordered set function with a WITHIN GROUP clause that allows you to indicate the ordering specification.

Oracle, for example, implemented such a function (called LISTAGG), as an ordered set function. So, to query a table called Sales.Orders returning for each customer a string with all *orderid* values concatenated in *orderid ordering*, you use the following code:

```
SELECT custid,
  LISTAGG(orderid, ',') WITHIN GROUP(ORDER BY orderid) AS custorders
FROM Sales.Orders
GROUP BY custid;
```

```
custid  custorders
-------  -----------------------------------------------------------------------------------
1        10643,10692,10702,10835,10952,11011
2        10308,10625,10759,10926
3        10365,10507,10535,10573,10677,10682,10856
4        10355,10383,10453,10558,10707,10741,10743,10768,10793,10864,10920,10953,11016
5        10278,10280,10384,10444,10445,10524,10572,10626,10654,10672,10689,10733,10778,...
6        10501,10509,10582,10614,10853,10956,11058
7        10265,10297,10360,10436,10449,10559,10566,10584,10628,10679,10826
8        10326,10801,10970
9        10331,10340,10362,10470,10511,10525,10663,10715,10730,10732,10755,10827,10871,...
11       10289,10471,10484,10538,10539,10578,10599,10943,10947,11023
...
```

People use all kinds of alternative solutions in SQL Server to achieve ordered string concatenation. One of the more efficient techniques is based on XML manipulation using the FOR XML option with the PATH mode, like so:

```
SELECT custid,
  COALESCE(
    STUFF(
      (SELECT ',' + CAST(orderid AS VARCHAR(10)) AS [text()]
       FROM Sales.Orders AS O
       WHERE O.custid = C.custid
       ORDER BY orderid
       FOR XML PATH(''), TYPE).value('.', 'VARCHAR(MAX)'),
      1, 1, ''),
    '') AS custorders
FROM Sales.Customers AS C;
```

The innermost correlated subquery filters only the *orderid* values from the Orders table (aliased as *O*) that are associated with the current customer from the Customers table (aliased as *C*). With the FOR XML PATH('') option, you ask to generate a single XML string out of all of the values. Using the empty string as input to the PATH mode means that you don't want the wrapping elements to be produced, effectively giving you a concatenation of the values without any added tags. Because the subquery specifies *ORDER BY orderid*, the *orderid* values in the string are ordered. Note that you can order by anything at all—not necessarily by the values you're concatenating. The code also adds a comma as a separator before each *orderid* value, and then the STUFF function removes the first comma. Finally, the COALESCE function converts a NULL result to an empty string. So, it is possible to achieve ordered string concatenation in SQL Server, but it isn't pretty.

Summary

Ordered set functions are aggregate functions that have ordering relevance to the calculation. The standard defines some specific functions, but the concept is, in fact, general and can work for all kinds of aggregate calculations. I gave a few examples beyond what the standard supports, such as offset functions and string concatenation. SQL Server 2012 does not support ordered set functions, but I provided alternative methods to achieve similar calculations. I do hope very much to see SQL Server introducing support for such functions in the future—perhaps implementing the standard WITHIN GROUP clause and making it available to CLR user-defined aggregate functions that have ordering relevance.

CHAPTER 4

Optimization of Window Functions

This chapter describes the optimization of window functions in Microsoft SQL Server 2012. It assumes that you are familiar with analyzing graphical query-execution plans and with the core iterators such as Index Scan, Index Seek, Sort, Nested Loops, Parallelism, Compute Scalar, Filter, Stream Aggregate, and so on.

The chapter starts by introducing the data that will be used in the code samples. It then covers general indexing guidelines to support window functions of all kinds. Then I discuss the optimization of window ranking functions, which is followed by a discussion on improving parallel processing of window functions in general. The chapter then discusses optimization of aggregate and offset functions, first without window ordering and framing options and then with them. You will be introduced to the new Window Spool operator and discover how it does its magic. Finally, the chapter describes the optimization of distribution functions.

Note I'd like to thank Marc Friedman, Umachandar Jayachandran, Tobias Ternström, and Milan Stojic from the SQL Server development team for their help in understanding the optimization of window functions. It is much appreciated.

Sample Data

Most of the examples in the chapter query tables called Accounts and Transactions, which hold information about bank accounts and transactions within those accounts. For deposits, the transactions have a positive amount associated with them, and for withdrawals, they have a negative one. Run the following code to create the Accounts and Transactions tables in the TSQL2012 sample database:

```
SET NOCOUNT ON;
USE TSQL2012;

IF OBJECT_ID('dbo.Transactions', 'U') IS NOT NULL DROP TABLE dbo.Transactions;
IF OBJECT_ID('dbo.Accounts', 'U') IS NOT NULL DROP TABLE dbo.Accounts;

CREATE TABLE dbo.Accounts
(
  actid   INT         NOT NULL,
  actname VARCHAR(50) NOT NULL,
  CONSTRAINT PK_Accounts PRIMARY KEY(actid)
);
```

```
CREATE TABLE dbo.Transactions
(
  actid   INT    NOT NULL,
  tranid INT    NOT NULL,
  val     MONEY NOT NULL,
  CONSTRAINT PK_Transactions PRIMARY KEY(actid, tranid),
  CONSTRAINT FK_Transactions_Accounts
    FOREIGN KEY(actid)
    REFERENCES dbo.Accounts(actid)
);
```

The code samples and performance measures I provide in the chapter assume that the tables are populated with a large set of sample data. But if you need a small set of sample data just to test the logic of the solutions, you can use the following code to fill the tables:

```
INSERT INTO dbo.Accounts(actid, actname) VALUES
  (1,  'account 1'),
  (2,  'account 2'),
  (3,  'account 3');

INSERT INTO dbo.Transactions(actid, tranid, val) VALUES
  (1,  1,   4.00),
  (1,  2, -2.00),
  (1,  3,   5.00),
  (1,  4,   2.00),
  (1,  5,   1.00),
  (1,  6,   3.00),
  (1,  7, -4.00),
  (1,  8, -1.00),
  (1,  9, -2.00),
  (1, 10, -3.00),
  (2,  1,   2.00),
  (2,  2,   1.00),
  (2,  3,   5.00),
  (2,  4,   1.00),
  (2,  5, -5.00),
  (2,  6,   4.00),
  (2,  7,   2.00),
  (2,  8, -4.00),
  (2,  9, -5.00),
  (2, 10,   4.00),
  (3,  1, -3.00),
  (3,  2,   3.00),
  (3,  3, -2.00),
  (3,  4,   1.00),
  (3,  5,   4.00),
  (3,  6, -1.00),
  (3,  7,   5.00),
  (3,  8,   3.00),
  (3,  9,   5.00),
  (3, 10, -3.00);
```

As for producing a large set of sample data, first run the following code to create a helper function called *GetNums* (which you can get details about in Chapter 5, "T-SQL Solutions Using Window Functions"), which generates a sequence of integers in the requested range:

```
IF OBJECT_ID('dbo.GetNums', 'IF') IS NOT NULL DROP FUNCTION dbo.GetNums;
GO
CREATE FUNCTION dbo.GetNums(@low AS BIGINT, @high AS BIGINT) RETURNS TABLE
AS
RETURN
  WITH
    L0   AS (SELECT c FROM (VALUES(1),(1)) AS D(c)),
    L1   AS (SELECT 1 AS c FROM L0 AS A CROSS JOIN L0 AS B),
    L2   AS (SELECT 1 AS c FROM L1 AS A CROSS JOIN L1 AS B),
    L3   AS (SELECT 1 AS c FROM L2 AS A CROSS JOIN L2 AS B),
    L4   AS (SELECT 1 AS c FROM L3 AS A CROSS JOIN L3 AS B),
    L5   AS (SELECT 1 AS c FROM L4 AS A CROSS JOIN L4 AS B),
    Nums AS (SELECT ROW_NUMBER() OVER(ORDER BY (SELECT NULL)) AS rownum
             FROM L5)
  SELECT @low + rownum - 1 AS n
  FROM Nums
  ORDER BY rownum
  OFFSET 0 ROWS FETCH FIRST @high - @low + 1 ROWS ONLY;
GO
```

And then use the following code to fill the Accounts table with 100 accounts and the Transactions table with 20,000 transactions per account—a total of 2,000,000 transactions:

```
DECLARE
  @num_partitions     AS INT = 100,
  @rows_per_partition AS INT = 20000;

TRUNCATE TABLE dbo.Transactions;
DELETE FROM dbo.Accounts;

INSERT INTO dbo.Accounts WITH (TABLOCK) (actid, actname)
  SELECT n AS actid, 'account ' + CAST(n AS VARCHAR(10)) AS actname
  FROM dbo.GetNums(1, @num_partitions) AS P;

INSERT INTO dbo.Transactions WITH (TABLOCK) (actid, tranid, val)
  SELECT NP.n, RPP.n,
    (ABS(CHECKSUM(NEWID())%2)*2-1) * (1 + ABS(CHECKSUM(NEWID())%5))
  FROM dbo.GetNums(1, @num_partitions) AS NP
    CROSS JOIN dbo.GetNums(1, @rows_per_partition) AS RPP;
```

Feel free to adjust the number of partitions (accounts) and rows per partition (transactions per account) as needed, but keep in mind that I used the preceding inputs in my tests.

Indexing Guidelines

The plan iterators that compute the result of a window function will be described in detail later in the chapter. For now, it suffices to say that they need the input rows to be sorted by the partitioning columns (if a window partition clause exists), followed by the ordering columns (assuming a window order clause is relevant). If no index exists that holds the data in the required order, a sort operation will be required before the window function iterators can do their jobs.

POC Index

The general indexing guidelines to support window functions follow a concept I like to think of as *POC*, which is short for *Partitioning*, *Ordering*, and *Covering*. It's also sometimes referred to as POCo. A POC index's keys should be the window partition columns followed by the window order columns, and the index should include in the leaf the rest of the columns that the query refers to. The inclusion can be achieved either with an explicit INCLUDE clause of a nonclustered index or by means of the index being clustered—in which case, it needs to include all table columns in the leaf rows.

Absent a POC index, the plan includes a Sort iterator, and with large input sets, it can be quite expensive. Sorting has $N * LOG(N)$ complexity, which is worse than linear. This means that with more rows, you pay more per row. For example $1000 * LOG(1000) = 3000$ and $10000 * LOG(10000) = 40000$. This means that 10 times more rows results in 13 times more work, and it gets worse the further you go. As an example, consider the following query:

```
SELECT actid, tranid, val,
  ROW_NUMBER() OVER(PARTITION BY actid ORDER BY val) AS rownum
FROM dbo.Transactions;
```

The plan for this query is shown in Figure 4-1.

FIGURE 4-1 Plan with a Sort iterator.

At the moment, there's no POC index in place. The clustered index is scanned without an ordering requirement (that is, the *Ordered* property of the scan is *False*), and then an expensive Sort iterator is used to sort the data. The query ran for four seconds on my system against hot cache, with results discarded. (To discard results, open the Query Options context menu, choose Grid under Results, and select the Discard Results After Execution option.) Next, run the following code to create a POC index:

```
CREATE INDEX idx_actid_val_i_tranid
  ON dbo.Transactions(actid /* P */, val /* O */)
  INCLUDE(tranid /* C */);
```

As you can see, the first part of the key list is the window partition column (*actid* in our case), followed by the window order columns (*val* in our case), and then the rest of the columns referenced by the query *(tranid* in our case). Rerun the following query:

```
SELECT actid, tranid, val,
  ROW_NUMBER() OVER(PARTITION BY actid ORDER BY val) AS rownum
FROM dbo.Transactions;
```

The plan for this query is shown in Figure 4-2.

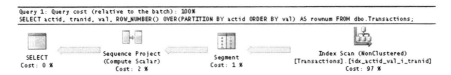

```
Query 1: Query cost (relative to the batch): 100%
SELECT actid, tranid, val, ROW_NUMBER() OVER(PARTITION BY actid ORDER BY val) AS rownum FROM dbo.Transactions;
```

SELECT   Sequence Project   Segment   Index Scan (NonClustered)
Cost: 0 %   (Compute Scalar)   Cost: 1 %   [Transactions].[idx_actid_val_i_tranid]
                Cost: 2 %   Cost: 97 %

FIGURE 4-2 Plan without a Sort iterator.

The Sort iterator is removed. The plan performs an ordered scan of the POC index to satisfy the ordering requirement of the iterators that compute the window function's result. This time the query ran for two seconds even though a serial plan was used, compared with four seconds for the previous parallel plan with the sort. With larger sets, the difference can be greater.

If the query also involves equality filters—for example, *WHERE col1 = 5 AND col2 = 'ABC'*—you can address both the filtering needs and the window function's ordering needs with the same index by putting the filtered columns first in the index key list. You can then think of the index as an FPOC index, with *FPO* as the key list and *C* as the include list.

If you have multiple window functions in the query, as long as they have the same window specification, they can usually rely on the same ordered data without the need to add a Sort iterator for each. Note also that when specifying multiple window functions with different window ordering (and possibly also presentation ordering), their order of appearance in the SELECT list can affect the number of sorts that will take place in the plan.

Backward Scans

The pages in each level of an index, including the leaf, are connected with a doubly linked list; so technically, the index can be scanned either ordered forward or ordered backward. When rows need to be consumed in index key order, but in the exact reverse direction to that of the index, often the optimizer will have the logic to perform an ordered backward scan. But there are curious aspects of backward scans and the ability to rely on those to compute window functions that are interesting to know and that can affect your choices.

The first curious aspect is that ordered forward scans can benefit from parallelism, whereas ordered backward scans cannot. Parallel backward scans are just not implemented in the storage engine at the moment. To demonstrate that forward scans can be parallelized, run the following query and request the actual execution plan:

```
SELECT actid, tranid, val,
  ROW_NUMBER() OVER(ORDER BY actid, val) AS rownum
FROM dbo.Transactions
WHERE tranid < 1000;
```

Figure 4-3 has the plan for this query, showing that a parallel scan was used.

FIGURE 4-3 Parallel plan.

Next, run the following query, where the direction of the window order columns is reversed:

```
SELECT actid, tranid, val,
  ROW_NUMBER() OVER(ORDER BY actid DESC, val DESC) AS rownum
FROM dbo.Transactions
WHERE tranid < 1000;
```

The execution plan for the query is shown in Figure 4-4.

Query 1: Query cost (relative to the batch): 100%
SELECT actid, tranid, val, ROW_NUMBER() OVER(ORDER BY actid DESC, val DESC) AS rownum FROM dbo.Transactions WHERE t

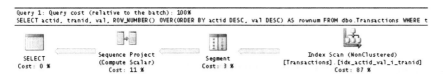

FIGURE 4-4 Serial plan.

The optimizer did choose to use an ordered scan of the same index used before, in a backward fashion, and thus the plan is serial.

You might have noticed that the last two queries have only a window ordering clause but are missing a window partition clause. Still, the index created earlier satisfies the aforementioned POC guidelines, only the *P* is irrelevant here. It's not by chance that I chose not to include a window partition clause in these examples. And this leads me to the second curious aspect of optimization of window functions.

It turns out that if the function has a window partition clause, to perform an ordered scan of an index and avoid a sort, the partitioning values must be read in ascending order even though there's no logical reasoning behind it. There's an exception to this rule, but I'll get to that later.

Consider the following query, which was already used in a previous example:

```
SELECT actid, tranid, val,
  ROW_NUMBER() OVER(PARTITION BY actid ORDER BY val) AS rownum
FROM dbo.Transactions;
```

The plan for this query was shown earlier in Figure 4-2, where you saw that the POC index was scanned in an ordered fashion and a sort was avoided.

Next, try a similar query, only this time reverse the direction of the ordering column, like so:

```
SELECT actid, tranid, val,
  ROW_NUMBER() OVER(PARTITION BY actid ORDER BY val DESC) AS rownum
FROM dbo.Transactions;
```

The plan for this query is shown in Figure 4-5, where you will find a Sort iterator.

FIGURE 4-5 Plan with a Sort iterator for descending order.

The index that was used in the previous example is used here as well because it does cover this query, but its ordering is not relied on here. You can verify this by looking at the *Ordered* property of the Index Scan iterator, and you will find that in this case it is *False*, whereas in the previous case it was *True*. That's an optimization shortcoming. The order in which the distinct partition column values are scanned shouldn't matter. What matters is that the values within each partition need to be scanned in exactly the order defined by the window order clause. So scanning the index in backward order should provide the values to the window function in the right order. But alas, the optimizer doesn't realize this.

There are two indexes that can prevent the need to sort: one with the key list (*actid, val DESC*) and another with the exact inverse directions (*actid DESC, val*), both with the same include list as before (*tranid*). In the former case, an ordered forward scan will be used; in the latter case, an ordered backward one will be used.

But what's even more curious—and thanks to Brad Schulz for this tip—is what happens if you add a presentation ORDER BY clause that requests to order the rows by the partitioning column in descending order. Suddenly, the iterators that compute the window function are willing to consume the partitioning values in descending order and can rely on index ordering for this. So simply adding a presentation ORDER BY clause with *tranid DESC* to our last query removes the need for a Sort iterator. Here's the revised query:

```
SELECT actid, tranid, val,
  ROW_NUMBER() OVER(PARTITION BY actid ORDER BY val DESC) AS rownum
FROM dbo.Transactions
ORDER BY actid DESC;
```

The plan for this query is shown in Figure 4-6.

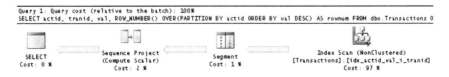

FIGURE 4-6 Plan without a Sort iterator for descending order.

Observe that the Sort iterator was removed. The plan performs an ordered backward scan of the index. Remember that a backward scan will not be parallelized in cases where a forward scan normally would. Still, it's remarkable to identify a case where adding a presentation ORDER BY clause to a query improves performance!

Columnstore Indexes

Columnstore indexes are new in SQL Server 2012. They group and store the data for each column (as opposed to doing it by row as the traditional indexes do), and then join the columns to provide the related data. They can achieve a high level of compression using a technology called VertiPaq. For certain types of queries, especially in data warehouses, columnstore indexes can provide significant performance improvements compared with the traditional indexes. The performance benefits are due to the compression (reduced I/O) and a new batch-mode processing of the data, as opposed to the traditional row-mode processing.

Queries that can benefit from columnstore indexes are, for example, queries that involve filtering, grouping, and star joins. However, there are no special benefits in columnstore indexes that can produce faster computation of window functions. Some queries with window functions might perform better (for example, due to the compression that results in reduced I/O); however, the processing of the iterators involved in the window functions usually will still be done in row mode. In other words, to get good performance for your window functions, you typically want to focus on creating traditional, POC indexes, which will help you avoid the need to sort the data.

Ranking Functions

This section describes the optimization of the ranking functions: ROW_NUMBER, NTILE, RANK, and DENSE_RANK. The iterators computing the ranking functions need to consume the rows one partition at a time, and in order based on the window order clause. Therefore, you need to follow the POC guidelines described earlier if you want to avoid unnecessary sorts. In my examples I'll assume that the index *idx_actid_val_i_tranid*, which you created in the previous section, still exists. If it doesn't, make sure you create it first so that you get similar results to mine.

The two key iterators that help compute the ranking functions are Segment and Sequence Project. Segment is used to send one segment of rows at a time to the next iterator. It has a Group By property that defines the list of expressions to segment by. Its output in each row is a flag called *SegmentN* (with *N* representing some number of the expression—for example, *Segment1004*), indicating whether the row is the first in the segment or not.

The Sequence Project iterator is responsible for the actual computation of the ranking function. By evaluating the flags produced by the preceding Segment iterators, it will reset, keep, or increment the ranking value produced for the previous row. The output of the Sequence Project iterator holding the ranking value is named *ExpressionN* (again, with *N* representing some number of the expression—for example, *Expr1003*).

ROW_NUMBER

I'll use the following query to describe the optimization of the ROW_NUMBER function:

```
SELECT actid, tranid, val,
  ROW_NUMBER() OVER(PARTITION BY actid ORDER BY val) AS rownum
FROM dbo.Transactions;
```

The plan for this query is shown in Figure 4-7.

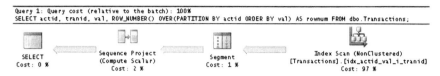

FIGURE 4-7 Plan for ROW_NUMBER.

Because there is a POC index in place, it is scanned in an ordered fashion. Without such an index, remember that an expensive Sort iterator would be added. Next, the Segment iterator creates groups of rows based on the partitioning column *actid*, producing a flag (*SegmentN*) that indicates whether a new partition starts. Whenever *SegmentN* indicates that a new partition starts, the Sequence Project iterator generates the row number value 1 (and calls it *ExprN*); otherwise, it increments the previous value by 1.

There's an interesting aspect of the window ordering of ranking functions that can be an obstacle in certain cases. The window order clause of ranking functions is mandatory, and it cannot be based on a constant. Usually it's not a problem because normally you do need to produce ranking values based on some ordering requirements that map to some table attributes or expressions based on them. However, sometimes you just need to produce unique values in no particular order. You could argue that if ordering makes no difference, it shouldn't matter if you specify some attribute just to satisfy the requirement. But then you need to remember that the plan will involve a Sort iterator if a POC index doesn't exist, or it will be forced to use an ordered index scan if one does exist. You want to allow a scan of the data that is not required to be done in index order for potential performance improvement, and certainly you want to avoid sorting.

As mentioned, a window order clause is mandatory, and SQL Server doesn't allow the ordering to be based on a constant—for example, ORDER BY NULL. But surprisingly, when passing an expression based on a subquery that returns a constant—for example, ORDER BY (SELECT NULL)—SQL Server will accept it. At the same time, the optimizer un-nests, or expands, the expression and realizes that the ordering is the same for all rows. Therefore, it removes the ordering requirement from the input data. Here's a complete query demonstrating this technique:

```
SELECT actid, tranid, val,
  ROW_NUMBER() OVER(ORDER BY (SELECT NULL)) AS rownum
FROM dbo.Transactions;
```

The execution plan for this query is shown in Figure 4-8.

FIGURE 4-8 Plan for ROW_NUMBER with arbitrary ordering.

Observe in the properties of the Index Scan iterator that the *Ordered* property is *False*, meaning that the iterator is not required to return the data in index key order.

NTILE

As a reminder from the discussions in Chapter 2, "A Detailed Look at Window Functions," NTILE is a computation that is conceptually based on two elements: the row number and the count of rows in the partition. If both are known for any given row, you can then apply a formula to compute the tile number. From the previous section, you already know how a row number is computed and optimized. The tricky part is to compute the count of rows in the respective partition. I say "tricky" because a single pass over the data cannot be sufficient. This is because the partition's row count is needed for each individual row, and this count cannot be known until the scanning of all partition rows has been completed. To see how the optimizer handles this problem, consider the following query:

```
SELECT actid, tranid, val,
  NTILE(100) OVER(PARTITION BY actid ORDER BY val) AS rownum
FROM dbo.Transactions;
```

The plan for this query is shown in Figure 4-9.

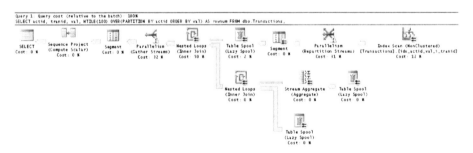

FIGURE 4-9 Plan for NTILE.

The optimizer's answer to our problem is to perform the following steps:

- Read the rows from a POC index if one exists. (One does exist in our case.)

- Segment the rows by the partitioning element (*actid* in our case).

- Store one partition's rows at a time in a work table (represented by the upper Table Spool iterator in the plan).

- Read the spool twice (see the two bottom Table Spool iterators in the plan)—once to compute the count with a Stream Aggregate iterator, and another to get the detail rows.

- Join the aggregate and detail rows to get the count and detail in the same target row.

- Segment the data again by the partitioning element (*actid* in our case).

- Use the Sequence Project iterator to compute the tile number.

Note that the Table Spool iterator represents a work table in tempdb. Even though the percentages associated with it in the plan seem to be low, it actually has quite high overhead. To give you a sense, the same query with a ROW_NUMBER function runs on my system for two seconds, whereas the one with the NTILE function runs for 45 seconds. Later in this chapter when I discuss aggregate functions without ordering and framing, I explain ways to avoid expensive spooling.

RANK and DENSE_RANK

The RANK and DENSE_RANK functions perform computations very similar to ROW_NUMBER, only they are sensitive to ties in the ordering values. Recall that RANK computes one more than the number of rows that have a lower ordering value than the current one, and DENSE_RANK computes one more than the number of distinct ordering values that are lower than the current one. So in addition to needing the segment flag that indicates whether a new partition starts, the Sequence Project operator also needs to know whether the ordering value has changed. Recall that the plan shown earlier for the ROW_NUMBER function has a single Segment iterator that is grouped by the partitioning element. The plans for RANK and DENSE_RANK are similar, but they require a second Segment iterator that is grouped by both the partitioning and ordering elements.

As an example, the following query invokes the RANK function:

```
SELECT actid, tranid, val,
  RANK() OVER(PARTITION BY actid ORDER BY val) AS rownum
FROM dbo.Transactions;
```

The plan for this query is shown in Figure 4-10.

FIGURE 4-10 Plan for RANK.

The first Segment iterator is grouped by *actid*, returning the flag *Segment1004*, and the second is grouped by *actid, val*, returning the flag *Segment1005*. When *Segment1004* indicates that the row is the first in the partition, Sequence Project returns a 1. Otherwise, when *Segment1005* indicates that the ordering value has changed, Sequence Project returns the respective row number. If the ordering value hasn't changed, Sequence Project returns the same value as the previous rank.

The DENSE_RANK function is computed in a similar way. Here's a query you can use as an example:

```
SELECT actid, tranid, val,
  DENSE_RANK() OVER(PARTITION BY actid ORDER BY val) AS rownum
FROM dbo.Transactions;
```

The plan for this query is shown in Figure 4-11.

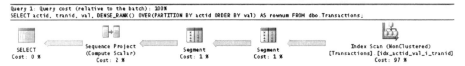

FIGURE 4-11 Plan for DENSE_RANK.

The main difference here is in what the Sequence Project iterator computes. When *Segment1005* indicates that the ordering value has changed, Sequence Project adds 1 to the previous dense rank value.

Because the plans for RANK and DENSE_RANK are so similar to the plan for ROW_NUMBER, the performance you get is also very similar. In my system, all three queries ran for two seconds.

Improved Parallelism with APPLY

This section describes a technique I learned from Adam Machanic—the book's technical editor—that can improve, sometimes dramatically, the way parallelism is handled when optimizing queries with window functions.

Before I describe the technique, I should note that I ran the examples in this book against a system with eight logical CPUs. SQL Server does consider, among other things, the number of logical CPUs when deciding between a parallel plan and a serial plan. So if you have fewer logical CPUs in your environment than eight, you might not get parallel plans in all the cases I did.

Tip If for test purposes you want to mimic an environment with a different number of CPUs than the actual one, there are a couple of ways to go about doing this. One option is to use the startup parameter *–Pn*, where *n* represents the number of schedulers you want SQL Server to start with. Say you have four logical CPUs in your machine and you start the SQL Server Service with the startup parameter *–P8*. SQL Server will start with eight schedulers, and the optimizer will produce plans based on this number, as if it were running in an environment with eight logical CPUs. The degree of parallelism (DOP) for execution will typically be eight for parallel plans.

The second method is one I learned from Eladio Rincón. You can use an undocumented DBCC command called DBCC OPTIMIZER_WHATIF. As a first argument indicate 1, and as a second argument use the number of CPUs you want the optimizer to assume when creating the plan. For example, DBCC OPTIMIZER_WHATIF(1, 8) makes the optimizer assume eight CPUs when creating the plan. Note that this command will not change the number of schedulers that SQL Server starts with; hence, it also won't change the DOP for execution from the actual number of schedulers. But it will create a plan as if there were eight CPUs in the machine. You might also need to add OPTION(RECOMPILE) to force SQL Server to create a new plan after running this command.

Say that, for some query Q, SQL Server normally generates a serial plan when there are four CPUs in the machine and a parallel plan when there are eight. At the moment, you have four CPUs in the machine. Normally, SQL Server generates a serial plan in that system for Q. Using the startup parameter *–P8*, SQL Server will generate a parallel plan with DOP for execution 8. With DBCC OPTIMIZER_WHATIF(1, 8), SQL Server will generate a parallel plan with DOP for execution 4. Also, the startup parameter has a global impact on the entire instance, whereas the DBCC command has a local impact only on the current session. Either way, remember that these options aren't documented officially and hence should be used only for test purposes.

Back to the parallel APPLY technique: it is mainly useful when there's a window partition clause involved and the built-in parallelism doesn't produce an optimal result, or simply isn't used. A good example where the built-in parallel processing of window functions isn't always optimal is when Sort iterators are involved. Consider the following query as an example:

```
SELECT actid, tranid, val,
  ROW_NUMBER() OVER(PARTITION BY actid ORDER BY val) AS rownumasc,
  ROW_NUMBER() OVER(PARTITION BY actid ORDER BY val DESC) AS rownumdesc
FROM dbo.Transactions;
```

This query ran for seven seconds on my system. The plan for this query is shown in Figure 4-12.

FIGURE 4-12 Plan without APPLY.

Because two ROW_NUMBER functions are invoked, with different window specifications, they cannot both rely on POC indexes even if both existed. Only one function can benefit from an ordered scan of a POC index; the other function will require a Sort iterator to arrange the data in the desired order. Because a sort is involved here and the number of rows is quite large, the optimizer decides to use a parallel plan.

Parallel plans for queries with window functions need to partition the rows by the same elements as the window partitioning elements if the Segment and Sequence Project iterators are in a parallel zone. If you look at the properties of the Parallelism (Redistribute Streams) exchange iterator, it uses Hash partitioning and partitions the rows by *actid*. This iterator redistributes the rows from the source threads used for the parallel scan of the data to the target threads that actually compute the first window function's result. Then the rows are sorted based on the ordering requirements of the second window function. A Parallelism (Gather Streams) exchange iterator handles the gathering of the streams. Finally, the second window function's result is computed.

There are a number of bottlenecks in such a plan:

- **The repartitioning of the streams**   Moving data between threads is an expensive operation. In this case, it might have even been better if the storage engine used a serial scan and then distributed the streams directly thereafter.

- **The sort**   Currently, the DOP determines how many rows each thread will process. For example, on a DOP 8 query, each thread will process about 250,000 rows. Conversely, letting each thread work on only rows related to one account would mean 20,000 rows per sort. (Remember, there are 100 accounts, each with about 20,000 transactions.) This makes the existing sorts approximately 20 percent less efficient than they could be: *(((20000 * log(20000)) * 100) / ((250000 * log(250000)) * 8))*.

- **The second Segment and Sequence Project iterators**   These iterators are in a serial zone. Although these are not extremely expensive iterators, they do have a cost, and Amdahl's Law applies quite well. (This law states that the overall speed-up of a parallel algorithm will be limited by serial sections.)

All of these bottlenecks are eliminated by the solution using the parallel APPLY technique, which is implemented as follows:

1. Query the table that holds the distinct partitioning values (Accounts in our case).

2. Use the APPLY operator to apply to each left row the logic of the original query (against Transactions in our case), filtered by the current distinct partitioning value.

As an example, the previous query should be rewritten as shown in Listing 4-1.

LISTING 4-1 Parallel APPLY Technique

```
SELECT C.actid, A.*
FROM dbo.Accounts AS C
  CROSS APPLY (SELECT tranid, val,
                  ROW_NUMBER() OVER(ORDER BY val) AS rownumasc,
                  ROW_NUMBER() OVER(ORDER BY val DESC) AS rownumdesc
              FROM dbo.Transactions AS T
              WHERE T.actid = C.actid) AS A;
```

Observe that because the derived table A handles only one partition's rows, the window partition clause was removed from the window specification.

This query ran for three seconds on my system—less than half the run time of the previous query. The plan for the new query is shown in Figure 4-13.

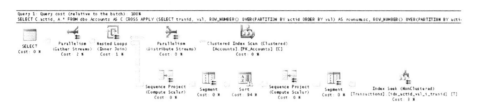

FIGURE 4-13 Plan with APPLY.

The plan starts by scanning the clustered index of the Accounts table. Then a Parallelism (Distribute Streams) exchange iterator is used to distribute the rows to multiple threads using a basic round-robin partitioning type (next packet to next thread). So each thread at the bottom part of the Nested Loops join iterator gets to work on a subset of one partition's rows only, but without the bottlenecks described earlier. The tradeoff is the number of index seek operations (and their associated logical reads) required to satisfy the query. When the partitioning column has very low density (for example, 200,000 partitions, each with 10 rows), you end up with a large number of seek operations, and the APPLY technique is not that efficient anymore.

I will use the parallel APPLY technique in a number of cases later in the chapter as well, and I recommend you consider it whenever you do not get optimal results from the built-in parallel treatment of window functions.

Aggregate and Offset Functions

The optimization of aggregate and offset functions varies significantly depending on whether ordering and framing are applicable or not. Therefore, I cover the two cases separately, starting with window aggregate functions without ordering and framing options.

Without Ordering and Framing

When a window aggregate function doesn't indicate ordering and framing options, the applicable frame of rows is basically the entire partition. For example, consider the following query:

```
SELECT actid, tranid, val,
    MAX(val) OVER(PARTITION BY actid) AS mx
FROM dbo.Transactions;
```

The query is asking for detail elements from each transaction (*actid*, *tranid*, and *val*) to be returned, as well as the maximum value of the current account. Both detail and aggregate elements are supposed to be returned in the same target row. As explained earlier in the "NTILE" section, a single scan of the data cannot be sufficient in this case. As you scan the detail rows, you don't know what the result of the aggregate of the partition is going to be until you finish scanning the partition. The optimizer's answer to this problem is to spool each partition's rows in a work table in tempdb and then read the spool twice—once for the aggregate computation and another for the detail rows.

The plan for this query is shown in Figure 4-14.

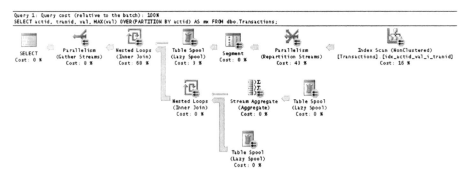

FIGURE 4-14 Plan for a window aggregate with just partitioning.

The plan performs the following steps:

- Read the rows from the POC index.

- Segment the rows by the partitioning element (*actid*).

- Store one partition's rows at a time in a work table. (This step is represented by the upper Table Spool iterator in the plan.)

- Read the spool twice (represented by the two bottom Table Spool iterators in the plan)—once to compute the MAX aggregate with a Stream Aggregate iterator, and another to get the detail rows.

- Join the aggregate and detail rows to get both in the same target row.

The spooling part doesn't use some kind of an optimized in-memory work table; rather, it uses an on-disk one in tempdb. The writes to and reads from the spool have a high overhead. This query ran for 10 seconds on my system.

If you need to filter the rows based on the result of the window function, recall that you cannot do this directly in the query's WHERE clause. You have to define a table expression based on the original query, and then handle the filtering in the outer query, like so:

```
WITH C AS
(
  SELECT actid, tranid, val,
    MAX(val) OVER(PARTITION BY actid) AS mx
  FROM dbo.Transactions
)
SELECT actid, tranid, val
FROM C
WHERE val = mx;
```

The plan for this query is shown in Figure 4-15.

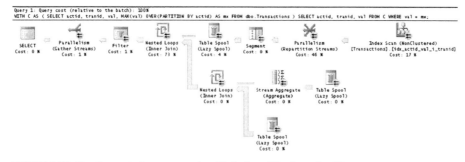

FIGURE 4-15 Plan for a window aggregate with just partitioning, plus filter.

Compared to the previous plan, this one adds a Filter iterator prior to the gathering of the streams. This query ran for 12 seconds on my system.

Due to the high overhead of the on-disk spooling in these plans, you can actually achieve much better performance if you use a grouped query that computes the aggregate and then join its result with the base table, like so:

```
WITH Aggs AS
(
  SELECT actid, MAX(val) AS mx
  FROM dbo.Transactions
  GROUP BY actid
)
```

```
SELECT T.actid, T.tranid, T.val, A.mx
FROM dbo.Transactions AS T
  JOIN Aggs AS A
    ON T.actid = A.actid;
```

The plan for this query is shown in Figure 4-16.

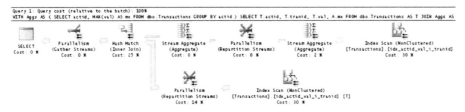

FIGURE 4-16 Plan for a grouped aggregate.

Observe that the covering index is scanned twice directly—once to compute the aggregate and another for the detail—and the results are joined using a Hash join iterator. No spooling takes place, and this translates to a query that finishes in two seconds.

Next, like before, add a filter based on the aggregate:

```
WITH Aggs AS
(
  SELECT actid, MAX(val) AS mx
  FROM dbo.Transactions
  GROUP BY actid
)
SELECT T.actid, T.tranid, T.val
FROM dbo.Transactions AS T
  JOIN Aggs AS A
    ON T.actid = A.actid
    AND T.val = A.mx;
```

The plan for this query is shown in Figure 4-17.

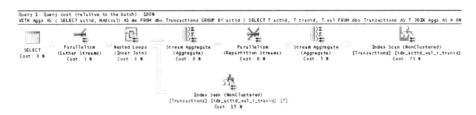

FIGURE 4-17 Plan for a grouped aggregate, plus filter.

Now a Nested Loops join iterator is used to match the related detail rows to each aggregated account group. This query finishes in less than one second.

With Ordering and Framing

Window aggregate and offset functions with ordering and framing options are new in SQL Server 2012, and the optimization of those involves new and enhanced iterators—specifically, a new, magical Window Spool iterator and an enhanced Stream Aggregate iterator.

I'll discuss three cases of optimization with ordering and framing: using a window frame extent with a lower bound UNBOUNDED PRECEDING, expanding all frame rows, and computing two cumulative values.

UNBOUNDED PRECEDING: The Fast-Track Case

When you use a window frame extent with UNBOUNDED PRECEDING as the lower bound, the optimizer uses a highly optimized strategy. I refer to this case as the *fast-track* case. But I'll get to that shortly. Let me first describe the roles of the Window Spool and Stream Aggregate iterators. By the way, internally the two iterators are implemented as one iterator, but they are presented in the plan as two.

The purpose of the Window Spool iterator is to expand each source row to its applicable frame rows—that's at least what happens in the worst-case scenario. The iterator generates an attribute identifying the window frame and calls it *WindowCountN*. The Stream Aggregate iterator groups the rows by *WindowCountN* and computes the aggregate. Now there's a problem of where to obtain the detail row's elements once the data has been grouped; for this, the current row is always added to the Window Spool, and the Stream Aggregate iterator has the logic to return the detail elements from that row.

As mentioned, each source row is expanded to all of its applicable frame rows only in the worst-case scenario, and I'll get to that later. In this section, I want to discuss special optimization for cases in which the low bound of the window frame is UNBOUNDED PRECEDING. In such a case, instead of expanding each source row to all applicable frame rows and then grouping and aggregating, the two iterators were coded with logic to just keep accumulating the values. So for each source row, the Window Spool iterator will have two rows—one with the cumulative information so far, and another with the current row. (Remember, this is needed for the detail elements.)

As an example, consider the following query:

```
SELECT actid, tranid, val,
  SUM(val) OVER(PARTITION BY actid
               ORDER BY tranid
               ROWS BETWEEN UNBOUNDED PRECEDING
                       AND CURRENT ROW) AS balance
FROM dbo.Transactions;
```

The plan is shown in Figure 4-18.

| SELECT Cost: 0 % | Compute Scalar Cost: 1 % | Stream Aggregate (Aggregate) Cost: 9 % | Window Spool Cost: 36 % | Segment Cost: 1 % | Sequence Project (Compute Scalar) Cost: 1 % | Segment Cost: 0 % | Clustered Index Scan (Clustered) [Transactions] [PK_Transactions] Cost: 50 % |
| 2000000 | | 4000000 | 2000000 | | | | |

FIGURE 4-18 Plan for ROWS.

The numbers below the arrows are row counts. The rows are scanned from the POC index in order. Then Segment and Sequence Project iterators compute a row number (call it *RowNumberN*). This row number is used for filtering of the right frame rows. Our case is a straightforward one, but think of cases that aren't (for example, ROWS BETWEEN 5 PRECEDING AND 2 FOLLOWING). Then another Segment iterator segments the data by *actid* for the computation of the window aggregate function. The Window Spool and Stream Aggregate iterators then just keep accumulating the values within each segment. Remember that the Transactions table has 2,000,000 rows. That's the number of rows you see streaming into the Window Spool iterator, as well as the number streaming out of the Stream Aggregate iterator. As explained earlier, the Window Spool iterator generates two rows for each source row in our special optimized case of UNBOUNDED PRECEDING—one for the cumulative value so far, and another for the current row to get the detail elements. Therefore you see 4,000,000 rows streaming from the Window Spool iterator to the Stream Aggregate iterator.

Also, if the conditions are right—and I'll get to the specifics later—the Window Spool iterator uses a highly optimized, in-memory work table, without all of the usual overhead that exists with work tables in tempdb, such as I/O, locks, latches, and so forth. Our query did benefit from the in-memory work table, plus the query used UNBOUNDED PRECEDING; therefore, it wasn't required to expand all frame rows. The two optimization aspects combined resulted in only nine seconds of run time for the query on my system and 6,208 logical reads. This is not bad at all compared to any other reliable method to compute running totals. (See Chapter 5 for more details on running totals.)

A number of conditions will prevent the Window Spool iterator from using the in-memory work table and cause it to use the far more expensive on-disk work table, with a B-tree indexed by the row number. I'll describe those conditions in detail in the next section, as well as how to check which kind of work table was used. For now, I want to mention that one of those conditions is when SQL Server cannot compute ahead of time the number of rows in the frame. An example of this is when using the RANGE window frame units instead of ROWS.

Recall from Chapter 2 that when using RANGE BETWEEN UNBOUNDED PRECEDING AND CURRENT ROW, the frame of a given row can involve additional rows ahead of the current one. That's the case when the ordering values are not unique within the partition. Currently, the optimizer doesn't check whether there's uniqueness—in which case, it can technically convert the RANGE option to an equivalent ROWS. It just defaults to using an on-disk work table. This translates to significant performance degradation compared to the ROWS option.

The following query is the same as the last one, only I replaced the ROWS option with RANGE:

```
SELECT actid, tranid, val,
  SUM(val) OVER(PARTITION BY actid
               ORDER BY tranid
               RANGE BETWEEN UNBOUNDED PRECEDING
                         AND CURRENT ROW) AS balance
FROM dbo.Transactions;
```

The plan for this query is shown in Figure 4-19.

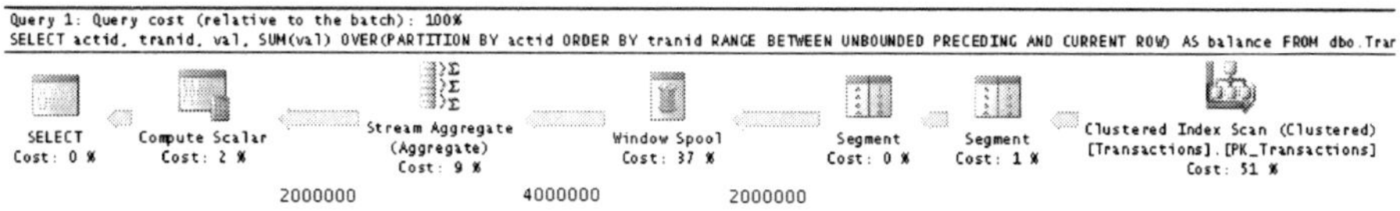

FIGURE 4-19 Plan for RANGE.

Nothing in the plan gives away the fact that an on-disk work table was used. In fact, it looks the same as the previous plan (minus the Sequence Project iterator), and the same number of rows stream between the iterators. The STATISTICS IO option is one way to tell that an on-disk work table was used. For the ROWS option, it reported zero reads against *Worktable* because it was an in-memory one. For the RANGE option, it reports millions of reads. A trace shows a total of 18,063,511 logical reads and 5,800 writes. This translates to 60 seconds of run time, compared with the nine seconds for ROWS.

The unfortunate part is that if you indicate a window order clause without an explicit window frame clause, the default according to the standard is RANGE BETWEEN UNBOUNDED PRECEDING AND CURRENT ROW, as in the following query:

```
SELECT actid, tranid, val,
  SUM(val) OVER(PARTITION BY actid
               ORDER BY tranid) AS balance
FROM dbo.Transactions;
```

It is highly likely that many people will use this form thinking it means by default ROWS BETWEEN UNBOUNDED PRECEDING AND CURRENT ROW, and they will not realize it actually translates to RANGE. This will incur the performance penalty, not to mention incorrect results if there are duplicates. I hope that in the future, at least in cases where there's uniqueness of the ordering values within each partition, that the optimizer will first translate the RANGE option to ROWS in this fast-track case.

Based on the details of the preceding discussions, you can improve the parallel processing of the RANGE query by using the parallel APPLY technique, like so:

```
SELECT C.actid, A.*
FROM dbo.Accounts AS C
  CROSS APPLY (SELECT tranid, val,
                 SUM(val) OVER(ORDER BY tranid
                              RANGE BETWEEN UNBOUNDED PRECEDING
                                        AND CURRENT ROW) AS balance
              FROM dbo.Transactions AS T
              WHERE T.actid = C.actid) AS A;
```

This query now gets a parallel plan that runs for 21 seconds—a third of the time of the query without APPLY. Still, it's much slower than the version with ROWS. So you can consider it a best practice to use the ROWS option whenever possible—certainly when there's uniqueness and the two are conceptually equivalent in the fast-track case.

Expanding All Frame Rows

In the previous section, I described a fast-track case that is used when the low bound of the frame is UNBOUNDED PRECEDING. In that case, SQL Server doesn't expand all frame rows for each source row; rather, it just keeps accumulating the values. As mentioned, the Window Spool iterator produces only two rows for each source row—one with the accumulation of values so far, and another with the base row for the detail elements.

When the low bound of the frame isn't UNBOUNDED PRECEDING, the fast-track case doesn't apply. In these cases, the optimizer will choose between one of two strategies. One strategy, which is the focus of this section, is to expand all frame rows for each source row. Another strategy, which is the focus of the next section, is to compute two cumulative values—*CumulativeBottom* and *CumulativeTop*—and derive the result based on the two.

To use the second strategy, the aggregate has to be a cumulative one (SUM, COUNT, COUNT_BIG, AVG, STDEV, STDEVP, VAR, or VARP), and there needs to be more than four rows in the frame to justify it. If the aggregate isn't a cumulative one (MIN, MAX, FIRST_VALUE, LAST_VALUE, or CHECKSUM_AGG) or the number of rows in the frame is four or less, the first strategy (in which all frame rows are expanded for each source row) will be used.

Note Internally LAG and LEAD are converted to the LAST_VALUE function with only one row in the frame; therefore, I won't discuss LAG and LEAD separately. As an example, LAG(x, 6) OVER(ORDER BY y) is translated to LAST_VALUE(x) OVER(ORDER BY y ROWS BETWEEN 6 PRECEDING AND 6 PRECEDING).

Consider the following example:

```
SELECT actid, tranid, val,
  SUM(val) OVER(PARTITION BY actid
                ORDER BY tranid
                ROWS BETWEEN 5 PRECEDING
                        AND 2 PRECEDING) AS sumval
FROM dbo.Transactions;
```

The plan for this query is shown in Figure 4-20. It took 14 seconds for the query to complete.

Query 1: Query cost (relative to the batch) 100%
SELECT actid, tranid, val, SUM(val) OVER(PARTITION BY actid ORDER BY tranid ROWS BETWEEN 5 PRECEDING AND 2 PRECEDING) AS sumval FROM dbo.Transactions;

SELECT	Compute Scalar	Stream Aggregate (Aggregate)	Window Spool	Segment	Compute Scalar	Sequence Project (Compute Scalar)	Segment	Clustered Index Scan (Clustered) [Transactions].[PK_Transactions]
Cost: 0 %	Cost: 1 %	Cost: 12 %	Cost: 46 %	Cost: 1 %	Cost: 1 %	Cost: 1 %	Cost: 0 %	Cost: 38 %
		2000000	9998600	2000000				

FIGURE 4-20 Plan expanding all frame rows.

The query uses a cumulative aggregate (SUM), but the frame has only four rows. Therefore, all frame rows are expanded. With four rows in each frame, plus the current row that is added for the detail elements, the Window Spool will produce five rows for each source row. Therefore, the plan shows that the Window Spool iterator generates almost 10,000,000 rows out of the 2,000,000 source rows. The frames for the first few rows in each partition have fewer than four rows; hence, the plan shows that the Window Spool iterator generates a bit less than 10,000,000 rows.

The Window Spool iterator needs to know which target rows to store in its work table for each source row, as well as generate a frame identifier in the target rows so that the Stream Aggregate iterator has something to group the rows by.

To figure out which rows to produce in each frame, the plan starts by computing a row number to each source row (using the first Segment and Sequence Project iterators). The row number is computed using the same partitioning and ordering as those of the original window function. The plan then uses a Compute Scalar iterator to compute for each source row the two row numbers—*BottomRowNumberN* and *TopRowNumberN*—that are supposed to bind the frame. For example, suppose that the current row has row number 10. The row numbers of the respective frame bounds are *TopRowNumberN* = 10 – 5 = 5 and *BottomRowNumber* = 10 – 2 = 8. The work table that the Window Spool creates is indexed by that row number. So if the rows with the row numbers 5 through 8 already exist in the work table, they will be queried and added to the work table associated with the new frame. If some rows are missing, the plan will keep requesting more rows and feed the spool until the bottom row number is reached. The Window Spool iterator generates for each target row an attribute it calls *WindowCountN* that identifies the frame. That's the attribute that the Stream Aggregate iterator groups the rows by.

In addition to computing the aggregate of interest, the Stream Aggregate iterator computes the count of rows in the frame, and then the Compute Scalar iterator that follows will return a NULL if the frame is empty.

As long as the number of rows in the frame is four or less, regardless of which window function you use, all frame rows will be expanded. Additional examples that will be treated in this manner are the following: 2 PRECEDING AND 1 FOLLOWING, 2 FOLLOWING AND 5 FOLLOWING, and so on.

If the current row is one of the boundary points of the frame, the plan won't need to compute both the top and bottom row numbers. It will compute only one row number–based boundary in addition to the existing *RowNumberN*. For example, for the frame 3 PRECEDING AND CURRENT ROW, it will compute only *TopRowNumberN (RowNumberN – 3)*, and for the frame CURRENT ROW AND 3

FOLLOWING, it will compute *BottomRowNumberN (RowNumberN + 3)*. The other boundary point will simply be *RowNumberN*.

When the window function you're using isn't a cumulative one (MIN, MAX, FIRST_VALUE, LAST_VALUE, or CHECKSUM_AGG), regardless of the number of rows in the frame, all frame rows will be expanded. Consider the following example:

```
SELECT actid, tranid, val,
  MAX(val) OVER(PARTITION BY actid
                ORDER BY tranid
                ROWS BETWEEN 100 PRECEDING
                         AND   2 PRECEDING) AS maxval
FROM dbo.Transactions;
```

The plan for this query is shown in Figure 4-21.

FIGURE 4-21 Plan for MAX aggregate.

Because the MAX aggregate is used, all frame rows get expanded. That's 99 rows per frame; multiply that by the number of rows in the table, and you end up with quite a large number of rows returned by the Window Spool iterator (close to 200,000,000 rows). It took this query 75 seconds to complete.

You can see that SQL Server decided to use a parallel plan. I explained earlier the issues with the way parallelism is handled natively for window functions and suggested that you try using the parallel APPLY technique instead. Here's the parallel APPLY version:

```
SELECT C.actid, A.*
FROM dbo.Accounts AS C
  CROSS APPLY (SELECT tranid, val,
                  MAX(val) OVER(ORDER BY tranid
                                ROWS BETWEEN 100 PRECEDING
                                         AND   2 PRECEDING) AS maxval
               FROM dbo.Transactions AS T
               WHERE T.actid = C.actid) AS A;
```

On my machine, this query finishes in 31 seconds.

The Window Spool iterator prefers to use a new optimized in-memory work table. However, if any of the following conditions is met, it will have no choice but to resort to the much slower on-disk work table with all of the associated overhead (for example, locking, latches, and I/O):

■ If the distance between the two extreme points among the current, top, and bottom row numbers exceeds 10,000

■ If it can't compute the number of rows in the frame—for example, when using RANGE

■ When using LAG or LEAD with an expression as the offset

There are a couple of techniques you can use to test whether in practice SQL Server used an on-disk work table or an in-memory one. The first technique is to use the STATISTICS IO option; the second technique is to use an Extended Event designed exactly for this purpose.

Using the STATISTICS IO option, you know that the in-memory work table was used when the number of reads reported against the work table is 0. When it's greater than 0, the on-disk one was used. As an example, the following code turns STATISTICS IO ON and runs two queries using the MAX window aggregate function:

```
SET STATISTICS IO ON;

SELECT actid, tranid, val,
  MAX(val) OVER(PARTITION BY actid
               ORDER BY tranid
               ROWS BETWEEN 9999 PRECEDING
                        AND 9999 PRECEDING) AS maxval
FROM dbo.Transactions;

SELECT actid, tranid, val,
  MAX(val) OVER(PARTITION BY actid
               ORDER BY tranid
               ROWS BETWEEN 10000 PRECEDING
                        AND 10000 PRECEDING) AS maxval
FROM dbo.Transactions;
```

The first query uses the following frame:

```
ROWS BETWEEN 9999 PRECEDING AND 9999 PRECEDING
```

The distance in terms of number of rows between the extreme points (remember, the current row is also considered for this purpose) is 10,000; hence, the in-memory work table can be used. This query finished in six seconds.

The second query uses the following frame:

```
ROWS BETWEEN 10000 PRECEDING AND 10000 PRECEDING
```

This time, the distance between the extreme points is 10,001; hence, the on-disk work table is used. This query finished in 33 seconds.

Here's the output of STATISTICS IO for the two queries:

```
-- 9999 PRECEDING AND 9999 PRECEDING, 6 seconds
Table 'Worktable'. Scan count 0, logical reads 0, physical reads 0, read-ahead reads 0, lob
logical reads 0, lob physical reads 0, lob read-ahead reads 0.
Table 'Transactions'. Scan count 1, logical reads 6208, physical reads 0, read-ahead reads 0,
lob logical reads 0, lob physical reads 0, lob read-ahead reads 0.

-- 10000 PRECEDING AND 10000 PRECEDING, 33 seconds
Table 'Worktable'. Scan count 2000100, logical reads 12086700, physical reads 0, read-ahead
reads 0, lob logical reads 0, lob physical reads 0, lob read-ahead reads 0.
Table 'Transactions'. Scan count 1, logical reads 6208, physical reads 0, read-ahead reads 0,
lob logical reads 0, lob physical reads 0, lob read-ahead reads 0.
```

Observe that for the first query, 0 reads are reported, whereas for the second query, 12,086,700 reads are reported.

Before I describe the second technique, run the following code to turn the STATISTICS IO option to OFF:

```
SET STATISTICS IO OFF;
```

The second technique to identify whether an on-disk work table was used is with an Extended Event called *window_spool_ondisk_warning*. Run the following code to create an event session using an asynchronous file target and start the session:

```
CREATE EVENT SESSION xe_window_spool ON SERVER
ADD EVENT sqlserver.window_spool_ondisk_warning
  ( ACTION (sqlserver.plan_handle, sqlserver.sql_text) )
ADD TARGET package0.asynchronous_file_target
  ( SET FILENAME  = N'c:\temp\xe_xe_window_spool.xel',
    metadatafile  = N'c:\temp\xe_xe_window_spool.xem' );

ALTER EVENT SESSION xe_window_spool ON SERVER STATE = START;
```

Rerun the preceding queries, and then open the file c:\temp\xe_xe_window_spool.xel from SQL Server Management Studio (SSMS). You will find information about the queries for which an on-disk work table was used, including the plan handle and the query text.

When you're done, run the following code for cleanup:

```
DROP EVENT SESSION xe_window_spool ON SERVER;
```

Computing Two Cumulative Values

When the window function is a cumulative one (SUM, COUNT, COUNT_BIG, AVG, STDEV, STDEVP, VAR, or VARP) and there are more than four rows in the frame, the optimizer uses a specialized strategy that doesn't involve expanding all frame rows. It computes two cumulative values, and then derives the result from the two. Consider the following query as an example:

```
SELECT actid, tranid, val,
  SUM(val) OVER(PARTITION BY actid
                ORDER BY tranid
                ROWS BETWEEN 100 PRECEDING
                         AND  2 PRECEDING) AS sumval
FROM dbo.Transactions;
```

The plan for this query is shown in Figure 4-22. The query took 14 seconds to complete.

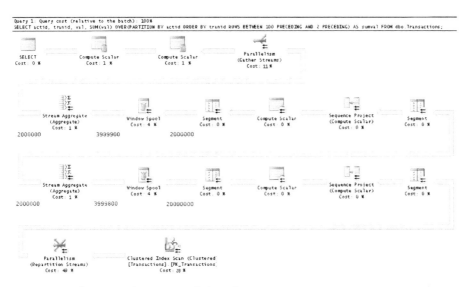

Query 1: Query cost (relative to the batch): 100%
SELECT actid, tranid, val, SUM(val) OVER(PARTITION BY actid ORDER BY tranid ROWS BETWEEN 100 PRECEDING AND 2 PRECEDING) AS sumval FROM dbo.Transactions;

FIGURE 4-22 Plan computing two cumulative values.

The optimizer decided to use a parallel plan. The plan uses a parallel scan of the POC index followed by an exchange iterator that repartitions the streams by the window-partitioning element (*actid* in our case). Then the plan uses a sequence of iterators (Segment, Sequence Project, Compute Scalar, Segment, Window Spool, and Stream Aggregate) to compute the cumulative bottom SUM and COUNT aggregate values (which we'll call *CumulativeBottomSum* and *CumulativeBottomCount*). The rows that were accumulated to compute the cumulative bottom aggregates are those from the beginning of the partition up to the row with the current row number minus 2. The technique used to compute the cumulative aggregates is the one I described in the "UNBOUNDED PRECEDING: The Fast-Track Case" section. Hence, you see that the Window Spool iterator generates only two rows for each source row—one with the accumulated values, and the current row for the detail elements.

Next, the plan uses another sequence of iterators (Segment, Sequence Project, Compute Scalar, Segment, Window Spool, and Stream Aggregate) to compute the cumulative top SUM and COUNT aggregate values (which we'll call *CumulativeTopSum* and *CumulativeTopCount*). The rows that were accumulated to compute those values are those from the beginning of the partition up to the row with the current row number minus 101.

Then a Compute Scalar iterator computes the window frame SUM as *CumulativeBottomSum* – *CumulativeTopSum* and the window frame COUNT as *CumulativeBottomCount* – *CumulativeTopCount*. Finally, the last Compute Scalar iterator evaluates the count of rows in the window frame, and if the count is 0, it returns a NULL.

As mentioned, this query took 14 seconds to complete on my system. That's using the built-in parallel handling of window functions. Here, as well, you can try using the parallel APPLY technique, as shown next.

```
SELECT C.actid, A.*
FROM dbo.Accounts AS C
  CROSS APPLY (SELECT tranid, val,
                   SUM(val) OVER(ORDER BY tranid
                          ROWS BETWEEN 100 PRECEDING
                                   AND  2 PRECEDING) AS sumval
             FROM dbo.Transactions AS T
             WHERE T.actid = C.actid) AS A;
```

The run time on my system decreased to eight seconds.

Distribution Functions

This section describes the optimization of distribution functions. I'll start with rank distribution functions and then continue with inverse distribution functions. If you don't remember the logic behind these computations, make sure you first review the section covering distribution functions in Chapter 2.

Rank Distribution Functions

Rank distribution functions are PERCENT_RANK and CUME_DIST. Recall that the PERCENT_RANK function is computed as $(rk - 1) / (nr - 1)$, where rk is the rank of the row and nr is the count of rows in the partition. Computing the count of rows in the respective partition involves using a Table Spool iterator as described earlier in the chapter. Computing the rank involves using the Sequence Project iterator. The plan that computes PERCENT_RANK simply incorporates both techniques.

Consider the following query as an example:

```
SELECT testid, studentid, score,
  PERCENT_RANK() OVER(PARTITION BY testid ORDER BY score) AS percentrank
FROM Stats.Scores;
```

The plan for this query is shown in Figure 4-23.

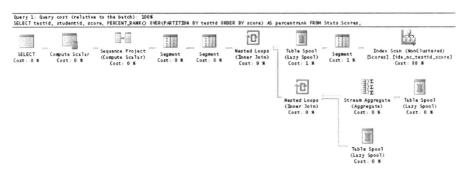

FIGURE 4-23 Plan for PERCENT_RANK.

The first part is scanning the data and segmenting it by *testid*. Then, one partition at a time, the partition rows are written to a spool, and the spool is read twice—once to compute the count (*nr*), and a second time to obtain the detail rows. Then the detail rows and the aggregates are joined. Next, the Segment and the Sequence Project iterators are used to compute the rank (*rk*). Finally, the Compute Scalar iterator computes the result of the PERCENT_RANK function as *(rk – 1) / (nr – 1)*.

As for CUME_DIST, the computation is *np / nr*, where *nr* is the same as before (the count of rows in the partition) and *np* is the count of rows that precede or are peers of the current row.

Consider the following query as an example:

```
SELECT testid, studentid, score,
  CUME_DIST()    OVER(PARTITION BY testid ORDER BY score) AS cumedist
FROM Stats.Scores;
```

The plan for this query is shown in Figure 4-24.

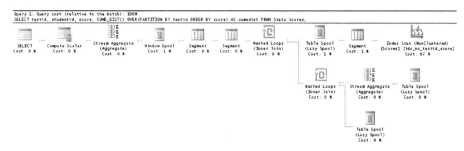

FIGURE 4-24 Plan for CUME_DIST.

The first part, which computes *nr*, is the same as in the plan for PERCENT_RANK. The second part is a bit trickier. To calculate *np*, SQL Server might need to look ahead of the current row. Also, here the plan uses two Segment iterators—the first iterator segments the rows by the partitioning element (*testid*), and the second iterator segments the rows by the partitioning plus ordering elements (*testid* and *score*). However, instead of using a Sequence Project iterator, it uses the new Window Spool and Stream Aggregate iterators in the fast-track mode to count the number of rows that precede or are peer of the current one. Finally, the Compute Scalar iterator computes the CUME_DIST value as *np / nr*.

Inverse Distribution Functions

The optimization of inverse distribution functions, PERCENTILE_CONT and PERCENTILE_DISC, is more involved than that of rank distribution functions. I'll start with PERCENTILE_DISC. Consider the following query:

```
SELECT testid, score,
  PERCENTILE_DISC(0.5) WITHIN GROUP(ORDER BY score)
    OVER(PARTITION BY testid) AS percentiledisc
FROM Stats.Scores;
```

The plan for this query appears in Figure 4-25.

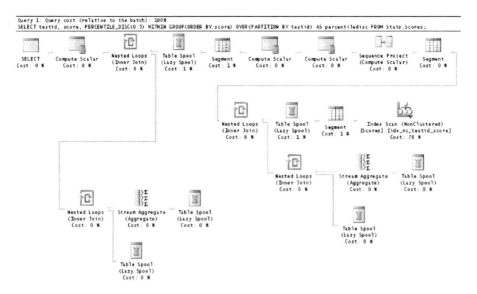

FIGURE 4-25 Plan for PERCENTILE_DISC.

The plan involves the following steps:

■ The first set of eight iterators that appear in the bottom-right section of Figure 4-25 are responsible for computing the count of rows for each row in the respective *testid* partition. The plan names this count *PartitionSizeN*.

■ The Segment and Sequence Project iterators that follow compute a row number within the *testid* partition, based on score ordering. The plan calls this row number *RowNumberN*.

■ The first Compute Scalar iterator computes the row number of the row that holds the percentile for the partition. It does so with the expression (simplified): *CeilingTargetRowN = ceiling(@pct * PartitionSize1013)*, where *@pct* is the input percent to the function (0.5 in our case).

■ The second Compute Scalar iterator computes an expression called *PartialSumN*. This expression returns the desired percentile score if the current row's row number (*RowNumberN*) is equal to *MIN(1, CeilingTargetRowN)*; otherwise, it returns a NULL. In simplified terms, *PartialSumN* will have the score only if it is the desired percentile; otherwise, it returns a NULL.

■ The last part needs to pull from each partition the non-NULL percentile (*PartialSumN*) and associate it with each detail row. For this, the plan again uses a Table Spool iterator. The plan segments the data by *testid* and, one partition at a time, stores the current partition's rows in a spool. Then the plan reads the spool twice—once to retrieve the non-NULL percentile using a *MAX(PartialSumN)* aggregate (call the result *PercentileResultN*), and another time to retrieve the detail. The plan then joins the detail and the aggregates.

■ The last part is checking the partition size. If it's 0, it returns NULL; otherwise, it returns *PercentileResultN*.

As for the PERCENTILE_CONT function, I'll use the following query to discuss the plan:

```
SELECT testid, score,
  PERCENTILE_CONT(0.5) WITHIN GROUP(ORDER BY score)
    OVER(PARTITION BY testid) AS percentilecont
FROM Stats.Scores;
```

The plan for this query is shown in Figure 4-26.

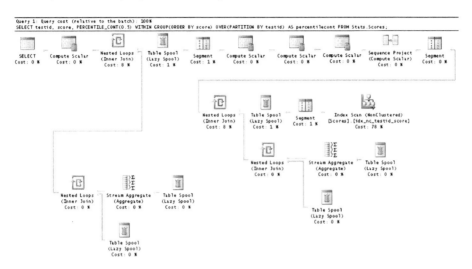

FIGURE 4-26 Plan for PERCENTILE_CONT.

As you can see, the general layout of the plan is similar to that for the PERCENTILE_DISC function. There are a couple of main differences, though. One difference is in the Compute Scalar iterators that appear right after the computation of the row number, and the other difference is in the second Stream Aggregate iterator. I'll start with the Compute Scalar iterators:

- The first Compute Scalar iterator computes the target row number, including the fraction: *TargetRowN = 1 + @pct * (PartitionSizeN – 1)*.

- The second Compute Scalar iterator computes the floor and ceiling of *TargetRowN*, naming them *FloorTargetRowN* and *CeilingTargetRowN*, respectively.

- The third Compute Scalar iterator computes an expression called *PartialSumN*. If no interpolation is needed, *PartialSumN* returns the percentile score if the current row is the target row and 0 otherwise. If an interpolation is needed, *PartialSumN* returns the parts of the interpolated score if the current row is either the floor or the ceiling of the target row; otherwise, it returns 0. The full computation of *PartialSumN* is quite convoluted; in case you have the stomach for it, here it is (simplified):

```
CASE
  -- when no interpolation is needed:
  --   return the current score if current row is target row, else 0
  WHEN CeilingTargetRowN = FloorTargetRowN AND CeilingTargetRowN = TargetRowN
```

```
        THEN CASE
            WHEN RowNumberN = TargetRowN
                THEN score
            ELSE 0
        END
-- when interpolation is needed:
--    return the parts of the interpolated value if current row
--    is either the floor or the ceiling of the target row
ELSE
  CASE
    WHEN RowNumberN = FloorTargetRowN
      THEN score * (CeilingTargetRowN - TargetRowN)
    ELSE
      CASE
        WHEN RowNumberN = CeilingTargetRowN
          THEN score * (TargetRowN - FloorTargetRowN)
        ELSE 0
      END
  END
END
```

The second difference from the plan for PERCENTILE_DISC is that the second Stream Aggregate iterator in the plan uses the SUM aggregate instead of MAX. It does so because this time more than one element could be relevant, and the parts that make the interpolated value need to be summed up.

Summary

This chapter covered SQL Server's optimization of window functions. There were a lot of details to cover, and I hope you didn't get lost in those. What are especially interesting are the new optimized Window Spool iterator and the enhanced Stream Aggregate iterator, as well as the optimized in-memory work table they use. There are still some glitches in optimization, especially ones that have to do with seemingly unnecessary sorts, but I expect those will be improved in the future. It's hard to get perfection, but it's important to strive for it. At any rate, when compared with alternative methods to compute the same calculations, SQL Server handles window functions very efficiently.

The next chapter gets into practical uses of window functions and, in some cases, compares solutions based on those with more traditional alternatives, demonstrating how much more efficient the new functions and functionality are.

CHAPTER 5

T-SQL Solutions Using Window Functions

The first four chapters of this book described window functions in detail, including both their logical aspects and their optimization aspects. In this fifth and last chapter of the book, I'm going to show how to solve a wide range of querying problems using window functions. What could be surprising to some is the large number of solutions that rely on the ROW_NUMBER function—by far the most commonly used of the bunch.

The solutions covered in this chapter are Virtual Auxiliary Table of Numbers, Sequences of Date and Time Values, Sequences of Keys, Paging, Removing Duplicates, Pivoting, Top N Per Group, Mode, Running Totals, Max Concurrent Intervals, Packing Intervals, Gaps and Islands, Median, Conditional Aggregate, and Sorting Hierarchies.

Note This chapter covers only a sample of solutions to show the usefulness and practicality of window functions. You will probably find many other ways to use window functions to solve problems more elegantly and efficiently than with alternative methods.

Virtual Auxiliary Table of Numbers

An auxiliary table of numbers is a helper table filled with a sequence of integers you can use to address many different querying tasks. There are many uses for such a numbers table, such as generating a sequence of date and time values and splitting separated lists of values. Normally, it is recommended to keep such a permanent table in your database, fill it with as many numbers as you will ever need, and then query it as needed. However, in some environments you don't have an option to create and populate new tables, and you need to get by with just querying logic.

To generate a large sequence of integers efficiently using querying logic, you can use cross joins. You start off with a query that generates a result set with two rows using a table value constructor, like so:

```
SELECT c FROM (VALUES(1),(1)) AS D(c);
```

This code generates the following output:

```
c
-----------
1
1
```

Next, define a common table expression (CTE)—call it *L0* for *level 0*—based on the previous query, and then cross two instances of the CTE to square the number of rows, getting four rows, like so:

```
WITH
   L0    AS(SELECT c FROM (VALUES(1),(1)) AS D(c))
SELECT 1 AS c FROM L0 AS A CROSS JOIN L0 AS B;
```

```
c
-----------
1
1
1
1
```

In a similar way, you can define a CTE (call it *L1* for *level 1*) based on the last query, and cross two instances of the new CTE to again square the number of rows, getting 16 rows, like so:

```
WITH
   L0    AS (SELECT c FROM (VALUES(1),(1)) AS D(c)),
   L1    AS (SELECT 1 AS c FROM L0 AS A CROSS JOIN L0 AS B)
SELECT 1 AS c FROM L1 AS A CROSS JOIN L1 AS B;
```

```
c
-----------
1
1
1
1
1
1
1
1
1
1
1
1
1
1
1
1
```

You can keep adding CTEs, each crossing two instances of the last CTE, squaring the number of rows. With *L* levels (starting the count with 0), the total number of rows you get is 2^{2^L} (read, two to the power of two to the power of *L*). For instance, with five levels, you get 4,294,967,296 rows. So with five levels of CTEs besides level 0, this method gives you over four billion rows. You will hardly ever need that many rows in a numbers table, but using the OFFSET/FETCH option in Microsoft SQL Server 2012, or TOP in previous versions of SQL Server, you can cap the number of rows based on user input. Using the ROW_NUMBER function with ORDER BY (SELECT NULL), you can generate the actual numbers without worrying about any sorting cost. Putting it all together, to generate a sequence of numbers in the range @low to @high, you can use the following code in SQL Server 2012:

```
WITH
  L0   AS (SELECT c FROM (VALUES(1),(1)) AS D(c)),
  L1   AS (SELECT 1 AS c FROM L0 AS A CROSS JOIN L0 AS B),
  L2   AS (SELECT 1 AS c FROM L1 AS A CROSS JOIN L1 AS B),
  L3   AS (SELECT 1 AS c FROM L2 AS A CROSS JOIN L2 AS B),
  L4   AS (SELECT 1 AS c FROM L3 AS A CROSS JOIN L3 AS B),
  L5   AS (SELECT 1 AS c FROM L4 AS A CROSS JOIN L4 AS B),
  Nums AS (SELECT ROW_NUMBER() OVER(ORDER BY (SELECT NULL)) AS rownum
           FROM L5)
SELECT @low + rownum - 1 AS n
FROM Nums
ORDER BY rownum
OFFSET 0 ROWS FETCH FIRST @high - @low + 1 ROWS ONLY;
```

The beauty in this approach is that SQL Server's optimizer realizes that there's no need to actually generate more rows than @high – @low + 1, so the query processor simply stops as soon as this number is reached. So if you need a sequence of only 10 numbers, it will generate only 10 and stop. If you want avoid repeating this code every time you need a sequence of numbers, you can encapsulate it in an inline table-valued function, like so:

```
USE TSQL2012;
IF OBJECT_ID('dbo.GetNums', 'IF') IS NOT NULL DROP FUNCTION dbo.GetNums;
GO
CREATE FUNCTION dbo.GetNums(@low AS BIGINT, @high AS BIGINT) RETURNS TABLE
AS
RETURN
  WITH
    L0   AS (SELECT c FROM (VALUES(1),(1)) AS D(c)),
    L1   AS (SELECT 1 AS c FROM L0 AS A CROSS JOIN L0 AS B),
    L2   AS (SELECT 1 AS c FROM L1 AS A CROSS JOIN L1 AS B),
    L3   AS (SELECT 1 AS c FROM L2 AS A CROSS JOIN L2 AS B),
    L4   AS (SELECT 1 AS c FROM L3 AS A CROSS JOIN L3 AS B),
    L5   AS (SELECT 1 AS c FROM L4 AS A CROSS JOIN L4 AS B),
    Nums AS (SELECT ROW_NUMBER() OVER(ORDER BY (SELECT NULL)) AS rownum
             FROM L5)
  SELECT @low + rownum - 1 AS n
  FROM Nums
  ORDER BY rownum
  OFFSET 0 ROWS FETCH FIRST @high - @low + 1 ROWS ONLY;
GO
```

Remember that the OFFSET/FETCH option was added in SQL Server 2012. If you need to define such a function in previous versions of SQL Server, use the TOP option instead, like so:

```
IF OBJECT_ID('dbo.GetNums', 'IF') IS NOT NULL
  DROP FUNCTION dbo.GetNums;
GO
CREATE FUNCTION dbo.GetNums(@low AS BIGINT, @high AS BIGINT) RETURNS TABLE
AS
RETURN
```

```
WITH
  L0  AS (SELECT c FROM (VALUES(1),(1)) AS D(c)),
  L1  AS (SELECT 1 AS c FROM L0 AS A CROSS JOIN L0 AS B),
  L2  AS (SELECT 1 AS c FROM L1 AS A CROSS JOIN L1 AS B),
  L3  AS (SELECT 1 AS c FROM L2 AS A CROSS JOIN L2 AS B),
  L4  AS (SELECT 1 AS c FROM L3 AS A CROSS JOIN L3 AS B),
  L5  AS (SELECT 1 AS c FROM L4 AS A CROSS JOIN L4 AS B),
  Nums AS (SELECT ROW_NUMBER() OVER(ORDER BY (SELECT NULL)) AS rownum
           FROM L5)
SELECT TOP(@high - @low + 1) @low + rownum - 1 AS n
FROM Nums
ORDER BY rownum;
GO
```

Both functions are optimized the same way, so performance is not a factor in determining which of the two is better to use. One factor that might matter to you is compatibility with systems running SQL Server versions prior to 2012—in which case, you might prefer to use the version with TOP. Then again, TOP isn't standard, whereas OFFSET-FETCH is; so, if using standard code when possible is a priority, you might prefer to use the latter in systems running SQL Server 2012.

As an example for using the *GetNums* function, the following code generates a sequence of numbers in the range 11 through 20:

```
SELECT n FROM dbo.GetNums(11, 20);
```

```
n
--------------------
11
12
13
14
15
16
17
18
19
20
```

To get a sense of how fast this method is, I tested it on a moderately equipped laptop after choosing the Discard Results After Execution query option from the Query Options dialog. It took only six seconds for the following request to generate a sequence of 10,000,000 numbers:

```
SELECT n FROM dbo.GetNums(1, 10000000);
```

The downside of the function is that plans for queries that use it are elaborate and can be a bit hard to follow. That's especially the case when multiple sequences are involved. Plans for queries against a real table of numbers, naturally, produce much simpler plans.

In this chapter, you will see a number of solutions that rely on the *GetNums* function.

Sequences of Date and Time Values

Various scenarios related to data manipulation require you to generate a sequence of date and time values between some input *@start* and *@end* points, with some interval (for example, 1 day, 12 hours, and so on). Examples for such scenarios include populating a time dimension in a data warehouse, scheduling applications, and others. An efficient tool that can be used for this purpose is the *GetNums* function described in the previous section. You accept the *@start* and *@end* date and time values as inputs, and using the DATEDIFF function, calculate how many intervals of the unit of interest there are between the two. Invoke the *GetNums* function with inputs *0* as *@low* and the aforementioned difference as *@high*. Finally, to generate the result date and time values, add *n* times the temporal interval to *@start*.

Here's an example for generating a sequence of dates in the range February 1, 2012 to February 12, 2012:

```
DECLARE
  @start AS DATE = '20120201',
  @end   AS DATE = '20120212';

SELECT DATEADD(day, n, @start) AS dt
FROM dbo.GetNums(0, DATEDIFF(day, @start, @end)) AS Nums;

dt
----------
2012-02-01
2012-02-02
2012-02-03
2012-02-04
2012-02-05
2012-02-06
2012-02-07
2012-02-08
2012-02-09
2012-02-10
2012-02-11
2012-02-12
```

If the interval is a product of some temporal unit—for example, 12 hours—use that unit (hour in this case) when calculating the difference between *@start* and *@end*, and divide the result by 12 to calculate *@high*; then multiply *n* by 12 to get the number of hours that need to be added to *@start* when calculating the result date and time values. As an example, the following code generates a sequence of date and time values between February 12, 2012 and February 18, 2012, with 12-hour intervals between the sequence values:

```
DECLARE
  @start AS DATETIME2 = '2012-02-12 00:00:00.0000000',
  @end   AS DATETIME2 = '2012-02-18 12:00:00.0000000';

SELECT DATEADD(hour, n*12, @start) AS dt
FROM dbo.GetNums(0, DATEDIFF(hour, @start, @end)/12) AS Nums;
```

```
dt
--------------------------
2012-02-12 00:00:00.0000000
2012-02-12 12:00:00.0000000
2012-02-13 00:00:00.0000000
2012-02-13 12:00:00.0000000
2012-02-14 00:00:00.0000000
2012-02-14 12:00:00.0000000
2012-02-15 00:00:00.0000000
2012-02-15 12:00:00.0000000
2012-02-16 00:00:00.0000000
2012-02-16 12:00:00.0000000
2012-02-17 00:00:00.0000000
2012-02-17 12:00:00.0000000
2012-02-18 00:00:00.0000000
2012-02-18 12:00:00.0000000
```

Sequences of Keys

In various scenarios you might need to generate a sequence of unique integer keys when updating or inserting data in a table. SQL Server 2012 introduces support for sequence objects, enabling you to create solutions for some of those needs. However, sequence objects are not available in versions prior to SQL Server 2012. Furthermore, SQL Server will not undo the generation of sequence values if the transaction where new sequence values were generated fails, meaning that you can end up with gaps between sequence values. (This is the same situation with IDENTITY.) If you need to guarantee there will be no gaps between the generated keys, you cannot use sequence objects. In this section, I will show you how to address a number of needs for sequence values without the new sequence objects.

Update a Column with Unique Values

The first scenario I'll describe involves the need to deal with data-quality issues. Run the following code to create and populate a table called MyOrders that I will use as sample data:

```
IF OBJECT_ID('Sales.MyOrders', 'U') IS NOT NULL
  DROP TABLE Sales.MyOrders;
GO

SELECT 0 AS orderid, custid, empid, orderdate
INTO Sales.MyOrders
FROM Sales.Orders;

SELECT * FROM Sales.MyOrders;
```

```
orderid      custid       empid        orderdate
-----------  -----------  -----------  -----------------------
0            85           5            2006-07-04 00:00:00.000
0            79           6            2006-07-05 00:00:00.000
0            34           4            2006-07-08 00:00:00.000
0            84           3            2006-07-08 00:00:00.000
```

0	76	4	2006-07-09 00:00:00.000
0	34	3	2006-07-10 00:00:00.000
0	14	5	2006-07-11 00:00:00.000
0	68	9	2006-07-12 00:00:00.000
0	88	3	2006-07-15 00:00:00.000
0	35	4	2006-07-16 00:00:00.000

. . .

Suppose that due to data-quality issues the table MyOrders doesn't have unique values in the *orderid* attribute. You are tasked with updating all rows with unique integers starting with 1 in arbitrary order. To address this need, you can define a CTE based on a query against MyOrders, returning the *orderid* attribute as well as a ROW_NUMBER calculation. If there's no ordering requirement for the calculation of row numbers, you can use (SELECT NULL) in the window order clause. Then, in the outer query against the CTE, use an UPDATE statement that sets *orderid* to the result of the ROW_NUMBER calculation, like so:

```
WITH C AS
(
  SELECT orderid, ROW_NUMBER() OVER(ORDER BY (SELECT NULL)) AS rownum
  FROM Sales.MyOrders
)
UPDATE C
  SET orderid = rownum;
```

Query MyOrders after the update, and observe that the *orderid* values are now unique:

```
SELECT * FROM Sales.MyOrders;
```

orderid	custid	empid	orderdate
1	85	5	2006-07-04 00:00:00.000
2	79	6	2006-07-05 00:00:00.000
3	34	4	2006-07-08 00:00:00.000
4	84	3	2006-07-08 00:00:00.000
5	76	4	2006-07-09 00:00:00.000
6	34	3	2006-07-10 00:00:00.000
7	14	5	2006-07-11 00:00:00.000
8	68	9	2006-07-12 00:00:00.000
9	88	3	2006-07-15 00:00:00.000
10	35	4	2006-07-16 00:00:00.000

. . .

At this point, it's a good idea to add a primary key constraint to enforce uniqueness in the table.

Applying a Range of Sequence Values

Suppose that you need a sequencing mechanism that guarantees no gaps. You can't rely on the identity column property or the sequence object because both mechanisms will have gaps when the operation that generates the sequence value fails or just doesn't commit. One of the common ways to implement a sequencing mechanism that guarantees there will be no gaps is to store the last-used value in a table, and whenever you need a new value, increment the stored value and use the new one.

As an example, the following code creates a table called MySequence and populates it with one row with the value *0* in the *val* column:

```
IF OBJECT_ID('dbo.MySequence', 'U') IS NOT NULL DROP TABLE dbo.MySequence;
CREATE TABLE dbo.MySequence(val INT);
INSERT INTO dbo.MySequence VALUES(0);
```

You can then use a stored procedure such as the following whenever you need to generate and use a new sequence value:

```
IF OBJECT_ID('dbo.GetSequence', 'P') IS NOT NULL DROP PROC dbo.GetSequence;
GO

CREATE PROC dbo.GetSequence
  @val AS INT OUTPUT
AS
UPDATE dbo.MySequence
  SET @val = val += 1;
GO
```

The procedure updates the row in MySequence, incrementing the current value by 1, and stores the incremented value in the output parameter *@val*. Whenever you need a new sequence value, you execute the procedure and collect the new value from the output parameter, like so:

```
DECLARE @key AS INT;
EXEC dbo.GetSequence @val = @key OUTPUT;
SELECT @key;
```

If you run this code twice (in the same transaction, of course), you will get the sequence value 1 first and 2 second.

Suppose that sometimes you need to allocate a whole range of sequence values—for example, for use in a multirow insertion into some table. First, you need to alter the procedure to accept an input parameter (call it *@n*) that indicates the range size. Then the procedure can increment the *val* column in MySequence by *@n* and return the first value in the new range as the output parameter. Here's the altered definition of the procedure:

```
ALTER PROC dbo.GetSequence
  @val AS INT OUTPUT,
  @n   AS INT = 1
AS
UPDATE dbo.MySequence
  SET @val = val + 1,
      val += @n;
GO
```

You still need to figure out how to associate the individual sequence values in the range with rows in the result set of the query. Suppose that the following query returning customers from the UK represents the set you need to insert into the target table:

```
SELECT custid
FROM Sales.Customers
WHERE country = N'UK';

custid
-----------
4
11
16
19
38
53
72
```

You are supposed to generate surrogate keys for these customers and, ultimately, insert those into a customer dimension in your data warehouse. You can first populate a table variable with this result set along with the result of a ROW_NUMBER function that will generate unique integers starting with 1. (Call this column *rownum*.) Then you can collect the number of affected rows from the @@*rowcount* function into a local variable (call it @*rc*). Then you can invoke the procedure, passing @*rc* as the size of the range to allocate, and collect the first key in the range and put it into a local variable (call it @*firstkey*). Finally, you can query the table variable and compute the individual sequence values with the expression @*firstkey* + *rownum* − *1*. Here's the T-SQL code with the complete solution:

```
DECLARE @firstkey AS INT, @rc AS INT;

DECLARE @CustsStage AS TABLE
(
  custid INT,
  rownum INT
);

INSERT INTO @CustsStage(custid, rownum)
  SELECT custid, ROW_NUMBER() OVER(ORDER BY (SELECT NULL))
  FROM Sales.Customers
  WHERE country = N'UK';

SET @rc = @@rowcount;

EXEC dbo.GetSequence @val = @firstkey OUTPUT, @n = @rc;

SELECT custid, @firstkey + rownum - 1 AS keycol
FROM @CustsStage;

custid      keycol
----------- -----------
4           3
11          4
16          5
19          6
38          7
53          8
72          9
```

Of course, normally the last part inserts the result of this query into the target table. Also, observe that I use ORDER BY (SELECT NULL) in the window order clause of the ROW_NUMBER function to get an arbitrary order for the row numbers. If you need the sequence values to be assigned in a certain order (for example, *custid* ordering), make sure you revise the window order clause accordingly.

Next run a similar process, this time querying source customers from France:

```
DECLARE @firstkey AS INT, @rc AS INT;

DECLARE @CustsStage AS TABLE
(
  custid INT,
  rownum INT
);

INSERT INTO @CustsStage(custid, rownum)
  SELECT custid, ROW_NUMBER() OVER(ORDER BY (SELECT NULL))
  FROM Sales.Customers
  WHERE country = N'France';

SET @rc = @@rowcount;

EXEC dbo.GetSequence @val = @firstkey OUTPUT, @n = @rc;

SELECT custid, @firstkey + rownum - 1 AS keycol
FROM @CustsStage;
```

```
custid       keycol
-----------  -----------
7            10
9            11
18           12
23           13
26           14
40           15
41           16
57           17
74           18
84           19
85           20
```

Notice in the result that the sequence values generated simply continued right after the end of the previously allocated range.

When you're done, run the following code for cleanup:

```
IF OBJECT_ID('dbo.GetSequence', 'P') IS NOT NULL DROP PROC dbo.GetSequence;
IF OBJECT_ID('dbo.MySequence', 'U') IS NOT NULL DROP TABLE dbo.MySequence;
```

Paging

Paging is a common need in applications. You want to allow the user to get one portion of rows at a time from a result set of a query so that the result can more easily fit in the target web page, UI, or screen. The ROW_NUMBER function can be used for paging purposes. You assign row numbers to the result rows based on the desired ordering, and then filter the right range of row numbers based on given page-number and page-size arguments. For optimal performance, you want to have an index defined on the window ordering elements as the index keys and include in the index the rest of the attributes that appear in the query for coverage purposes.

As an example, suppose you want to allow paging through orders from the Sales.Orders table based on *orderdate, orderid* ordering (from least to most recent), and return in the result set the attributes *orderid, orderdate, custid*, and *empid*. Following the indexing guidelines I just mentioned, you arrange the following index:

```
CREATE UNIQUE INDEX idx_od_oid_i_cid_eid
  ON Sales.Orders(orderdate, orderid)
  INCLUDE(custid, empid);
```

Then, given a page number and a page size as inputs, you use the following code to filter the correct page of rows. For example, the following code returns the third page with a page size of 25 rows, meaning the rows with row numbers 51 through 75:

```
DECLARE
  @pagenum  AS INT = 3,
  @pagesize AS INT = 25;

WITH C AS
(
  SELECT ROW_NUMBER() OVER( ORDER BY orderdate, orderid ) AS rownum,
    orderid, orderdate, custid, empid
  FROM Sales.Orders
)
SELECT orderid, orderdate, custid, empid
FROM C
WHERE rownum BETWEEN (@pagenum - 1) * @pagesize + 1
                AND @pagenum * @pagesize
ORDER BY rownum;
```

orderid	orderdate	custid	empid
10298	2006-09-05 00:00:00.000	37	6
10299	2006-09-06 00:00:00.000	67	4
10300	2006-09-09 00:00:00.000	49	2
10301	2006-09-09 00:00:00.000	86	8
10302	2006-09-10 00:00:00.000	76	4
10303	2006-09-11 00:00:00.000	30	7
10304	2006-09-12 00:00:00.000	80	1
10305	2006-09-13 00:00:00.000	55	8
10306	2006-09-16 00:00:00.000	69	1
10307	2006-09-17 00:00:00.000	48	2
10308	2006-09-18 00:00:00.000	2	7

10309	2006-09-19 00:00:00.000	37	3
10310	2006-09-20 00:00:00.000	77	8
10311	2006-09-20 00:00:00.000	18	1
10312	2006-09-23 00:00:00.000	86	2
10313	2006-09-24 00:00:00.000	63	2
10314	2006-09-25 00:00:00.000	65	1
10315	2006-09-26 00:00:00.000	38	4
10316	2006-09-27 00:00:00.000	65	1
10317	2006-09-30 00:00:00.000	48	6
10318	2006-10-01 00:00:00.000	38	8
10319	2006-10-02 00:00:00.000	80	7
10320	2006-10-03 00:00:00.000	87	5
10321	2006-10-03 00:00:00.000	38	3
10322	2006-10-04 00:00:00.000	58	7

Figure 5-1 shows the execution plan for this query.

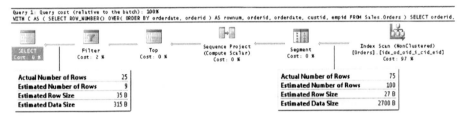

FIGURE 5-1 Execution plan for a query with ROW_NUMBER.

Observe that because there was an index to support the ROW_NUMBER calculation, SQL Server didn't really need to scan all rows from the table. Rather, it scanned only the first 75 rows in the index and then filtered the rows with row numbers 51 through 75. As you can imagine, without such an index in place, SQL Server would have no choice but to scan all rows, sort, assign row numbers, and then filter. So indexing here is critical for good performance.

You can use the aforementioned technique based on row numbers in SQL Server 2005 and later. If you're using SQL Server 2012, an alternative solution to paging is to use the new OFFSET/FETCH filtering option. This option is similar to TOP, except that it's standard, it supports skipping rows, and it's part of the ORDER BY clause. Here's the code you use to filter the right page of rows using the OFFSET/FETCH option given the page number and page size as inputs:

```
DECLARE
  @pagenum  AS INT = 3,
  @pagesize AS INT = 25;

SELECT orderid, orderdate, custid, empid
FROM Sales.Orders
ORDER BY orderdate, orderid
OFFSET (@pagenum - 1) * @pagesize ROWS FETCH NEXT @pagesize ROWS ONLY;
```

The execution plan for this query is shown in Figure 5-2.

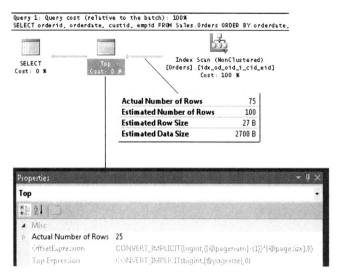

Query 1: Query cost (relative to the batch): 100%
SELECT orderid, orderdate, custid, empid FROM Sales.Orders ORDER BY orderdate,

SELECT Cost: 0 %	Top Cost: 0 %	Index Scan (NonClustered) [Orders].[idx_od_oid_i_cid_eid] Cost: 100 %

Actual Number of Rows	75
Estimated Number of Rows	100
Estimated Row Size	27 B
Estimated Data Size	2700 B

Properties

Top

▲ Misc
▷ Actual Number of Rows 25
  OffsetExpression   CONVERT_IMPLICIT(bigint,[@pagenum]-(1))*[@pagesize],0)
  Top Expression   CONVERT_IMPLICIT(bigint,[@pagesize],0)

FIGURE 5-2 Execution plan for a query with OFFSET/FETCH.

Observe in the execution plan that the optimization is similar to that of the technique based on row numbers—in the sense that SQL Server scans only the first 75 rows in the index and filters the last 25. As a result, the work, in terms of number of reads, is similar in both cases.

When you're done, run the following code for cleanup:

```
DROP INDEX idx_od_oid_i_cid_eid ON Sales.Orders;
```

Removing Duplicates

De-duplication of data is a common need, especially when dealing with data-quality issues in environments that end up with duplicate rows due to lack of enforcement of uniqueness with constraints. As an example, the following code prepares sample data with duplicate orders in a table called MyOrders:

```
IF OBJECT_ID('Sales.MyOrders') IS NOT NULL DROP TABLE Sales.MyOrders;
GO

SELECT * INTO Sales.MyOrders FROM Sales.Orders
UNION ALL
SELECT * FROM Sales.Orders
UNION ALL
SELECT * FROM Sales.Orders;
```

Suppose that you need to de-duplicate the data, keeping only one occurrence of each unique *orderid* value. You mark the duplicate number using the ROW_NUMBER function, partitioned by what's supposed to be unique (*orderid* in our case), and using arbitrary ordering if you don't care which row is kept and which is removed. Here's the code with the ROW_NUMBER function marking the duplicates:

```
SELECT orderid,
  ROW_NUMBER() OVER(PARTITION BY orderid
                    ORDER BY (SELECT NULL)) AS n
FROM Sales.MyOrders;
```

```
orderid     n
----------- --------------------
10248       1
10248       2
10248       3
10249       1
10249       2
10249       3
10250       1
10250       2
10250       3
```

Next, you consider different options depending on the number of rows that need to be deleted, the percent of table cardinality that number represents, the production activity, and so on. When a small number of the rows need to be deleted, it's usually OK to use a fully logged delete operation that removes all occurrences where the row number is greater than 1, like so:

```
WITH C AS
(
  SELECT orderid,
    ROW_NUMBER() OVER(PARTITION BY orderid
                      ORDER BY (SELECT NULL)) AS n
  FROM Sales.MyOrders
)
DELETE FROM C
WHERE n > 1;
```

If, however, you have a large number of rows that need to be deleted—especially when this number represents a large percentage of the rows in the table—the fully logged delete can prove too slow. In such a case, one of the options to consider is using a minimally logged operation, like SELECT INTO, to copy distinct rows (rows with row number 1) into a different table name; drop the original table; rename the new table to the original table name; then re-create constraints, indexes, and triggers on the target table. Here's the code with the complete solution:

```
WITH C AS
(
  SELECT *,
    ROW_NUMBER() OVER(PARTITION BY orderid
                      ORDER BY (SELECT NULL)) AS n
  FROM Sales.MyOrders
)
SELECT orderid, custid, empid, orderdate, requireddate, shippeddate,
  shipperid, freight, shipname, shipaddress, shipcity, shipregion,
  shippostalcode, shipcountry
INTO Sales.OrdersTmp
FROM C
```

```
WHERE n = 1;

DROP TABLE Sales.MyOrders;
EXEC sp_rename 'Sales.OrdersTmp', 'MyOrders';
-- recreate indexes, constraints, triggers
```

To keep things simple, I didn't include any transaction control in this example, but you should always remember that multiple users can interact with the data. If you implement this technique in production you should be sure to do the following:

1. Open a transaction.

2. Take a lock on the table.

3. Perform the SELECT INTO.

4. Drop and rename the objects.

5. Re-create indexes, constraints, and triggers.

6. Commit the transaction.

There's another option that I learned from Javier Loria to filter either just the distinct rows or all but the distinct rows. You compute both ROW_NUMBER and RANK based on *orderid* ordering, like so:

```
SELECT orderid,
  ROW_NUMBER() OVER(ORDER BY orderid) AS rownum,
  RANK() OVER(ORDER BY orderid) AS rnk
FROM Sales.MyOrders;
```

```
orderid     rownum                rnk
----------- --------------------- --------------------
10248       1                     1
10248       2                     1
10248       3                     1
10249       4                     4
10249       5                     4
10249       6                     4
10250       7                     7
10250       8                     7
10250       9                     7
```

Observe in the result that only in one row for each unique *orderid* value are the row number and rank the same. For example, if you have a small percentage of rows to delete, you encapsulate the previous query in a CTE definition and, in the outer statement, issue a DELETE where the row number is different than the rank, like so:

```
WITH C AS
(
  SELECT orderid,
    ROW_NUMBER() OVER(ORDER BY orderid) AS rownum,
    RANK() OVER(ORDER BY orderid) AS rnk
  FROM Sales.MyOrders
)
DELETE FROM C
WHERE rownum <> rnk;
```

The preceding solutions are not the only ones. For example, there are scenarios where you will want to split a large delete into batches using the TOP option. But here I wanted to focus on solutions using window functions.

When you're done, run the following code for cleanup:

```
IF OBJECT_ID('Sales.MyOrders') IS NOT NULL DROP TABLE Sales.MyOrders;
```

Pivoting

Pivoting is a technique to aggregate and rotate data from a state of rows to columns. When pivoting data, you need to identify three elements: the element you want to see on rows (the grouping element), the element you want to see on columns (the spreading element), and the element you want to see in the data portion (the aggregation element).

As an example, suppose that you need to query the Sales.OrderValues view and return a row for each order year, a column for each order month, and the sum of order values for each year and month intersection. In this request, the *on rows*, or grouping, element is *YEAR(orderdate)*; the *on cols*, or spreading, element is *MONTH(orderdate)*; the distinct spreading values are 1, 2, 3, 4, 5, 6, 7, 8, 9, 10, 11, and 12; and the *data*, or aggregation, element is *SUM(val)*.

To achieve pivoting, you first want to prepare a table expression such as a CTE, where you return only the three elements that are involved in your pivoting task. Then, in the outer statement, you query the table expression and use the PIVOT operator to handle the pivoting logic, like so (output wrapped):

```
WITH C AS
(
  SELECT YEAR(orderdate) AS orderyear, MONTH(orderdate) AS ordermonth, val
  FROM Sales.OrderValues
)
SELECT *
FROM C
  PIVOT(SUM(val)
    FOR ordermonth IN ([1],[2],[3],[4],[5],[6],[7],[8],[9],[10],[11],[12])) AS P;
```

orderyear	1	2	3	4	5	6
2007	61258.08	38483.64	38547.23	53032.95	53781.30	36362.82
2008	94222.12	99415.29	104854.18	123798.70	18333.64	NULL
2006	NULL	NULL	NULL	NULL	NULL	NULL

orderyear	7	8	9	10	11	12
2007	51020.86	47287.68	55629.27	66749.23	43533.80	71398.44
2008	NULL	NULL	NULL	NULL	NULL	NULL
2006	27861.90	25485.28	26381.40	37515.73	45600.05	45239.63

In this case, all three pivoting elements are known, including the distinct values in the spreading element (the months). But there are certain pivoting tasks where the spreading element doesn't exist in the source and needs to be computed. For example, consider a request to return, for each customer, the order IDs of its five most recent orders. You want to see the customer IDs on rows and the order IDs in the data part, but there's nothing common to the order IDs across customers that you can use as your spreading element.

The solution is to use a ROW_NUMBER function that assigns ordinals to the order IDs within each customer partition, based on the desired ordering—*orderdate DESC, orderid DESC* in our case. Then the attribute representing that row number can be used as the spreading element and the ordinals can be calculated as the spreading values.

So first, here's the code that generates the row numbers for each customer's orders from most recent to least recent:

```
SELECT custid, val,
  ROW_NUMBER() OVER(PARTITION BY custid
                    ORDER BY orderdate DESC, orderid DESC) AS rownum
FROM Sales.OrderValues;
```

custid	val	rownum
1	933.50	1
1	471.20	2
1	845.80	3
1	330.00	4
1	878.00	5
1	814.50	6
2	514.40	1
2	320.00	2
2	479.75	3
2	88.80	4
3	660.00	1
3	375.50	2
3	813.37	3
3	2082.00	4
3	1940.85	5
3	749.06	6
3	403.20	7

...

Now you can define a CTE based on the previous query, and then in the outer query handle the pivoting logic, with *rownum* being used as the spreading element:

```
WITH C AS
(
  SELECT custid, val,
    ROW_NUMBER() OVER(PARTITION BY custid
                      ORDER BY orderdate DESC, orderid DESC) AS rownum
  FROM Sales.OrderValues
)
SELECT *
FROM C
  PIVOT(MAX(val) FOR rownum IN ([1],[2],[3],[4],[5])) AS P;
```

```
custid  1         2         3         4         5
-------  --------  --------  --------  --------  ---------
1        933.50    471.20    845.80    330.00    878.00
2        514.40    320.00    479.75    88.80     NULL
3        660.00    375.50    813.37    2082.00   1940.85
4        491.50    4441.25   390.00    282.00    191.10
5        1835.70   709.55    1096.20   2048.21   1064.50
6        858.00    677.00    625.00    464.00    330.00
7        730.00    660.00    450.00    593.75    1761.00
8        224.00    3026.85   982.00    NULL      NULL
9        792.75    360.00    1788.63   917.00    1979.23
10       525.00    1309.50   877.73    1014.00   717.50
...
```

If you need to concatenate into one string the order IDs of the five most recent orders for each customer, you can use SQL Server 2012's new CONCAT function, like so:

```
WITH C AS
(
  SELECT custid, CAST(orderid AS VARCHAR(11)) AS sorderid,
    ROW_NUMBER() OVER(PARTITION BY custid
                      ORDER BY orderdate DESC, orderid DESC) AS rownum
  FROM Sales.OrderValues
)
SELECT custid, CONCAT([1], ','+[2], ','+[3], ','+[4], ','+[5]) AS orderids
FROM C
  PIVOT(MAX(sorderid) FOR rownum IN ([1],[2],[3],[4],[5])) AS P;
```

```
custid      orderids
----------  -------------------------------------------------------------
1           11011,10952,10835,10702,10692
2           10926,10759,10625,10308
3           10856,10682,10677,10573,10535
4           11016,10953,10920,10864,10793
5           10924,10875,10866,10857,10837
6           11058,10956,10853,10614,10582
7           10826,10679,10628,10584,10566
8           10970,10801,10326
9           11076,10940,10932,10876,10871
10          11048,11045,11027,10982,10975
...
```

The CONCAT function automatically replaces a NULL with an empty string. To achieve the same thing in versions prior to SQL Server 2012, you need to use the + concatenation operator and the COALESCE function to replace a NULL with an empty string, like so:

```
WITH C AS
(
  SELECT custid, CAST(orderid AS VARCHAR(11)) AS sorderid,
    ROW_NUMBER() OVER(PARTITION BY custid
                      ORDER BY orderdate DESC, orderid DESC) AS rownum
  FROM Sales.OrderValues
)
```

```
SELECT custid,
  [1] + COALESCE(','+[2], '')
      + COALESCE(','+[3], '')
      + COALESCE(','+[4], '')
      + COALESCE(','+[5], '') AS orderids
FROM C
  PIVOT(MAX(sorderid) FOR rownum IN ([1],[2],[3],[4],[5])) AS P;
```

TOP N Per Group

The Top-N-per-Group problem is a common querying problem that involves filtering a requested number of rows from each group, or partition, of rows, based on some defined ordering. A request to query the Sales.Orders table and return, for each customer, the three most recent orders is an example for the Top-N-per-Group problem. In this case, the partitioning element is *custid*; the ordering specification is *orderdate DESC, orderid DESC* (most recent); and *N* is 3. Both TOP and the newer OFFSET/FETCH filtering options do support indicating the number of rows to filter and ordering specification, but they don't support a partition clause. Imagine how nice it would be if you could indicate both a partition clause and an order clause as part of the filter specification—something like this:

```
SELECT
  TOP (3) OVER(
    PARTITION BY custid
    ORDER BY orderdate DESC, orderid DESC)
  custid, orderdate, orderid, empid
FROM Sales.Orders;
```

Unfortunately, such syntax doesn't exist, and you have to figure out other solutions to this need.

Note I submitted a request to Microsoft to support the TOP OVER syntax. You can find the request here: *http://connect.microsoft.com/SQLServer/feedback/details/254390/over-clause-enhancement-request-top-over.*

Indexing guidelines, regardless of the solution you use, follow the POC concept. (POC stands for *Partioning, Ordering, Covering*; see Chapter 4, "Optimization of Window Functions," for more information.) The index key list is defined based on the partitioning columns (*custid* in our case) followed by the ordering columns (*orderdate DESC, orderid DESC* in our case), and it includes the rest of the columns that appear in the query for coverage purposes. Of course, if the index is a clustered index, all table columns are covered anyway, so you don't need to worry about the C part of the POC index. Here's the code to generate the POC index for our task, assuming *empid* is the only remaining column you need to return from the query other than *custid*, *orderdate*, and *orderid*:

```
CREATE UNIQUE INDEX idx_cid_odD_oidD_i_empid
  ON Sales.Orders(custid, orderdate DESC, orderid DESC)
  INCLUDE(empid);
```

Assuming you have a POC index in place, there are two strategies to address the task: one using the ROW_NUMBER function, and another using the APPLY operator and OFFSET/FETCH or TOP. What determines which of the two is most efficient is the density of the partitioning column (*custid* in our case). With low density—namely, a large number of distinct customers, each with a small number of orders—a solution based on the ROW_NUMBER function is optimal. You assign row numbers based on the same partitioning and ordering requirements as those in the request, and then filter only the rows with row numbers that are less than or equal to the number of rows you need to filter for each group. Here's the complete solution implementing this approach:

```
WITH C AS
(
  SELECT custid, orderdate, orderid, empid,
    ROW_NUMBER() OVER(
      PARTITION BY custid
      ORDER BY orderdate DESC, orderid DESC) AS rownum
  FROM Sales.Orders
)
SELECT *
FROM C
WHERE rownum <= 3
ORDER BY custid, rownum;
```

Figure 5-3 shows the execution plan for this query.

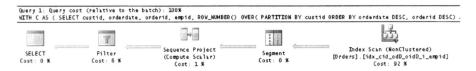

FIGURE 5-3 Execution plan for a query with low density.

What makes this strategy so efficient when the partitioning column has low density (remember, that's a large number of distinct customers, each with a small number of orders) is that the plan involves only one ordered scan of the POC index. In such a case, you do not want a plan that performs a seek operation in the index for each distinct partitioning value (customer). However, when the partitioning column has high density (a small number of distinct customers, each with a large number of orders), a plan that performs a seek in the index for each customer becomes a more efficient strategy than a full scan of the index leaf. The way to achieve such a plan is to query the table that holds the distinct partitioning values (Sales.Customers in our case) and use the APPLY operator to invoke a query with OFFSET/FETCH or TOP for each customer, like so:

```
SELECT C.custid, A.*
FROM Sales.Customers AS C
  CROSS APPLY (SELECT orderdate, orderid, empid
              FROM Sales.Orders AS O
              WHERE O.custid = C.custid
              ORDER BY orderdate DESC, orderid DESC
              OFFSET 0 ROWS FETCH FIRST 3 ROWS ONLY) AS A;
```

The plan for this query is shown in Figure 5-4.

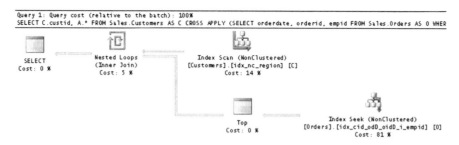

```
Query 1: Query cost (relative to the batch): 100%
SELECT C.custid, A.* FROM Sales.Customers AS C CROSS APPLY (SELECT orderdate, orderid, empid FROM Sales.Orders AS O WHER
```

FIGURE 5-4 Execution plan for a query with high density.

Observe in the plan that an index on the Customers table is scanned to retrieve all customer IDs. Then, for each customer, the plan performs a seek operation in our POC index (going to the beginning of the current customer's section in the index leaf), and then scans three rows in the leaf for the three most recent orders.

Remember that the OFFSET/FETCH was added in SQL Server 2012. In earlier versions of SQL Server, you can use the TOP option instead:

```
SELECT C.custid, A.*
FROM Sales.Customers AS C
  CROSS APPLY (SELECT TOP (3) orderdate, orderid, empid
               FROM Sales.Orders AS O
               WHERE O.custid = C.custid
               ORDER BY orderdate DESC, orderid DESC) AS A;
```

Note that to perform well, both strategies require a POC index. If you don't have an index in place and either cannot or do not want to create one, there's a third strategy that tends to perform better than the other two. However, this third strategy works only when *N* equals *1*.

At this point, you can drop the POC index:

```
DROP INDEX idx_cid_odD_oidD_i_empid ON Sales.Orders;
```

The third strategy implements a technique you can think of as a *carry-along sort*. I introduced this technique earlier in the book in Chapter 3, "Ordered Set Functions," when discussing offset functions. The idea is to form a single string for each partition where you concatenate first the ordering attributes and then all of the nonkey attributes you need in the result. It's important to use a concatenation technique that results in a string that sorts the same as the ordering elements are supposed to sort. For example, in our case the ordering is based on *orderdate DESC* and *orderid DESC*.

The first element is a date. To get a charter string representation of a date that sorts the same as the original date, you need to convert the date to the form YYYYMMDD. To achieve this, use the CONVERT function with style 112. As for the *orderid* element, it's a positive integer. To have a character string form of the number sort the same as the original integer, you need to format the value as a fixed-length string with leading spaces or zeros. You can format the value as a fixed-length string with leading spaces using the STR function.

The solution involves grouping the rows by the partitioning column and calculating the maximum concatenated string per group. That maximum string represents the concatenated elements from the row you need to return. Next, you define a CTE based on the last query. Then, in the outer query, use SUBSTRING functions to extract the individual elements you originally concatenated and convert them back to their original types. Here's what the complete solution looks like:

```
WITH C AS
(
  SELECT custid,
    MAX(CONVERT(CHAR(8), orderdate, 112)
        + STR(orderid, 10)
        + STR(empid, 10) COLLATE Latin1_General_BIN2) AS mx
  FROM Sales.Orders
  GROUP BY custid
)
SELECT custid,
  CAST(SUBSTRING(mx,  1,  8) AS DATETIME) AS orderdate,
  CAST(SUBSTRING(mx,  9, 10) AS INT)      AS custid,
  CAST(SUBSTRING(mx, 19, 10) AS INT)      AS empid
FROM C;
```

The query isn't pretty, but its plan involves only one scan of the data, and it tends to outperform the other solutions when the POC index doesn't exist. Remember that if you can afford such an index, you don't want to use this solution; rather, you should use one of the other two strategies, depending on the density of the partitioning column.

Mode

Mode is a statistical calculation that returns the most frequently occurring value in the population. Consider, for example, the Sales.Orders table, which holds order information. Each order was placed by some customer and handled by some employee. Suppose you want to know, for each customer, which employee handled the most orders. That employee is the mode because she appears most frequently in the customer's orders.

Naturally there is the potential for ties if there are multiple employees who handled the most orders for a given customer. Depending on your needs, you either return all ties or break the ties. I will cover solutions to both cases. If you do want to break the ties, suppose the tiebreaker is the highest employee ID number—if multiple employees handled the most orders for a given customer, return the one with the highest employee ID number among those.

Indexing is straightforward here; you want an index defined on (*custid, empid*):

```
CREATE INDEX idx_custid_empid ON Sales.Orders(custid, empid);
```

I'll start with a solution that relies on the ROW_NUMBER function. The first step is to group the orders by *custid* and *empid*, and then return for each group the count of orders, like so:

```
SELECT custid, empid, COUNT(*) AS cnt
FROM Sales.Orders
GROUP BY custid, empid;
```

custid	empid	cnt
1	1	2
3	1	1
4	1	3
5	1	4
9	1	3
10	1	2
11	1	1
14	1	1
15	1	1
17	1	2

. . .

The next step is to add a ROW_NUMBER calculation partitioned by *custid* and ordered by *COUNT(*) DESC, empid DESC*. For each customer, the row with the highest count (and, in the case of ties, the highest employee ID number) will be assigned row number 1:

```
SELECT custid, empid, COUNT(*) AS cnt,
  ROW_NUMBER() OVER(PARTITION BY custid
                    ORDER BY COUNT(*) DESC, empid DESC) AS rn
FROM Sales.Orders
GROUP BY custid, empid;
```

custid	empid	cnt	rn
1	4	2	1
1	1	2	2
1	6	1	3
1	3	1	4
2	3	2	1
2	7	1	2
2	4	1	3
3	3	3	1
3	7	2	2
3	4	1	3
3	1	1	4

. . .

Finally, you need to filter only the rows where the row number is equal to 1 using a CTE, like so:

```
WITH C AS
(
  SELECT custid, empid, COUNT(*) AS cnt,
    ROW_NUMBER() OVER(PARTITION BY custid
                      ORDER BY COUNT(*) DESC, empid DESC) AS rn
  FROM Sales.Orders
  GROUP BY custid, empid
)
SELECT custid, empid, cnt
FROM C
WHERE rn = 1;
```

```
custid        empid         cnt
-----------   -----------   -----------
1             4             2
2             3             2
3             3             3
4             4             4
5             3             6
6             9             3
7             4             3
8             4             2
9             4             4
10            3             4
...
```

Because the window-ordering specification includes *empid DESC* as a tiebreaker, you get to return only one row per customer when implementing the tiebreaker requirements of the task. If you do not want to break the ties, use the RANK function instead of ROW_NUMBER and remove *empid* from the window order clause, like so:

```
WITH C AS
(
  SELECT custid, empid, COUNT(*) AS cnt,
    RANK() OVER(PARTITION BY custid
                ORDER BY COUNT(*) DESC) AS rn
  FROM Sales.Orders
  GROUP BY custid, empid
)
SELECT custid, empid, cnt
FROM C
WHERE rn = 1;
```

```
custid        empid         cnt
-----------   -----------   -----------
1             1             2
1             4             2
2             3             2
3             3             3
4             4             4
5             3             6
6             9             3
7             4             3
8             4             2
9             4             4
10            3             4
11            6             2
11            4             2
11            3             2
...
```

Remember that the RANK function is sensitive to ties, unlike the ROW_NUMBER function. This means that given the same ordering value—*COUNT(*)* in our case—you get the same rank. So all rows with the greatest count per customer get rank 1, and hence all are kept. Observe, for example, that in the case of customer 1, two different employees—with IDs 1 and 4—handled the most orders—two in number—and hence both were returned.

Perhaps you realized that the Mode problem is a version of the previously discussed Top-N-per-Group problem. And recall that in addition to the solution that is based on window functions, you can also use a solution based on the carry-along-sort concept. But this concept works only as long as N equals 1, which in our case means you do want to implement a tiebreaker.

To implement the carry-along-sort concept in this case, you need to form a concatenated string with the count as the first part and the employee ID as the second part, like so:

```
SELECT custid,
  STR(COUNT(*), 10) + STR(empid, 10) COLLATE Latin1_General_BIN2 AS cntemp
FROM Sales.Orders
GROUP BY custid, empid;
```

```
custid      cntemp
----------- ---------------------
1                    2         1
3                    1         1
4                    3         1
5                    4         1
9                    3         1
10                   2         1
11                   1         1
14                   1         1
15                   1         1
17                   2         1
...
```

Observe that I used fixed-length segments for the count and the *empid* with leading spaces so that the strings would sort the same as the original integer values. The conversion to a binary collation will allow more efficient comparisons between the strings.

The next step is to define a CTE based on this query, and then, in the outer query, group the rows by customer and calculate the maximum concatenated string per group. Finally, extract the different parts from the maximum concatenated string and convert back to the original types, like so:

```
WITH C AS
(
  SELECT custid,
    STR(COUNT(*), 10) + STR(empid, 10) COLLATE Latin1_General_BIN2 AS cntemp
  FROM Sales.Orders
  GROUP BY custid, empid
)
SELECT custid,
  CAST(SUBSTRING(MAX(cntemp), 11, 10) AS INT) AS empid,
  CAST(SUBSTRING(MAX(cntemp),  1, 10) AS INT) AS cnt
FROM C
GROUP BY custid;
```

```
custid      empid       cnt
----------- ----------- -----------
1           4           2
2           3           2
3           3           3
4           4           4
5           3           6
```

6	9	3
7	4	3
8	4	2
9	4	4
10	3	4
...		

As mentioned in the "TOP N Per Group" section, the solution based on window functions performs well when there is an index in place, so there's no reason to use the more complicated carry-along-sort one. But when there's no index to support the solution, the latter tends to perform better.

When you're done, run the following code for cleanup:

```
DROP INDEX idx_custid_empid ON Sales.Orders;
```

Running Totals

Calculating running totals is a very common need. The basic idea is to keep accumulating the values in one attribute (the aggregated element) based on ordering defined by another attribute or attributes (the ordering element), possibly within partitions of rows defined by yet another attribute or attributes (the partitioning element). There are many examples in life for calculating running totals, including calculating bank account balances, tracking product stock levels in a warehouse, tracking cumulative sales values, and so on.

Prior to SQL Server 2012, the set-based solutions used to calculate running totals were extremely expensive. Therefore, people often resorted to iterative solutions that weren't very fast but in certain data distribution scenarios were faster than the set-based solutions. With the enhanced support for window functions in SQL Server 2012, you can now calculate running totals with simple set-based code that performs much better than all of the older T-SQL solutions—which were set-based and iterative. I could have just showed you the new solution here and moved on to the next section in the chapter, but to help you really appreciate the greatness of the new solution, I will describe the older ones and compare their performance. Feel free, of course, to read only the first section covering the new solution and skip the rest if that's what you prefer.

I will use the bank account balances in my examples to demonstrate the different solutions. Here's code you can use to create and populate the Transactions table with a small set of sample data:

```
SET NOCOUNT ON;
USE TSQL2012;

IF OBJECT_ID('dbo.Transactions', 'U') IS NOT NULL DROP TABLE dbo.Transactions;

CREATE TABLE dbo.Transactions
(
  actid  INT   NOT NULL,          -- partitioning column
  tranid INT   NOT NULL,          -- ordering column
  val    MONEY NOT NULL,          -- measure
  CONSTRAINT PK_Transactions PRIMARY KEY(actid, tranid)
);
```

```
-- small set of sample data
INSERT INTO dbo.Transactions(actid, tranid, val) VALUES
  (1,  1,   4.00),
  (1,  2,  -2.00),
  (1,  3,   5.00),
  (1,  4,   2.00),
  (1,  5,   1.00),
  (1,  6,   3.00),
  (1,  7,  -4.00),
  (1,  8,  -1.00),
  (1,  9,  -2.00),
  (1, 10,  -3.00),
  (2,  1,   2.00),
  (2,  2,   1.00),
  (2,  3,   5.00),
  (2,  4,   1.00),
  (2,  5,  -5.00),
  (2,  6,   4.00),
  (2,  7,   2.00),
  (2,  8,  -4.00),
  (2,  9,  -5.00),
  (2, 10,   4.00),
  (3,  1,  -3.00),
  (3,  2,   3.00),
  (3,  3,  -2.00),
  (3,  4,   1.00),
  (3,  5,   4.00),
  (3,  6,  -1.00),
  (3,  7,   5.00),
  (3,  8,   3.00),
  (3,  9,   5.00),
  (3, 10,  -3.00);
```

Each row in the table represents a transaction in some bank account. When the transaction is a deposit, the amount in the *val* column is positive; when it's a withdrawal, the amount is negative. Your task is to compute the account balance at each point by accumulating the amounts in the *val* column based on ordering defined by the *tranid* column, within each account independently. The desired results should look like this for the small set of sample data:

actid	tranid	val	balance
1	1	4.00	4.00
1	2	-2.00	2.00
1	3	5.00	7.00
1	4	2.00	9.00
1	5	1.00	10.00
1	6	3.00	13.00
1	7	-4.00	9.00
1	8	-1.00	8.00
1	9	-2.00	6.00
1	10	-3.00	3.00
2	1	2.00	2.00
2	2	1.00	3.00

2	3	5.00	8.00
2	4	1.00	9.00
2	5	-5.00	4.00
2	6	4.00	8.00
2	7	2.00	10.00
2	8	-4.00	6.00
2	9	-5.00	1.00
2	10	4.00	5.00
3	1	-3.00	-3.00
3	2	3.00	0.00
3	3	-2.00	-2.00
3	4	1.00	-1.00
3	5	4.00	3.00
3	6	-1.00	2.00
3	7	5.00	7.00
3	8	3.00	10.00
3	9	5.00	15.00
3	10	-3.00	12.00

To test the performance of the solutions, you need a larger set of sample data. You can use the following code to achieve this:

```
DECLARE
  @num_partitions     AS INT = 10,
  @rows_per_partition AS INT = 10000;

TRUNCATE TABLE dbo.Transactions;

INSERT INTO dbo.Transactions WITH (TABLOCK) (actid, tranid, val)
  SELECT NP.n, RPP.n,
    (ABS(CHECKSUM(NEWID())%2)*2-1) * (1 + ABS(CHECKSUM(NEWID())%5))
  FROM dbo.GetNums(1, @num_partitions) AS NP
    CROSS JOIN dbo.GetNums(1, @rows_per_partition) AS RPP;
```

Feel free to change the inputs as needed to control the number of partitions (accounts) and number of rows per partition (transactions).

Set-Based Solution Using Window Functions

I'll start with the new set-based solution that uses the SUM window aggregate function. The window specification is intuitive here; you need to partition the window by *actid*, order by *tranid*, and filter the frame of rows between no low boundary point (UNBOUNDED PRECEDING) and the current row. Here's the solution query:

```
SELECT actid, tranid, val,
  SUM(val) OVER(PARTITION BY actid
                ORDER BY tranid
                ROWS BETWEEN UNBOUNDED PRECEDING
                         AND CURRENT ROW) AS balance
FROM dbo.Transactions;
```

Not only is the code is simple and straightforward, it also performs very well. The plan for this query is shown in Figure 5-5.

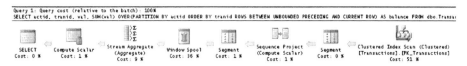

SELECT	Compute Scalar	Stream Aggregate (Aggregate)	Window Spool	Segment	Sequence Project (Compute Scalar)	Segment	Clustered Index Scan (Clustered) [Transactions].[PK_Transactions]
Cost: 0 %	Cost: 1 %	Cost: 9 %	Cost: 36 %	Cost: 1 %	Cost: 1 %	Cost: 0 %	Cost: 51 %

FIGURE 5-5 Execution plan for a query using window functions.

The table has a clustered index that follows the POC guidelines that window functions can benefit from. Namely, the index key list is based on the partitioning element (*actid*) followed by the ordering element (*tranid*), and it includes for coverage purposes all the rest of the columns in the query (*val*). The plan shows an ordered scan of the index, followed by a computation of a row number for internal purposes, and then the window aggregate. Because you arranged a POC index, the optimizer didn't need to add a sort operator in the plan. That's a very efficient plan. What's more, this plan scales linearly. Later, when I show the results of a benchmark I did, you'll see how much more efficient this solution is than the older ones.

Set-Based Solutions Using Subqueries or Joins

Traditional set-based solutions to running totals that were available prior to SQL Server 2012 used either subqueries or joins. Using a subquery, you can calculate the running total by filtering all rows that have the same *actid* value as in the outer row, and a *tranid* value that is less than or equal to the one in the outer row. Then you apply the aggregate to the filtered rows. Here's the solution query:

```
SELECT actid, tranid, val,
  (SELECT SUM(T2.val)
   FROM dbo.Transactions AS T2
   WHERE T2.actid = T1.actid
     AND T2.tranid <= T1.tranid) AS balance
FROM dbo.Transactions AS T1;
```

A similar approach can be implemented using joins. You use the same predicate as the one used in the WHERE clause of the subquery in the ON clause of the join. This way, for the *N*th transaction of some account A in the instance you refer to as T1, you will find *N* matches in the instance T2, with transactions 1 through *N*. The row in T1 is repeated in the result for each of its matches, so you need to group the rows by all elements from T1 to get the current transaction info and apply the aggregate to the *val* attribute from T2 to calculate the running total. The solution query looks like this:

```
SELECT T1.actid, T1.tranid, T1.val,
  SUM(T2.val) AS balance
FROM dbo.Transactions AS T1
  JOIN dbo.Transactions AS T2
    ON T2.actid = T1.actid
    AND T2.tranid <= T1.tranid
GROUP BY T1.actid, T1.tranid, T1.val;
```

Figure 5-6 shows the plans for both solutions.

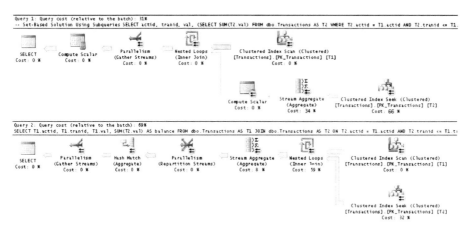

FIGURE 5-6 Execution plans for queries using subqueries and joins.

Observe that in both cases the clustered index is scanned in full representing the instance T1. Then, for each row, the plan performs a seek operation in the index to get to the beginning of the current account's section in the index leaf, and then it scans all transactions where *T2.tranid* is less than or equal to *T1.tranid*. Then the point where the aggregate of those rows takes place is a bit different in the two plans, but the number of rows scanned is the same.

To realize how many rows get scanned, consider the elements involved in the data. Let p be the number of partitions (accounts), and let r be the number of rows per partition (transactions). Then the number of rows in the table is roughly pr, assuming an even distribution of transactions per account. So the upper scan of the clustered index involves scanning pr rows. But the work at the inner part of the Nested Loops iterator is what we're most concerned with. For each partition, the plan scans $1 + 2 + \ldots + r$ rows, which is equal to $(r + r^2) / 2$. In total, the number of rows processed in these plans is $pr + p(r + r^2) / 2$. This means that with respect to partition size, the scaling of this plan is quadratic; that is, if you increase the partition size by a factor of f, the work involved increases by a factor of close to f^2. That's bad. As examples, 100 rows have a "cost" of 10,000 rows, 1,000 rows have a "cost" of 1,000,000, and so on. Simply put, it translates to very slow queries when the partition size is not tiny because the squared effect is very dramatic. It's OK to use these solutions for up to a few dozen rows per partition, but not many more.

Cursor-Based Solution

Using a cursor-based solution to running totals is straightforward. You declare a cursor based on a query that orders the data by *actid* and *tranid*. You then iterate through the cursor records. Whenever you hit a new account, you reset the variable holding the aggregate. In each iteration, you add to the variable the value of the new transaction; you then store a row in a table variable with the current transaction information plus the running total so far. When you're done iterating, you return the result to the caller by querying the table variable. Here's the complete solution code:

```
DECLARE @Result AS TABLE
(
  actid   INT,
  tranid  INT,
  val     MONEY,
  balance MONEY
);

DECLARE
  @actid    AS INT,
  @prvactid AS INT,
  @tranid   AS INT,
  @val      AS MONEY,
  @balance  AS MONEY;

DECLARE C CURSOR FAST_FORWARD FOR
  SELECT actid, tranid, val
  FROM dbo.Transactions
  ORDER BY actid, tranid;

OPEN C

FETCH NEXT FROM C INTO @actid, @tranid, @val;

SELECT @prvactid = @actid, @balance = 0;

WHILE @@fetch_status = 0
BEGIN
  IF @actid <> @prvactid
    SELECT @prvactid = @actid, @balance = 0;

  SET @balance = @balance + @val;

  INSERT INTO @Result VALUES(@actid, @tranid, @val, @balance);

  FETCH NEXT FROM C INTO @actid, @tranid, @val;
END

CLOSE C;

DEALLOCATE C;

SELECT * FROM @Result;
```

The plan for the query that the cursor is based on is shown in Figure 5-7.

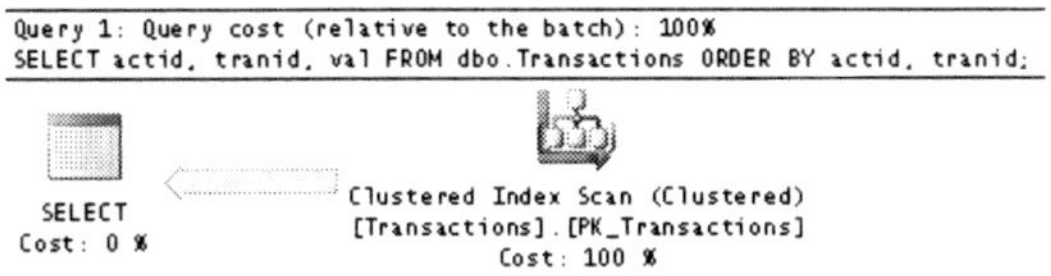

FIGURE 5-7 Execution plan for the query used by the cursor.

This plan has linear scaling because the data from the index is scanned only once, in order. Also, each fetching of a row from the cursor has a constant cost per row. If you call the cursor overhead per row o, you can express the cost of this solution as $pr + pro$ (keeping in mind that p is the number of partitions and r is the number of rows per partition). So you can see that if you increase the number of rows per partition by a factor of f, the work involved becomes $prf + prfo$, meaning that you get linear scaling. The overhead per row is high; however, because the scaling is linear, from a certain partition size on, this solution will perform better than the solutions based on subqueries and joins due to their quadratic scaling. Benchmark studies that I did show that the point where the cursor solution becomes faster is around a few hundred rows per partition.

Despite the performance gains cursor solutions provide, in general you should avoid using them because they are not relational.

CLR-Based Solution

One possible Common Language Runtime (CLR) solution is basically another form of a cursor-based solution. The difference is that instead of using a T-SQL cursor that involves a high amount of overhead for each fetch and slow iterations, you use a .NET *SQLDataReader* and .NET iterations, which are much faster. One of the things that make the CLR option faster is that you don't need to store the result rows in a temporary table—the results are streamed right back to the caller. The logic of the CLR-based solution is similar to that of the T-SQL cursor-based solution. Here's the .NET code defining the solution's stored procedure:

```
using System;
using System.Data;
using System.Data.SqlClient;
using System.Data.SqlTypes;
using Microsoft.SqlServer.Server;

public partial class StoredProcedures
{
    [Microsoft.SqlServer.Server.SqlProcedure]
    public static void AccountBalances()
    {
        using (SqlConnection conn = new SqlConnection("context connection=true;"))
        {
            SqlCommand comm = new SqlCommand();
            comm.Connection = conn;
            comm.CommandText = @"" +
                "SELECT actid, tranid, val " +
                "FROM dbo.Transactions " +
                "ORDER BY actid, tranid;";

            SqlMetaData[] columns = new SqlMetaData[4];
            columns[0] = new SqlMetaData("actid"  , SqlDbType.Int);
            columns[1] = new SqlMetaData("tranid" , SqlDbType.Int);
            columns[2] = new SqlMetaData("val"    , SqlDbType.Money);
            columns[3] = new SqlMetaData("balance", SqlDbType.Money);

            SqlDataRecord record = new SqlDataRecord(columns);
```

```
        SqlContext.Pipe.SendResultsStart(record);

        conn.Open();

        SqlDataReader reader = comm.ExecuteReader();

        SqlInt32 prvactid = 0;
        SqlMoney balance = 0;

        while (reader.Read())
        {
            SqlInt32 actid = reader.GetSqlInt32(0);
            SqlMoney val = reader.GetSqlMoney(2);

            if (actid == prvactid)
            {
                balance += val;
            }
            else
            {
                balance = val;
            }

            prvactid = actid;

            record.SetSqlInt32(0, reader.GetSqlInt32(0));
            record.SetSqlInt32(1, reader.GetSqlInt32(1));
            record.SetSqlMoney(2, val);
            record.SetSqlMoney(3, balance);

            SqlContext.Pipe.SendResultsRow(record);
        }

        SqlContext.Pipe.SendResultsEnd();
    }
  }
};
```

To be able to execute the stored procedure in SQL Server, you first need to build an assembly called *AccountBalances* that is based on this code and deploy it in the TSQL2012 database. If you're not familiar with deployment of assemblies in SQL Server, you can read an article in Books Online titled "Deploying CLR Database Objects," which describes the process. You can find this article at *http://technet.microsoft.com/en-us/library/ms345099(SQL.110).aspx*.

Assuming you called the assembly *AccountBalances*, and the path to the assembly file is C:\AccountBalances\AccountBalances.dll, you can use the following code to load the assembly to the database and then register the stored procedure:

```
CREATE ASSEMBLY AccountBalances FROM 'C:\AccountBalances\AccountBalances.dll';
GO

CREATE PROCEDURE dbo.AccountBalances
AS EXTERNAL NAME AccountBalances.StoredProcedures.AccountBalances;
```

After the assembly has been deployed and the procedure has been registered, you can execute the procedure using the following code:

```
EXEC dbo.AccountBalances;
```

As mentioned, a *SQLDataReader* is just another form of a cursor, only the overhead of each fetch is less than that of a T-SQL cursor. Also, iterations in .NET are much faster than iterations in T-SQL. So the CLR-based solution also has linear scaling. In my benchmarks, this solution started performing better than the solutions using subqueries and joins at around 15 rows per partition.

When you're done, run the following code for cleanup:

```
DROP PROCEDURE dbo.AccountBalances;
DROP ASSEMBLY AccountBalances;
```

Nested Iterations

So far, I have shown you solutions that are either set based or iterative. The next solution, known as *nested iterations*, is a hybrid of iterative and set-based logic. The idea is to first copy into a temporary table the rows from the source table (bank account transactions in our case), along with a new attribute called *rownum* that is calculated by using the ROW_NUMBER function. The row numbers are partitioned by *actid* and ordered by *tranid*, so the first transaction in each account is assigned the row number 1, the second transaction is assigned row number 2, and so on. You then create a clustered index on the temporary table with the key list (*rownum*, *actid*). Then you use either a recursive CTE or your own loop to handle one row number at a time across all accounts in each iteration. The running total is then computed by adding the value associated with the current row number to the value associated with the previous row number.

Here's the implementation of this logic using a recursive CTE:

```
SELECT actid, tranid, val,
  ROW_NUMBER() OVER(PARTITION BY actid ORDER BY tranid) AS rownum
INTO #Transactions
FROM dbo.Transactions;

CREATE UNIQUE CLUSTERED INDEX idx_rownum_actid ON #Transactions(rownum, actid);

WITH C AS
(
  SELECT 1 AS rownum, actid, tranid, val, val AS sumqty
  FROM #Transactions
  WHERE rownum = 1

  UNION ALL

  SELECT PRV.rownum + 1, PRV.actid, PRV.tranid, CUR.val, PRV.sumqty + CUR.val
  FROM C AS PRV
    JOIN #Transactions AS CUR
      ON CUR.rownum = PRV.rownum + 1
      AND CUR.actid = PRV.actid
)
```

```
SELECT actid, tranid, val, sumqty
FROM C
OPTION (MAXRECURSION 0);

DROP TABLE #Transactions;
```

And here's the implementation of the same logic using an explicit loop:

```
SELECT ROW_NUMBER() OVER(PARTITION BY actid ORDER BY tranid) AS rownum,
  actid, tranid, val, CAST(val AS BIGINT) AS sumqty
INTO #Transactions
FROM dbo.Transactions;

CREATE UNIQUE CLUSTERED INDEX idx_rownum_actid ON #Transactions(rownum, actid);

DECLARE @rownum AS INT;
SET @rownum = 1;

WHILE 1 = 1
BEGIN
  SET @rownum = @rownum + 1;

  UPDATE CUR
    SET sumqty = PRV.sumqty + CUR.val
  FROM #Transactions AS CUR
    JOIN #Transactions AS PRV
      ON CUR.rownum = @rownum
      AND PRV.rownum = @rownum - 1
      AND CUR.actid = PRV.actid;

  IF @@rowcount = 0 BREAK;
END

SELECT actid, tranid, val, sumqty
FROM #Transactions;

DROP TABLE #Transactions;
```

This solution tends to perform well when there are a lot of partitions with a small number of rows per partition. This way, the number of iterations is small. And most of the work is handled by the set-based part of the solution that joins the rows associated with one row number with the rows associated with the previous row number.

Multirow UPDATE with Variables

The various techniques I showed so far for handling running totals are guaranteed to produce the correct result. The technique that is the focus of this section is a controversial one because it relies on observed behavior as opposed to documented behavior, and it also violates relational concepts. What makes it so appealing to some is that it is very fast.

The technique involves using an UPDATE statement with variables. An UPDATE statement can set a variable to an expression based on a column value, as well as set a column value to an expression based on a variable. The solution starts by creating a temporary table called #Transactions with the *actid, tranid, val,* and *balance* attributes and a clustered index based on the key list (*actid, tranid*). Then the solution populates the temp table with all rows from the source Transactions table, setting the balance column to 0.00 in all rows. The solution then invokes an UPDATE statement with variables against the temporary table to calculate the running totals and assign those to the balance column. It uses variables called *@prevaccount* and *@prevbalance*, and it sets the balance using the following expression:

```
SET @prevbalance = balance = CASE
                               WHEN actid = @prevaccount
                                 THEN @prevbalance + val
                               ELSE val
                             END
```

The CASE expression checks whether the current account ID is equal to the previous account ID; if the account IDs are equivalent, it returns the previous balance plus the current transaction value. If the account IDs are different, it returns the current transaction value. The balance is then set to the result of the CASE expression and also assigned to the *@prevbalance* variable. In a separate expression, the *@prevaccount* variable is set to the current account ID.

After the UPDATE statement, the solution presents the rows from the temporary table and then drops the table. Here's the complete solution code:

```
CREATE TABLE #Transactions
(
  actid        INT,
  tranid       INT,
  val          MONEY,
  balance      MONEY
);

CREATE CLUSTERED INDEX idx_actid_tranid ON #Transactions(actid, tranid);

INSERT INTO #Transactions WITH (TABLOCK) (actid, tranid, val, balance)
  SELECT actid, tranid, val, 0.00
  FROM dbo.Transactions
  ORDER BY actid, tranid;

DECLARE @prevaccount AS INT, @prevbalance AS MONEY;

UPDATE #Transactions
  SET @prevbalance = balance = CASE
                                 WHEN actid = @prevaccount
                                   THEN @prevbalance + val
                                 ELSE val
                               END,
      @prevaccount = actid
FROM #Transactions WITH(INDEX(1), TABLOCKX)
OPTION (MAXDOP 1);

SELECT * FROM #Transactions;

DROP TABLE #Transactions;
```

The plan for this solution is shown in Figure 5-8. The first part is the INSERT, the second part is the UPDATE, and the third part is the SELECT.

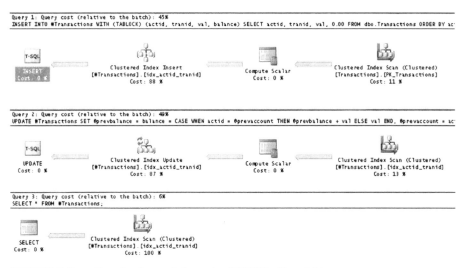

FIGURE 5-8 Execution plan for a solution using UPDATE with variables.

This solution makes an assumption that the UPDATE will always be optimized with an ordered scan of the clustered index, and it even uses a number of hints in an attempt to avoid situations that might prevent that—for example, parallelism. The problem is that there is no official guarantee that the optimizer will always scan the data in clustered index order. You're not supposed to make assumptions about physical processing aspects when trying to ensure the logical correctness of your code, unless there are logical elements in the code that are defined to guarantee such behavior. There's nothing in the logical aspects of the code that give any such guarantees. Of course, it's up to you to decide whether or not you want to use this technique. I think it's irresponsible to use it even if you run it a thousand times and the observed behavior is "It seems to work." The onus is not on people to find a case where it doesn't work; rather, it's on people to prove that it will never fail—of course, that's impossible because Microsoft doesn't guarantee that.

Fortunately in SQL Server 2012, the controversy around this technique becomes moot. With the extremely efficient solution of using a window aggregate function available, you don't need to worry about any other solutions.

Performance Benchmark

I ran a performance benchmark comparing the different techniques. Figures 5-9 and 5-10 show the results of that benchmark.

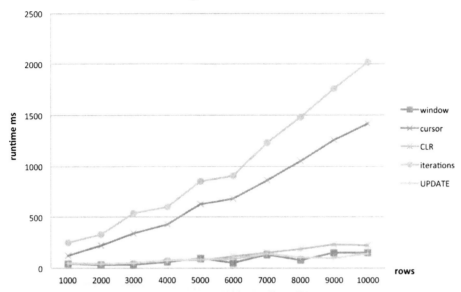

FIGURE 5-9 Benchmark of the running totals solutions, part I.

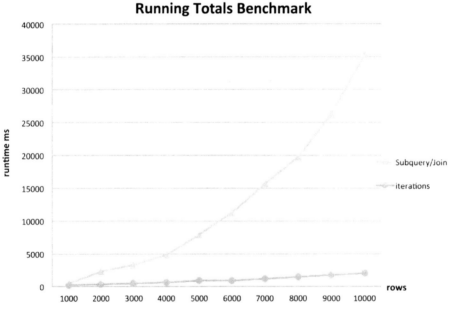

FIGURE 5-10 Benchmark of the running totals solutions, part II.

The reason for separating the results into two graphs was that the technique based on a subquery or join was so slow compared to the rest that I wanted to use a different scale for it. Regardless of the reason for doing it this way, observe that with respect to partition size, most solutions have linear scaling and only the one based on a subquery or join has quadratic scaling. Also, you can clearly see how efficient the new solution based on a window aggregate function is. The solution based on an UPDATE with variables is also very fast, but for the aforementioned reasons I recommended that you avoid it. The solution based on the CLR is also quite fast, but it involves writing all that .NET code and deploying an assembly in the database. From all perspectives, the set-based solution using a window aggregate is by far the most preferable one.

Max Concurrent Intervals

Consider a set of intervals representing things such as sessions, projects, calls, and so on. There's a classic problem known as *maximum concurrent intervals* where your task is to calculate the maximum number of intervals that were effective simultaneously. As an example, suppose that you're given a table called Sessions that holds data about user sessions for different applications. Your task is to write a solution that calculates, for each application, the maximum number of sessions that were active simultaneously. If one session ends exactly when another starts, assume that you're not supposed to consider them concurrent.

Here's the code to create the Sessions table and a couple of indexes to support your solutions:

```
SET NOCOUNT ON;
USE TSQL2012;

IF OBJECT_ID('dbo.Sessions', 'U') IS NOT NULL DROP TABLE dbo.Sessions;

CREATE TABLE dbo.Sessions
(
  keycol    INT         NOT NULL,
  app       VARCHAR(10) NOT NULL,
  usr       VARCHAR(10) NOT NULL,
  host      VARCHAR(10) NOT NULL,
  starttime DATETIME    NOT NULL,
  endtime   DATETIME    NOT NULL,
  CONSTRAINT PK_Sessions PRIMARY KEY(keycol),
  CHECK(endtime > starttime)
);
GO

CREATE UNIQUE INDEX idx_nc_app_st_et
  ON dbo.Sessions(app, starttime, keycol) INCLUDE(endtime);

CREATE UNIQUE INDEX idx_nc_app_et_st
  ON dbo.Sessions(app, endtime, keycol) INCLUDE(starttime);
```

Use the following code to populate the Sessions table with a small set of sample data to test the validity of your solution:

```
TRUNCATE TABLE dbo.Sessions;
```

```
INSERT INTO dbo.Sessions(keycol, app, usr, host, starttime, endtime) VALUES
  (2,  'app1', 'user1', 'host1', '20120212 08:30', '20120212 10:30'),
  (3,  'app1', 'user2', 'host1', '20120212 08:30', '20120212 08:45'),
  (5,  'app1', 'user3', 'host2', '20120212 09:00', '20120212 09:30'),
  (7,  'app1', 'user4', 'host2', '20120212 09:15', '20120212 10:30'),
  (11, 'app1', 'user5', 'host3', '20120212 09:15', '20120212 09:30'),
  (13, 'app1', 'user6', 'host3', '20120212 10:30', '20120212 14:30'),
  (17, 'app1', 'user7', 'host4', '20120212 10:45', '20120212 11:30'),
  (19, 'app1', 'user8', 'host4', '20120212 11:00', '20120212 12:30'),
  (23, 'app2', 'user8', 'host1', '20120212 08:30', '20120212 08:45'),
  (29, 'app2', 'user7', 'host1', '20120212 09:00', '20120212 09:30'),
  (31, 'app2', 'user6', 'host2', '20120212 11:45', '20120212 12:00'),
  (37, 'app2', 'user5', 'host2', '20120212 12:30', '20120212 14:00'),
  (41, 'app2', 'user4', 'host3', '20120212 12:45', '20120212 13:30'),
  (43, 'app2', 'user3', 'host3', '20120212 13:00', '20120212 14:00'),
  (47, 'app2', 'user2', 'host4', '20120212 14:00', '20120212 16:30'),
  (53, 'app2', 'user1', 'host4', '20120212 15:30', '20120212 17:00');
```

Here's the desired result for this small set of sample data:

```
app         mx
----------  -----------
app1        3
app2        4
```

To test the performance of your solution, you need a larger set of sample data, of course. The following code populates the table with 100,000 sessions with 10 distinct applications:

```
TRUNCATE TABLE dbo.Sessions;

DECLARE
  @numrows AS INT = 100000, -- total number of rows
  @numapps AS INT = 10;     -- number of applications

INSERT INTO dbo.Sessions WITH(TABLOCK)
    (keycol, app, usr, host, starttime, endtime)
  SELECT
    ROW_NUMBER() OVER(ORDER BY (SELECT NULL)) AS keycol,
    D.*,
    DATEADD(
      second,
      1 + ABS(CHECKSUM(NEWID())) % (20*60),
      starttime) AS endtime
  FROM
  (
    SELECT
      'app' + CAST(1 + ABS(CHECKSUM(NEWID())) % @numapps AS VARCHAR(10)) AS app,
      'user1' AS usr,
      'host1' AS host,
      DATEADD(
        second,
        1 + ABS(CHECKSUM(NEWID())) % (30*24*60*60),
        '20120101') AS starttime
    FROM dbo.GetNums(1, @numrows) AS Nums
  ) AS D;
```

Feel free to adjust the number of rows to populate the table with and the number of distinct applications according to your needs.

Before I show the efficient solutions that are based on window functions, I'll show a couple of solutions that do not use window functions and talk about their shortcomings. I'll first describe the traditional set-based solution.

Traditional Set-Based Solution

You can think of each session as being made of two events—a start event, which increases the count of active sessions, and an end event, which decreases that count. If you look at the timeline, the count of active sessions remains constant in sections between consecutive events where a session either starts or ends. What's more, because a start event increases the count of active sessions, the maximum count must fall on a start event. As an example, suppose that there were two sessions with a certain application named App1: one session started at point P1 and ended at point P3, and another session started at point P2 and ended at point P4. Here's the chronological order of events and the number of active sessions after each event:

- P1, start, 1 active session

- P2, start, 2 active sessions

- P3, end, 1 active session

- P4, end, 0 active sessions

The number of active sessions between two consecutive points remains constant. The maximum number falls on a start point—P2 in this example.

The approach that the traditional set-based solution takes relies on this logic. The solution implements the following steps:

1. Define a table expression called *TimePoints* based on a query against the Sessions table that returns *app* and *starttime* (aliased as *ts* for *timestamp*).

2. Use a second table expression called *Counts* to query *TimePoints* (aliased as *P*).

3. In the second table expression, use a subquery to count how many sessions you can find in the Sessions table (aliased as *S*), where *P.app* is equal to *S.app*, and *P.ts* is on or after *S.starttime* and before *S.endtime*. The subquery counts how many sessions are active during each application session's start point in time.

4. Finally, in the outer query against *Counts*, group the rows by *app* and return for each application the maximum count.

Here's the complete solution code:

```
WITH TimePoints AS
(
  SELECT app, starttime AS ts FROM dbo.Sessions
),
Counts AS
(
  SELECT app, ts,
    (SELECT COUNT(*)
     FROM dbo.Sessions AS S
     WHERE P.app = S.app
       AND P.ts >= S.starttime
       AND P.ts < S.endtime) AS concurrent
  FROM TimePoints AS P
)
SELECT app, MAX(concurrent) AS mx
FROM Counts
GROUP BY app;
```

The solution seems straightforward, and it's not immediately apparent there's a performance problem with it. But when you run it against the large set of sample data, it takes a long time to complete. To understand why it's so slow, examine the query's execution plan, shown in Figure 5-11.

FIGURE 5-11 Execution plan for a traditional set-based solution.

The Index Scan iterator in the top-right part of the plan (the outer input of the Nested Loops join) scans one of the covering indexes created earlier (*idx_nc_app_et_st*) to obtain all start points in time for each application. Using the symbols *p* for the number of partitions (applications) and *r* for the number of rows per partition (sessions per application), this part involves scanning roughly *pr* rows. Then the inner part of the Nested Loops join is an Index Seek iterator against *idx_nc_app_st_et* that gets executed for each row returned from the upper input. Its task is to identify the rows representing the sessions that were active for the current application during the current point in time in the outer row.

Now focus your attention on the work involved in each execution of the Index Seek iterator. For the current outer row's elements *P.app* (call it *myapp*) and *P.ts* (call it *myts*), it is looking for all rows where *S.app* = *myapp*, *S.starttime* <= *myts*, and *S.endtime* > *myts*. Because the first index key is *app*, the seek predicate can efficiently handle the filtering of the first part: *S.app* = *myapp*. The problem is with the other two parts: *S.starttime* <= *myts* and *S.endtime* > *myts*. There's no one index that can enable a seek predicate to scan only the rows that satisfy both conditions. This predicate is supposed to filter rows where a value is between two columns. That's very different than needing to filter rows where a column is between two values. The former can rely on an index on the filtered column to filter only the qualifying rows. The latter, however, can rely on index ordering only for one of the conditions. As mentioned, the optimizer chose to apply the Index Seek iterator to the index *idx_nc_app_st_et*. The seek is performed based on the seek predicate *S.starttime* <= *myts*, so only rows that satisfy this predicate are actually accessed. However, all remaining rows are scanned and, using the predicate *S.endtime* > *myts*, only the ones that satisfy this condition are returned.

You can see which part of the predicate was evaluated as a Seek Predicate versus Predicate in the properties of the Index Seek iterator. The Seek Predicate property is shown here:

```
Seek Keys[1]: Prefix: [TSQL2012].[dbo].[Sessions].app =
Scalar Operator([TSQL2012].[dbo].[Sessions].[app]), End: [TSQL2012].[dbo].[Sessions].starttime
<= Scalar Operator([TSQL2012].[dbo].[Sessions].[starttime])
```

And the Predicate property is the following:

```
[TSQL2012].[dbo].[Sessions].[starttime]<[TSQL2012].[dbo].[Sessions].[endtime] as [S].[endtime]
```

If it isn't clear by now, that's bad news. The seek predicate prevents reading nonqualifying rows, but the scan predicate doesn't. The rows must be read before the scan predicate can be applied. I already mentioned that the Index Scan iterator scans approximately *pr* rows. The Index Seek iterator scans, for each row, on average about half the rows in the partition. This means that for *r* rows in a partition, it scans $r^2 / 2$ rows per partition. In total, the number of rows being processed is $pr + pr^2 / 2$. This means that with respect to partition size, this plan has quadratic complexity. So if the number of rows per partition increases by a factor of *f*, the work increases by a factor of close to f^2. So beyond very small partition sizes, the query will perform very badly.

Cursor-Based Solution

The cursor-based solution relies on the following query, which organizes the session start and end events as one chronological sequence of events:

```
SELECT app, starttime AS ts, +1 AS type
FROM dbo.Sessions

UNION ALL

SELECT app, endtime, -1
FROM dbo.Sessions

ORDER BY app, ts, type;
```

app	ts	type
app1	2012-02-12 08:30:00.000	1
app1	2012-02-12 08:30:00.000	1
app1	2012-02-12 08:45:00.000	-1
app1	2012-02-12 09:00:00.000	1
app1	2012-02-12 09:15:00.000	1
app1	2012-02-12 09:15:00.000	1
app1	2012-02-12 09:30:00.000	-1

```
app1        2012-02-12 09:30:00.000 -1
app1        2012-02-12 10:30:00.000 -1
app1        2012-02-12 10:30:00.000 -1
...
```

As you can see, the query marks start events with a +1 event type because they increase the count of active sessions, and it marks end events with a –1 event type because they decrease the count. The query sorts the events chronologically by *app*, *ts*, and *type*. The reason to add the type to the ORDER BY list is to ensure that if a start event and an end event happen at the same time, the end event will be considered first. (Remember, in such a case, you're not supposed to consider the two sessions as concurrent.)

The plan for this query is shown in Figure 5-12.

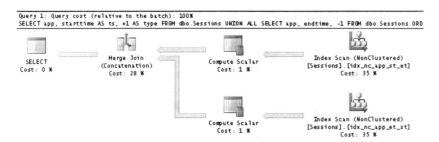

FIGURE 5-12 Execution plan for a cursor-based solution.

Observe that the plan is very efficient. It performs ordered scans of the two indexes created earlier, and it uses a Merge Join iterator to concatenate the results, thereby preserving index ordering and avoiding a sort operation.

The rest of the work is essentially calculating a running total of the type, within each application, based on this chronological order. The running total of the type is, in fact, the number of active sessions during each point. The cursor code performs just that, and in each application group, it keeps the maximum count found in a variable. When it's done with the group, it stores that maximum along with the application in a table variable. When done, the code just queries the table variable to present the result. Here's the complete solution code:

```
DECLARE
  @app AS varchar(10),
  @prevapp AS varchar (10),
  @ts AS datetime,
  @type AS int,
  @concurrent AS int,
  @mx AS int;

DECLARE @AppsMx TABLE
(
  app varchar (10) NOT NULL PRIMARY KEY,
  mx int NOT NULL
);
```

```
DECLARE sessions_cur CURSOR FAST_FORWARD FOR
  SELECT app, starttime AS ts, +1 AS type
  FROM dbo.Sessions

  UNION ALL

  SELECT app, endtime, -1
  FROM dbo.Sessions

  ORDER BY app, ts, type;

OPEN sessions_cur;

FETCH NEXT FROM sessions_cur
  INTO @app, @ts, @type;

SET @prevapp = @app;
SET @concurrent = 0;
SET @mx = 0;

WHILE @@FETCH_STATUS = 0
BEGIN
  IF @app <> @prevapp
  BEGIN
    INSERT INTO @AppsMx VALUES(@prevapp, @mx);
    SET @concurrent = 0;
    SET @mx = 0;
    SET @prevapp = @app;
  END

  SET @concurrent = @concurrent + @type;
  IF @concurrent > @mx SET @mx = @concurrent;

  FETCH NEXT FROM sessions_cur
    INTO @app, @ts, @type;
END

IF @prevapp IS NOT NULL
  INSERT INTO @AppsMx VALUES(@prevapp, @mx);

CLOSE sessions_cur;

DEALLOCATE sessions_cur;

SELECT * FROM @AppsMx;
```

The solution has the usual downsides of cursor-based solutions. In terms of performance, you pay extra for each row processing, but the scaling of the solution is linear. If the number of rows in the table is roughly pr, the cursor solution scans $2pr$ rows. In addition, with the per-row overhead of each cursor fetch (call it o), the total cost can be considered as $2pr + 2pro$. If the volume of data increases by a factor of f, the cost becomes $2prf + 2prfo$. So this solution is faster than the traditional set-based solution even from a very small partition size.

Solutions Based on Window Functions

I'll present two solutions based on window functions—the first is available only in SQL Server 2012 because it relies on new window aggregate capabilities, and the second has been available since SQL Server 2005 because it relies on the ROW_NUMBER function.

Consider the query used by the cursor in the previous solution. It arranges the start and end events as one sequence of events and marks start and end events with event types of +1 and –1. And then the calculation of the number of concurrent sessions during each point is done by a running total calculation. Prior to SQL Server 2012, a cursor was one of the more efficient solutions to running totals. But now that you have support for ordering and framing options in window aggregate functions, you can achieve a running total calculation far more efficiently.

The initial query and general principals of the solution that uses a window aggregate function are similar to those used by the cursor solution—only without the cursor and without the cursor overhead. Here's the complete solution code:

```
WITH C1 AS
(
  SELECT app, starttime AS ts, +1 AS type
  FROM dbo.Sessions

  UNION ALL

  SELECT app, endtime, -1
  FROM dbo.Sessions
),
C2 AS
(
  SELECT *,
    SUM(type) OVER(PARTITION BY app ORDER BY ts, type
                    ROWS BETWEEN UNBOUNDED PRECEDING AND CURRENT ROW) AS cnt
  FROM C1
)
SELECT app, MAX(cnt) AS mx
FROM C2
GROUP BY app;
```

The query in the CTE *C1* generates the unified sequence of start and end events. The query in the CTE *C2* computes the running total of the type, partitioned by *app* and ordered by *ts* and *type*. That's the count of active sessions during each point. Finally, the outer query groups the rows from *C2* by *app* and returns the maximum count for each *app*.

Observe how simple and elegant the solution ultimately is. It is also highly efficient and has linear scaling. Figure 5-13 shows the execution plan for this solution.

The first part is identical to the work in the plan for the query used by the cursor solution—namely, ordered scans of the indexes and a Merge Join (Concatenation) that preserves index ordering. Then this preserved ordering property is relied on when computing the window aggregate, so not even one sort operation is required in this plan.

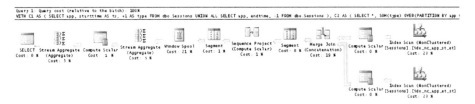

FIGURE 5-13 Execution plan for a solution using a window aggregate function.

The second solution based on window functions is available in versions of SQL Server prior to SQL Server 2012, relying mainly on the ROW_NUMBER function. I learned this elegant solution from Ben Flanaghan. Like the previous solution, it also unifies start and end events in a chronological sequence of events, marking start events as a +1 event type and end events as a –1 event type. Only the part that calculates how many intervals are active at any given point is handled differently. Here's the complete solution code:

```
WITH C1 AS
(
  SELECT app, starttime AS ts, +1 AS type, keycol,
    ROW_NUMBER() OVER(PARTITION BY app ORDER BY starttime, keycol) AS start_ordinal
  FROM dbo.Sessions

  UNION ALL

  SELECT app, endtime, -1, keycol, NULL
  FROM dbo.Sessions
),
C2 AS
(
  SELECT *,
    ROW_NUMBER() OVER(PARTITION BY app ORDER BY ts, type, keycol) AS start_or_end_ordinal
  FROM C1
)
SELECT app, MAX(start_ordinal - (start_or_end_ordinal - start_ordinal)) AS mx
FROM C2
GROUP BY app;
```

The query defining the CTE *C1* generates the chronological sequence of events. It also uses the ROW_NUMBER function to compute start ordinals for start events (with an attribute called *start_ordinal*). The *start_ordinal* attribute represents for each start event how many intervals have started so far. For end events, the second query uses a NULL as a placeholder for *start_ordinal* to allow unifying the start and end events.

The query defining the CTE *C2* queries *C1*, and it uses the ROW_NUMBER function to compute the *start_or_end_ordinal* attribute on top of the unified events, representing how many events—start or end—happened so far.

The magic happens in the outer query, which queries *C2*. Let *end_ordinal* be *start_or_end_ordinal* – *start_ordinal*. Then the count of active intervals is *start_ordinal* – *end_ordinal*. In other words, the count of active intervals is *start_ordinal* – (*start_or_end_ordinal* – *start_ordinal*). As you can see, the outer query is left to group the rows from *C2* by *app* and return, for each *app*, the maximum number of active intervals.

The plan for this solution is shown in Figure 5-14.

FIGURE 5-14 Execution plan for a solution using ROW_NUMBER.

Also in this plan, you can see that both ROW_NUMBER calculations—the one computing start ordinals, as well as the one computing start or end ordinals—rely on index ordering. The same applies to the aggregate operation. Hence, not even one sort operation is required in this plan.

Performance Benchmark

I ran a performance benchmark to compare the performance of the different solutions, and the results are shown in Figure 5-15.

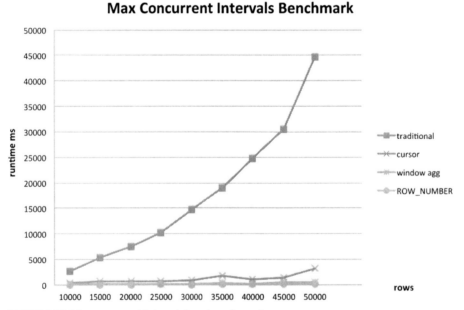

FIGURE 5-15 Max concurrent intervals benchmark results.

Observe how slow the traditional set-based solution is. You can see clearly its quadratic scaling. The cursor solution has linear scaling and is much better than the traditional set-based solution. The solutions based on window functions are by far the most efficient and also have linear scaling.

Packing Intervals

Packing intervals means grouping each set of contiguous intervals with which no other interval overlaps or is adjacent to (abutting), and returning the minimum start and maximum end for each group. Often, packing problems in SQL also involve a partitioning element (for example, a user, an application), where the packing is done for each partition independently.

The scenario I'll use to demonstrate solutions to the packing intervals problem involves user sessions for some application or service. Use the following code to create the Users and Sessions tables and to populate them with sample data to test the solution's validity:

```
SET NOCOUNT ON;
USE TSQL2012;

IF OBJECT_ID('dbo.Sessions') IS NOT NULL DROP TABLE dbo.Sessions;
IF OBJECT_ID('dbo.Users') IS NOT NULL DROP TABLE dbo.Users;

CREATE TABLE dbo.Users
(
  username  VARCHAR(14)  NOT NULL,
  CONSTRAINT PK_Users PRIMARY KEY(username)
);

INSERT INTO dbo.Users(username) VALUES('User1'), ('User2'), ('User3');

CREATE TABLE dbo.Sessions
(
  id        INT         NOT NULL IDENTITY(1, 1),
  username  VARCHAR(14) NOT NULL,
  starttime DATETIME2(3) NOT NULL,
  endtime   DATETIME2(3) NOT NULL,
  CONSTRAINT PK_Sessions PRIMARY KEY(id),
  CONSTRAINT CHK_endtime_gteq_starttime
    CHECK (endtime >= starttime)
);

INSERT INTO dbo.Sessions(username, starttime, endtime) VALUES
  ('User1', '20121201 08:00:00.000', '20121201 08:30:00.000'),
  ('User1', '20121201 08:30:00.000', '20121201 09:00:00.000'),
  ('User1', '20121201 09:00:00.000', '20121201 09:30:00.000'),
  ('User1', '20121201 10:00:00.000', '20121201 11:00:00.000'),
  ('User1', '20121201 10:30:00.000', '20121201 12:00:00.000'),
  ('User1', '20121201 11:30:00.000', '20121201 12:30:00.000'),
  ('User2', '20121201 08:00:00.000', '20121201 10:30:00.000'),
  ('User2', '20121201 08:30:00.000', '20121201 10:00:00.000'),
  ('User2', '20121201 09:00:00.000', '20121201 09:30:00.000'),
  ('User2', '20121201 11:00:00.000', '20121201 11:30:00.000'),
  ('User2', '20121201 11:32:00.000', '20121201 12:00:00.000'),
  ('User2', '20121201 12:04:00.000', '20121201 12:30:00.000'),
  ('User3', '20121201 08:00:00.000', '20121201 09:00:00.000'),
  ('User3', '20121201 08:00:00.000', '20121201 08:30:00.000'),
  ('User3', '20121201 08:30:00.000', '20121201 09:00:00.000'),
  ('User3', '20121201 09:30:00.000', '20121201 09:30:00.000');
```

Here's the desired result for the small set of sample data:

```
username  starttime                endtime
--------  -----------------------  -----------------------
User1     2012-12-01 08:00:00.000  2012-12-01 09:30:00.000
User1     2012-12-01 10:00:00.000  2012-12-01 12:30:00.000
User2     2012-12-01 08:00:00.000  2012-12-01 10:30:00.000
User2     2012-12-01 11:00:00.000  2012-12-01 11:30:00.000
User2     2012-12-01 11:32:00.000  2012-12-01 12:00:00.000
User2     2012-12-01 12:04:00.000  2012-12-01 12:30:00.000
User3     2012-12-01 08:00:00.000  2012-12-01 09:00:00.000
User3     2012-12-01 09:30:00.000  2012-12-01 09:30:00.000
```

Figure 5-16 is a graphical depiction of both the original intervals from the Sessions table (orange bars), as well as the packed intervals (red arrows).

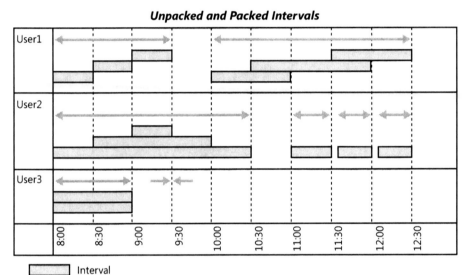

FIGURE 5-16 Unpacked and packed intervals.

You can use the following code to populate the Sessions table with a large set of sample data to test the performance of the solutions:

```
DECLARE
  @num_users          AS INT        = 2000,
  @intervals_per_user AS INT        = 2500,
  @start_period       AS DATETIME2(3) = '20120101',
  @end_period         AS DATETIME2(3) = '20120107',
  @max_duration_in_ms AS INT        = 3600000; -- 60 minutes

TRUNCATE TABLE dbo.Sessions;
TRUNCATE TABLE dbo.Users;
```

```
INSERT INTO dbo.Users(username)
  SELECT 'User' + RIGHT('000000000' + CAST(U.n AS VARCHAR(10)), 10) AS username
  FROM dbo.GetNums(1, @num_users) AS U;

WITH C AS
(
  SELECT 'User' + RIGHT('000000000' + CAST(U.n AS VARCHAR(10)), 10) AS username,
      DATEADD(ms, ABS(CHECKSUM(NEWID())) % 86400000,
        DATEADD(day, ABS(CHECKSUM(NEWID())) % DATEDIFF(day, @start_period, @end_period),
@start_period)) AS starttime
  FROM dbo.GetNums(1, @num_users) AS U
    CROSS JOIN dbo.GetNums(1, @intervals_per_user) AS I
)
INSERT INTO dbo.Sessions WITH (TABLOCK) (username, starttime, endtime)
  SELECT username, starttime,
    DATEADD(ms, ABS(CHECKSUM(NEWID())) % (@max_duration_in_ms + 1), starttime) AS endtime
  FROM C;
```

This code populates the Sessions table with 5,000,000 rows. I filled it with data for 2,000 users, each with 2,500 sessions during a period of a week, with each session lasting up to one hour. But the code allows you to change any element that you like to test the scaling of the solutions.

Traditional Set-Based Solution

The first solution I will cover is a classic solution that does the job, but very inefficiently. It will benefit from the following two indexes:

```
CREATE INDEX idx_user_start_end ON dbo.Sessions(username, starttime, endtime);
CREATE INDEX idx_user_end_start ON dbo.Sessions(username, endtime, starttime);
```

Here's the solution's code:

```
WITH StartTimes AS
(
  SELECT DISTINCT username, starttime
  FROM dbo.Sessions AS S1
  WHERE NOT EXISTS
    (SELECT * FROM dbo.Sessions AS S2
     WHERE S2.username = S1.username
       AND S2.starttime < S1.starttime
       AND S2.endtime >= S1.starttime)
),
EndTimes AS
(
  SELECT DISTINCT username, endtime
  FROM dbo.Sessions AS S1
  WHERE NOT EXISTS
    (SELECT * FROM dbo.Sessions AS S2
     WHERE S2.username = S1.username
       AND S2.endtime > S1.endtime
       AND S2.starttime <= S1.endtime)
)
```

```
SELECT username, starttime,
  (SELECT MIN(endtime) FROM EndTimes AS E
    WHERE E.username = S.username
      AND endtime >= starttime) AS endtime
FROM StartTimes AS S;
```

The CTE *StartTimes* isolates packed interval start times using a query that returns all interval start times for which you cannot find any interval by the same user that started before the current interval start and ended on or after the current interval start. The *EndTimes* CTE isolates packed interval end times using a query that returns all interval end times for which you cannot find any interval by the same user that ended after the current interval end and started on or before the current interval end. The outer query then matches to each packed interval start the nearest packed interval end and goes forward by returning the minimum end that is greater than or equal to the current start.

As mentioned, this solution is very inefficient. It took several hours to complete when run against the sample data with the 5,000,000 rows in the Sessions table.

Before continuing, run the following code to drop the indexes you created to support the last solution:

```
DROP INDEX idx_user_start_end ON dbo.Sessions;
DROP INDEX idx_user_end_start ON dbo.Sessions;
```

Solutions Based on Window Functions

Next, I'm going to cover two fairly new strategies based on window functions that are much faster than the traditional solution. You will want to create the following indexes to support the new solutions:

```
CREATE UNIQUE INDEX idx_user_start_id ON dbo.Sessions(username, starttime, id);
CREATE UNIQUE INDEX idx_user_end_id ON dbo.Sessions(username, endtime, id);
```

The first of the two new strategies relies mainly on the ROW_NUMBER function. The complete solution is shown in Listing 5-1. It runs for 47 seconds on my laptop when run against the sample data provided earlier with the 5,000,000 rows.

LISTING 5-1 Packing Intervals Using Row Numbers

```
WITH C1 AS
-- let e = end ordinals, let s = start ordinals
(
  SELECT id, username, starttime AS ts, +1 AS type, NULL AS e,
    ROW_NUMBER() OVER(PARTITION BY username ORDER BY starttime, id) AS s
  FROM dbo.Sessions

  UNION ALL
```

```
    SELECT id, username, endtime AS ts, -1 AS type,
      ROW_NUMBER() OVER(PARTITION BY username ORDER BY endtime, id) AS e,
      NULL AS s
    FROM dbo.Sessions
),
C2 AS
-- let se = start or end ordinal, namely, how many events (start or end) happened so far
(
    SELECT C1.*, ROW_NUMBER() OVER(PARTITION BY username ORDER BY ts, type DESC, id) AS se
    FROM C1
),
C3 AS
-- For start events, the expression s - (se - s) - 1 represents how many sessions were active
-- just before the current (hence - 1)
--
-- For end events, the expression (se - e) - e represents how many sessions are active
-- right after this one
--
-- The above two expressions are 0 exactly when a group of packed intervals
-- either starts or ends, respectively
--
-- After filtering only events when a group of packed intervals either starts or ends,
-- group each pair of adjacent start/end events
(
    SELECT username, ts,
      FLOOR((ROW_NUMBER() OVER(PARTITION BY username ORDER BY ts) - 1) / 2 + 1) AS grpnum
    FROM C2
    WHERE COALESCE(s - (se - s) - 1, (se - e) - e) = 0
)
SELECT username, MIN(ts) AS starttime, max(ts) AS endtime
FROM C3
GROUP BY username, grpnum;
```

The code in the CTE called *C1* unifies start events with end events in one chronological sequence of events (start or end). Start events are marked with a +1 event type because they increase the count of active sessions, and end events are marked with a –1 event type because they decrease the count of active sessions. Figure 5-17 shows the chronological sequence of unified events sorted by *username*, *ts*, *type DESC*, *id*, with green bars representing how many sessions are active before and after each event.

Observe that a packed interval always starts when the number of active sessions prior to a start event is zero, and it ends when the number of active sessions after an end event is zero. Therefore, with respect to each start event, you need to know how many sessions were active prior to it, and with respect to each end event, you need to know how many sessions are active after it. This information is calculated in steps.

id	username	ts	type	numintervals	
				0	
1	User1	2012-12-01 08:00	1	1	
2	User1	2012-12-01 08:30	1	2	
1	User1	2012-12-01 08:30	-1	1	
3	User1	2012-12-01 09:00	1	2	
2	User1	2012-12-01 09:00	-1	1	
3	User1	2012-12-01 09:30	-1	0	
				0	
4	User1	2012-12-01 10:00	1	1	
5	User1	2012-12-01 10:30	1	2	
4	User1	2012-12-01 11:00	-1	1	
6	User1	2012-12-01 11:30	1	2	
5	User1	2012-12-01 12:00	-1	1	
6	User1	2012-12-01 12:30	-1	0	
				0	
7	User2	2012-12-01 08:00	1	1	
8	User2	2012-12-01 08:30	1	2	
9	User2	2012-12-01 09:00	1	3	
9	User2	2012-12-01 09:30	-1	2	
8	User2	2012-12-01 10:00	-1	1	
7	User2	2012-12-01 10:30	-1	0	
				0	
10	User2	2012-12-01 11:00	1	1	
10	User2	2012-12-01 11:30	-1	0	
				0	
11	User2	2012-12-01 11:32	1	1	
11	User2	2012-12-01 12:00	-1	0	
				0	
12	User2	2012-12-01 12:04	1	1	
12	User2	2012-12-01 12:30	-1	0	
				0	
13	User3	2012-12-01 08:00	1	1	
14	User3	2012-12-01 08:00	1	2	
15	User3	2012-12-01 08:30	1	3	
14	User3	2012-12-01 08:30	-1	2	
13	User3	2012-12-01 09:00	-1	1	
15	User3	2012-12-01 09:00	-1	0	
				0	
16	User3	2012-12-01 09:30	1	1	
16	User3	2012-12-01 09:30	-1	0	

FIGURE 5-17 Start and end events ordered chronologically.

Observe that the code in the CTE *C1* calculates start ordinals for start events (an attribute called *s*), with NULLs used as placeholders in that attribute for end events, and it calculates end ordinals for end events (an attribute called *e*), with NULLs used as placeholders in that attribute for start events. The code in the CTE *C2* then simply adds an ordinal for start or end events (an attribute called *se*), partitioned by *username* and sorted by *ts*, *type DESC*, *id*. Following is the output of the code in *C2*, sorted by *username*, *ts*, *type DESC*, *id* (for readability, I marked the start event types as +1 instead of just 1 and replaced NULLs with blanks):

id	username	ts	type	e	s	se
1	User1	2012-12-01 08:00	+1		1	1
2	User1	2012-12-01 08:30	+1		2	2
1	User1	2012-12-01 08:30	-1	1		3
3	User1	2012-12-01 09:00	+1		3	4
2	User1	2012-12-01 09:00	-1	2		5
3	User1	2012-12-01 09:30	-1	3		6
4	User1	2012-12-01 10:00	+1		4	7
5	User1	2012-12-01 10:30	+1		5	8
4	User1	2012-12-01 11:00	-1	4		9
6	User1	2012-12-01 11:30	+1		6	10
5	User1	2012-12-01 12:00	-1	5		11
6	User1	2012-12-01 12:30	-1	6		12
7	User2	2012-12-01 08:00	+1		1	1
8	User2	2012-12-01 08:30	+1		2	2
9	User2	2012-12-01 09:00	+1		3	3
9	User2	2012-12-01 09:30	-1	1		4
8	User2	2012-12-01 10:00	-1	2		5
7	User2	2012-12-01 10:30	-1	3		6
10	User2	2012-12-01 11:00	+1		4	7
10	User2	2012-12-01 11:30	-1	4		8
11	User2	2012-12-01 11:32	+1		5	9
11	User2	2012-12-01 12:00	-1	5		10
12	User2	2012-12-01 12:04	+1		6	11
12	User2	2012-12-01 12:30	-1	6		12
13	User3	2012-12-01 08:00	+1		1	1
14	User3	2012-12-01 08:00	+1		2	2
15	User3	2012-12-01 08:30	+1		3	3
14	User3	2012-12-01 08:30	-1	1		4
13	User3	2012-12-01 09:00	-1	2		5
15	User3	2012-12-01 09:00	-1	3		6
16	User3	2012-12-01 09:30	+1		4	7
16	User3	2012-12-01 09:30	-1	4		8

The code in the CTE *C3* is where most of the magic is done. For each start event, you know how many sessions started so far (*s*), and you know how many sessions either started or ended so far (*se*). Therefore, you can easily calculate how many sessions ended so far (*se* − *s*). Now that you know how many sessions started and how many sessions ended, you can calculate how many sessions are active after the start event: *s* − *(se* − *s)*. Think of it just like calculating how many people are in a room if *x* people enter the room and *y* people leave the room. Finally, to find out how many sessions were active prior to the start event, simply subtract 1 from the calculation: *s* − *(se* − *s)* − 1.

In a similar way, you can calculate the number of active sessions after each end event. Having both the number of sessions that ended thus far (*e*) and the number of sessions that either started or ended (*se*), you can calculate how many sessions started as *se* − *e*. Then the number of active sessions is *(se* − *e)* − *e*.

Now, remember that you want to filter only start events where the number of active sessions prior to the event was zero, and end events where the number of active sessions after the event was zero. You can generalize the two filters into one:

```
WHERE COALESCE(s - (se - s) - 1, (se - e) - e) = 0
```

What you have left after filtering are pairs of adjacent start-end events, each representing the start and end of a packed interval. So you need to assign a group identifier to each pair to be able to later pivot each pair into one row. This can be achieved by assigning row numbers (call it n) and applying the calculation $(n - 1) / 2 + 1$, where / represents integer division. For n values 1, 2, 3, 4, ..., you get a result of 1, 1, 2, 2, ...

In SQL Server, the arithmetic operator / represents integer division when the operands are integers, but in Oracle you get a decimal division if you use this operator. I added a FLOOR function so that the code would run correctly on both platforms. So the code in the CTE *C3* generates the following output:

```
username  ts                grpnum
--------- ----------------- --------
User1     2012-12-01 08:00  1
User1     2012-12-01 09:30  1
User1     2012-12-01 10:00  2
User1     2012-12-01 12:30  2
User2     2012-12-01 08:00  1
User2     2012-12-01 10:30  1
User2     2012-12-01 11:00  2
User2     2012-12-01 11:30  2
User2     2012-12-01 11:32  3
User2     2012-12-01 12:00  3
User2     2012-12-01 12:04  4
User2     2012-12-01 12:30  4
User3     2012-12-01 08:00  1
User3     2012-12-01 09:00  1
User3     2012-12-01 09:30  2
User3     2012-12-01 09:30  2
```

What's left to the outer query to do is group the rows from *C3* by *username* and *grpnum*, and return the minimum *ts* as the packed interval's start time and the maximum *ts* as the end time.

The plan generated by SQL Server's optimizer for this query is highly efficient, given that you create the aforementioned indexes: *idx_user_start_id* and *idx_user_end_id*. The plan is shown in Figure 5-18.

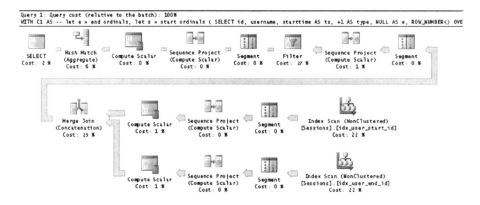

FIGURE 5-18 Plan for a solution using row numbers.

What's amazing about this plan is that it applies two ordered scans of the indexes created to support this solution (*idx_user_start_id* and *idx_user_end_id*), and it relies on the ordered scans to (take a deep breath now) do the following:

- Calculate the row numbers for start ordinals (*s*)

- Calculate row numbers for end ordinals (*e*)

- Perform a merge join to unify the results

- Calculate the start or end ordinals (*se*) on the unified sets

- Calculate the row numbers that are used to produce *grpnum* after filtering

And it does all this without requiring even one sort operator! It's truly remarkable to see an optimizer that so beautifully understands the concept of order preservation. Finally, a hash aggregate is used to group the data by *grpnum* (only the remaining rows after filtering). Because most of the operations used in this plan have linear complexity, this solution should scale close to linearly.

In total, this plan performs only two scans of the data (one of each index), in index order. As mentioned, this solution runs on my laptop for 47 seconds. The one thing that this solution doesn't exploit well is parallelism. That's where the second solution excels.

To exploit parallelism well, what you want is to encapsulate the logic from the solution in Listing 5-1 in a table expression that operates on a single customer and then apply that table expression to each user. I'm assuming here that you have a table holding the distinct users, which is a fair assumption to make. It is convenient, then, to encapsulate the logic from the solution in Listing 5-1 for a single user in an inline table function, as the following code shows:

```
IF OBJECT_ID('dbo.UserIntervals', 'IF') IS NOT NULL DROP FUNCTION dbo.UserIntervals;
GO

CREATE FUNCTION dbo.UserIntervals(@user AS VARCHAR(14)) RETURNS TABLE
AS
RETURN
  WITH C1 AS
  (
    SELECT id, starttime AS ts, +1 AS type, NULL AS e,
      ROW_NUMBER() OVER(ORDER BY starttime, id) AS s
    FROM dbo.Sessions
    WHERE username = @user

    UNION ALL

    SELECT id, endtime AS ts, -1 AS type,
      ROW_NUMBER() OVER(ORDER BY endtime, id) AS e,
      NULL AS s
    FROM dbo.Sessions
    WHERE username = @user
  ),
```

```
  C2 AS
  (
    SELECT C1.*, ROW_NUMBER() OVER(ORDER BY ts, type DESC, id) AS se
    FROM C1
  ),
  C3 AS
  (
    SELECT ts,
      FLOOR((ROW_NUMBER() OVER(ORDER BY ts) - 1) / 2 + 1) AS grpnum
    FROM C2
    WHERE COALESCE(s - (se - s) - 1, (se - e) - e) = 0
  )
  SELECT MIN(ts) AS starttime, max(ts) AS endtime
  FROM C3
  GROUP BY grpnum;
GO
```

And then finally, use the CROSS APPLY operator to apply the function to each user from the Users table, like so:

```
SELECT U.username, A.starttime, A.endtime
FROM dbo.Users AS U
  CROSS APPLY dbo.UserIntervals(U.username) AS A;
```

SQL Server generates the parallel plan shown in Figure 5-19 for this query.

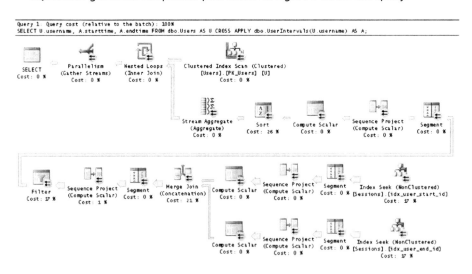

FIGURE 5-19 Plan for a solution using APPLY and row numbers.

As you can see, the plan uses a parallel scan of the clustered index on the Users table, and then it performs the work for each user in the inner branch of the Nested Loops join. The work done in this inner branch should look familiar—it's similar to the work done in the plan shown in Figure 5-18, only this time it's done for the data associated with one user. This inner branch, of course, is executed in parallel by multiple threads. This solution runs for six seconds on my laptop.

The second new solution that is based on window functions is shown in Listing 5-2. It uses the SUM window aggregate function, relying on elements in the window specifications that were introduced in SQL Server 2012.

LISTING 5-2 Solution Using Window Aggregate

```
WITH C1 AS
(
  SELECT username, starttime AS ts, +1 AS type, 1 AS sub
  FROM dbo.Sessions

  UNION ALL

  SELECT username, endtime AS ts, -1 AS type, 0 AS sub
  FROM dbo.Sessions
),
C2 AS
(
  SELECT C1.*,
    SUM(type) OVER(PARTITION BY username ORDER BY ts, type DESC
                  ROWS BETWEEN UNBOUNDED PRECEDING
                          AND CURRENT ROW) - sub AS cnt
  FROM C1
),
C3 AS
(
  SELECT username, ts,
    FLOOR((ROW_NUMBER() OVER(PARTITION BY username ORDER BY ts) - 1) / 2 + 1) AS grpnum
  FROM C2
  WHERE cnt = 0
)
SELECT username, MIN(ts) AS starttime, max(ts) AS endtime
FROM C3
GROUP BY username, grpnum;
```

This solution uses principles similar to those used by the previous solution, only instead of using row numbers to calculate the number of active sessions at any given point, it uses a window SUM aggregate. A running sum of the type (recall that +1 represents a start event and –1 represents an end event), partitioned by *username*, in chronological order, is the number of active sessions at any given point. Now, remember that for start events you need the number of active sessions prior to the event, and for end events you need the number after the event. Therefore, you need to subtract 1 from the count with start events and subtract nothing with end events. The solution generates an attribute called *sub*, with 1 for start events and 0 for end events, and it then subtracts that value from the running total, using the following expression:

```
SUM(type) OVER(PARTITION BY username ORDER BY ts, type DESC
              ROWS BETWEEN UNBOUNDED PRECEDING
                      AND CURRENT ROW) - sub AS cnt
```

The rest is similar to the logic of the previous solution. This solution generates the plan shown in Figure 5-20 and runs for 87 seconds on my laptop.

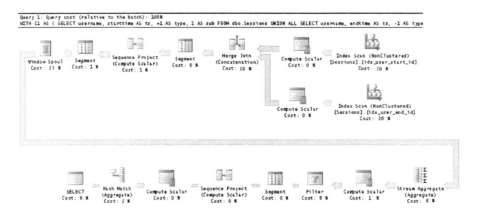

Query 1: Query cost (relative to the batch): 100%
WITH C1 AS (SELECT username, starttime AS ts, +1 AS type, 1 AS sub FROM dbo.Sessions UNION ALL SELECT username, endtime AS ts, -1 AS type

FIGURE 5-20 Plan for a solution using a window aggregate.

Just like you encapsulated the logic of the solution based on row numbers in an inline table function for a single user, and used the APPLY operator to invoke the function for each user from the Users table, you can do the same with the solution that uses the SUM window aggregate. Here's the code for the inline function's definition:

```
IF OBJECT_ID('dbo.UserIntervals', 'IF') IS NOT NULL DROP FUNCTION dbo.UserIntervals;
GO

CREATE FUNCTION dbo.UserIntervals(@user AS VARCHAR(14)) RETURNS TABLE
AS
RETURN
  WITH C1 AS
  (
    SELECT starttime AS ts, +1 AS type, 1 AS sub
    FROM dbo.Sessions
    WHERE username = @user

    UNION ALL

    SELECT endtime AS ts, -1 AS type, 0 AS sub
    FROM dbo.Sessions
    WHERE username = @user
  ),
  C2 AS
  (
    SELECT C1.*,
      SUM(type) OVER(ORDER BY ts, type DESC
                     ROWS BETWEEN UNBOUNDED PRECEDING
                             AND CURRENT ROW) - sub AS cnt
    FROM C1
  ),
  C3 AS
  (
    SELECT ts,
      FLOOR((ROW_NUMBER() OVER(ORDER BY ts) - 1) / 2 + 1) AS grpnum
    FROM C2
    WHERE cnt = 0
  )
```

```
  SELECT MIN(ts) AS starttime, max(ts) AS endtime
  FROM C3
  GROUP BY grpnum;
GO
```

And here's the query that applies the function to each user:

```
SELECT U.username, A.starttime, A.endtime
FROM dbo.Users AS U
  CROSS APPLY dbo.UserIntervals(U.username) AS A;
```

This code generates the plan shown in Figure 5-21 and runs for 13 seconds on my laptop.

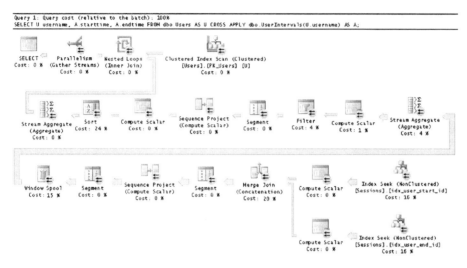

FIGURE 5-21 Plan for a solution using APPLY and a window aggregate.

Gaps and Islands

Gaps and Islands are classic problems in SQL that manifest themselves in practice in many forms. The basic concept is that you have some sort of sequence of numbers or date and time values where there's supposed to be a fixed interval between the entries, but some entries could be missing. Then the gaps problem involves identifying all ranges of missing values in the sequence, and the islands problem involves identifying all ranges of existing values. To demonstrate techniques to identify gaps and islands, I'll use a table called T1 with a numeric sequence in a column called *col1* with an interval of 1 integer, and a table called T2 with a date and time sequence in a column called *col1* with an interval of 1 day. Here's code to create T1 and T2 and fill them with some sample data:

```
SET NOCOUNT ON;
USE TSQL2012;

-- dbo.T1 (numeric sequence with unique values, interval: 1)
IF OBJECT_ID('dbo.T1', 'U') IS NOT NULL DROP TABLE dbo.T1;

CREATE TABLE dbo.T1
```

```
(
  col1 INT NOT NULL
    CONSTRAINT PK_T1 PRIMARY KEY
);
GO

INSERT INTO dbo.T1(col1)
  VALUES(2),(3),(7),(8),(9),(11),(15),(16),(17),(28);

-- dbo.T2 (temporal sequence with unique values, interval: 1 day)
IF OBJECT_ID('dbo.T2', 'U') IS NOT NULL DROP TABLE dbo.T2;

CREATE TABLE dbo.T2
(
  col1 DATE NOT NULL
    CONSTRAINT PK_T2 PRIMARY KEY
);
GO

INSERT INTO dbo.T2(col1) VALUES
  ('20120202'),
  ('20120203'),
  ('20120207'),
  ('20120208'),
  ('20120209'),
  ('20120211'),
  ('20120215'),
  ('20120216'),
  ('20120217'),
  ('20120228');
```

Gaps

As mentioned, the gaps problem involves identifying the ranges of missing values in the sequence. Using our sample data, here are the desired results for the numeric sequence in T1:

```
rangestart   rangeend
-----------  -----------
4            6
10           10
12           14
18           27
```

And here are the desired results for the temporal sequence in T2:

```
rangestart  rangeend
----------  ----------
2012-02-04  2012-02-06
2012-02-10  2012-02-10
2012-02-12  2012-02-14
2012-02-18  2012-02-27
```

In versions of SQL Server prior to SQL Server 2012, the techniques to handle gaps were quite expensive and sometimes complicated. But with the introduction of the LAG and LEAD functions, you can now handle this need simply and efficiently. Using the LEAD function, you can return for each current *col1* value (call it *cur*) the next value in the sequence (call it *nxt*). Then you can filter only pairs where the difference between the two is greater than the interval. Then add one interval to *cur* and subtract one interval from *nxt* to produce the actual gap information. Here's the complete solution with the numeric sequence followed by its execution plan (in Figure 5-22):

```
WITH C AS
(
  SELECT col1 AS cur, LEAD(col1) OVER(ORDER BY col1) AS nxt
  FROM dbo.T1
)
SELECT cur + 1 AS rangestart, nxt - 1 AS rangeend
FROM C
WHERE nxt - cur > 1;
```

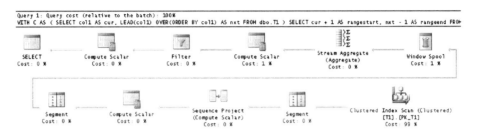

FIGURE 5-22 Plan for a solution to the gaps problem.

Observe how efficient the plan is, performing only one ordered scan of the index defined on *col1*. To apply the same technique to the temporal sequence, you simply use the DATEDIFF function to compute the difference between *cur* and *nxt*, and you use DATEADD to add or subtract an interval, like so:

```
WITH C AS
(
  SELECT col1 AS cur, LEAD(col1) OVER(ORDER BY col1) AS nxt
  FROM dbo.T2
)
SELECT DATEADD(day, 1, cur) AS rangestart, DATEADD(day, -1, nxt) rangeend
FROM C
WHERE DATEDIFF(day, cur, nxt) > 1;
```

Islands

The islands problem involves identifying ranges of existing values. Here's the desired output against the numeric sequence:

```
start_range end_range
----------- -----------
2           3
7           9
11          11
15          17
28          28
```

And here's the desired output against the temporal sequence:

```
start_range  end_range
-----------  ----------
2012-02-02   2012-02-03
2012-02-07   2012-02-09
2012-02-11   2012-02-11
2012-02-15   2012-02-17
2012-02-28   2012-02-28
```

One of the most efficient solutions to the islands problem involves using ranking calculations. You use the DENSE_RANK function to create a sequence of integers in *col1* ordering, and you calculate the difference between *col1* and the dense rank (*drnk*), like so:

```
SELECT col1,
  DENSE_RANK() OVER(ORDER BY col1) AS drnk,
  col1 - DENSE_RANK() OVER(ORDER BY col1) AS diff
FROM dbo.T1;
```

```
col1  drnk  diff
----- ----- -----
2     1     1
3     2     1
7     3     4
8     4     4
9     5     4
11    6     5
15    7     8
16    8     8
17    9     8
28    10    18
```

Observe that within an island the difference is the same, and that difference is unique for each island. That's because within an island, both *col1* and *drnk* keep advancing by the same interval. As soon as you jump to the next island, *col1* increases by more than one interval, whereas *drnk* keeps increasing by one. Therefore, the difference in each island is greater than the previous island's difference. Because this difference is the same within an island and unique for each island, you can use it as a group identifier. So what's left is just to group the rows by this difference and return the minimum and maximum *col1* values in each group, like so:

```
WITH C AS
(
  SELECT col1, col1 - DENSE_RANK() OVER(ORDER BY col1) AS grp
  FROM dbo.T1
)
SELECT MIN(col1) AS start_range, MAX(col1) AS end_range
FROM C
GROUP BY grp;
```

The plan for this solution is shown in Figure 5-23.

| SELECT Cost: 0 % | Stream Aggregate (Aggregate) Cost: 0 % | Sort Cost: 78 % | Compute Scalar Cost: 0 % | Sequence Project (Compute Scalar) Cost: 0 % | Segment Cost: 0 % | Segment Cost: 0 % | Clustered Index Scan (Clustered) [T1].[PK_T1] Cost: 22 % |

FIGURE 5-23 Plan for a solution to the islands problem.

The plan is very efficient because the computation of the dense rank value can rely on the ordering of the index on *col1*.

You might be wondering why we use the DENSE_RANK function and not ROW_NUMBER. This has to do with needing support for cases where the sequence values are not guaranteed to be unique. Using the ROW_NUMBER function, the technique works only when the sequence values are unique (which happens to be the case in our sample data), but it fails when duplicates are allowed. Using the DENSE_RANK function, the technique works both with unique and nonunique values; hence, I prefer to always use DENSE_RANK.

The technique can even work with temporal intervals, but it might not immediately be apparent. Remember that the technique involves producing a group identifier—namely, a value that is the same for all members of the same island and different than the values produced for other islands. With the temporal sequence, the *col1* values and dense rank values use different intervals—one uses an interval of 1 integer, and the other uses an interval of 1 day. To make the technique work, simply subtract from the *col1* value as many of the temporal interval as the dense rank value. You need to use the DATEADD function to achieve this. Then you will get a date and time value as a result that is the same for all members of the same island and different than the values produced for other islands. Here's the complete solution code:

```
WITH C AS
(
  SELECT col1, DATEADD(day, -1 * DENSE_RANK() OVER(ORDER BY col1), col1) AS grp
  FROM dbo.T2
)
SELECT MIN(col1) AS start_range, MAX(col1) AS end_range
FROM C
GROUP BY grp;
```

As you can see, instead of directly subtracting the result of the dense rank function from *col1*, you use DATEADD to subtract the dense rank multiplied by one day from *col1*.

There are querying problems where you need to use the islands technique, including availability reports, periods of activity, and others. You can even use the islands technique to handle a classic problem involving packing date intervals. Consider the following table that holds information about date intervals.

```
IF OBJECT_ID('dbo.Intervals', 'U') IS NOT NULL DROP TABLE dbo.Intervals;

CREATE TABLE dbo.Intervals
(
  id        INT  NOT NULL,
  startdate DATE NOT NULL,
  enddate   DATE NOT NULL
);

INSERT INTO dbo.Intervals(id, startdate, enddate) VALUES
  (1, '20120212', '20120220'),
  (2, '20120214', '20120312'),
  (3, '20120124', '20120201');
```

These date intervals could represent periods of activity, periods of validity, and many other types of date periods. Given some input period (the *@from* and *@to* parameters), your task is to pack the intervals within that period. In other words, you're supposed to merge intervals that overlap or are adjacent. Here's the desired result for the given sample data, assuming the input period is from January 1, 2012 to December 31, 2012:

```
rangestart rangeend
---------- ----------
2012-01-24 2012-02-01
2012-02-12 2012-03-12
```

The solution uses the *GetNums* function covered earlier in this chapter to generate a sequence of the dates that fall within the input period. The code defines a CTE called *Dates* representing this set of dates. The code then joins the CTE *Dates* (aliased as *D*) with the table Intervals (aliased as *I*), matching each date with the intervals that contain it using the following join predicate: *D.dt BETWEEN I.startdate AND I.enddate*. The code then uses the technique shown previously to compute a group identifier (call it *grp*) that identifies islands. The code defines a CTE called *Groups* that is based on this query. Finally, the outer query groups the rows by *grp* and returns the minimum and maximum dates within each island as the boundaries of the packed intervals. Here's the complete solution code:

```
DECLARE
  @from AS DATE = '20120101',
  @to   AS DATE = '20121231';

WITH Dates AS
(
  SELECT DATEADD(day, n-1, @from) AS dt
  FROM dbo.GetNums(1, DATEDIFF(day, @from, @to) + 1) AS Nums
),
Groups AS
(
  SELECT D.dt,
    DATEADD(day, -1 * DENSE_RANK() OVER(ORDER BY D.dt), D.dt) AS grp
  FROM dbo.Intervals AS I
    JOIN Dates AS D
      ON D.dt BETWEEN I.startdate AND I.enddate
)
SELECT MIN(dt) AS rangestart, MAX(dt) AS rangeend
FROM Groups
GROUP BY grp;
```

Note that this solution doesn't perform well when the intervals span long periods of time. That's understandable given that the solution unpacks each period to the individual dates involved.

There are versions of the islands problem that are more complicated than the fundamental one. For example, say you are supposed to ignore gaps of up to a certain size—for example, in our numeric sequence, say you are supposed to ignore gaps of up to 2. Then the desired output would be the following:

```
rangestart   rangeend
-----------  -----------
2            3
7            11
15           17
28           28
```

Observe that the values 7, 8, 9, and 11 are all part of one island starting with 7 and ending with 11. The gap between 9 and 11 is ignored because it isn't greater than 2.

You can use the LAG and LEAD functions to handle this task. You first define a CTE called *C1* based on a query against T1 computing the following two attributes: *isstart* and *isend*. The *isstart* attribute is a flag whose value is 1 when the sequence value is the first in the island and 0 when it isn't. A value is not the first value in the island if the difference between *col1* and the previous value (obtained using the LAG function) is less than or equal to 2; otherwise, it is the first value in the island. Similarly, a value is not the last value in the island if the difference between the next value (obtained using the LEAD function) and *col1* is less than or equal to 2; otherwise, it is the last value in the island.

Next, the code defines a CTE called *C2* that filters only rows where the sequence value is either a start or an end of an island. Using the LEAD function, the code matches to each island start value the island end value. This is achieved by using the expression *1-isend* as the offset for the LEAD function. This means that if the current row representing the start of an island also happens to represent its end, the offset will be 0; otherwise, it will be 1. Finally the outer query simply filters from *C2* only the rows where *isstart* is 1. Here's the complete solution code:

```
WITH C1 AS
(
  SELECT col1,
    CASE WHEN col1 - LAG(col1) OVER(ORDER BY col1)  <= 2 THEN 0 ELSE 1 END AS isstart,
    CASE WHEN LEAD(col1) OVER(ORDER BY col1) - col1 <= 2 THEN 0 ELSE 1 END AS isend
  FROM dbo.T1
),
C2 AS
(
  SELECT col1 AS rangestart, LEAD(col1, 1-isend) OVER(ORDER BY col1) AS rangeend, isstart
  FROM C1
  WHERE isstart = 1 OR isend = 1
)
SELECT rangestart, rangeend
FROM C2
WHERE isstart = 1;
```

The execution plan for this query is shown in Figure 5-24.

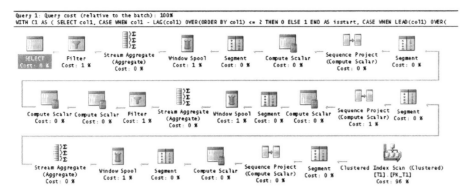

Query 1: Query cost (relative to the batch): 100%
WITH C1 AS (SELECT col1, CASE WHEN col1 - LAG(col1) OVER(ORDER BY col1) <= 2 THEN 0 ELSE 1 END AS isstart, CASE WHEN LEAD(col1) OVER(

FIGURE 5-24 Plan for a solution to the islands problem ignoring gaps up to 2.

For the next version of the islands problem, use the sample data generated by the following code:

```
IF OBJECT_ID('dbo.T1', 'U') IS NOT NULL DROP TABLE dbo.T1;

CREATE TABLE dbo.T1
(
  id  INT        NOT NULL PRIMARY KEY,
  val VARCHAR(10) NOT NULL
);
GO

INSERT INTO dbo.T1(id, val) VALUES
  (2, 'a'),
  (3, 'a'),
  (5, 'a'),
  (7, 'b'),
  (11, 'b'),
  (13, 'a'),
  (17, 'a'),
  (19, 'a'),
  (23, 'c'),
  (29, 'c'),
  (31, 'a'),
  (37, 'a'),
  (41, 'a'),
  (43, 'a'),
  (47, 'c'),
  (53, 'c'),
  (59, 'c');
```

This version of the islands problem involves identifying ranges of IDs where the value in the *val* attribute remains the same. Observe that there can be multiple islands associated with the same value in *val*. Here's the desired output for the given sample data:

mn	mx	val
2	5	a
7	11	b
13	19	a
23	29	c
31	43	a
47	59	c

The first step in the solution is to compute the difference between a row number based on *id* ordering and a row number based on *val, id* ordering (call it *grp*):

```
SELECT id, val,
  ROW_NUMBER() OVER(ORDER BY id)
    - ROW_NUMBER() OVER(ORDER BY val, id) AS grp
FROM dbo.T1;
```

id	val	grp
2	a	0
3	a	0
5	a	0
13	a	2
17	a	2
19	a	2
31	a	4
37	a	4
41	a	4
43	a	4
7	b	-7
11	b	-7
23	c	-4
29	c	-4
47	c	0
53	c	0
59	c	0

Observe that for each distinct value in the *val* attribute, *grp* is unique for each island. That's because the row numbers based on *id* ordering have gaps between the different islands, and row numbers based on *val, id* ordering don't. So for the same value in *val*, as you move from one island to the next, the difference becomes greater, while within an island it remains constant. To complete the solution, define a CTE based on the previous query and then, in the outer query, group the rows by *val, grp*, and return the minimum and maximum IDs for each *val*, like so:

```
WITH C AS
(
  SELECT id, val,
    ROW_NUMBER() OVER(ORDER BY id)
      - ROW_NUMBER() OVER(ORDER BY val, id) AS grp
  FROM dbo.T1
)
SELECT MIN(id) AS mn, MAX(id) AS mx, val
FROM C
GROUP BY val, grp
ORDER BY mn;
```

Median

In Chapters 2 and 3, I discussed how to compute percentiles. I mentioned that the 50th percentile—commonly known as the median—represents, loosely speaking, the value in the population that 50 percent of the values are less than. I provided solutions to calculating any percentile in both SQL Server 2012 and in previous versions of SQL Server. Here, I'll just remind you of the solution in SQL Server 2012 using the PERCENTILE_CONT function (CONT for the continuous distribution model) and then show interesting solutions specific to the median calculation used prior to SQL Server 2012.

For sample data, I'll use the Stats.Scores table, which holds student test scores. Suppose your task was to compute, for each test, the median score assuming continuous distribution model. If there's an odd number of student test scores for a given test, you're supposed to return the middle score. If there's an even number, you're supposed to return the average of the two middle scores. Here's the desired output for the given sample data:

```
testid      median
----------  -------
Test ABC    75
Test XYZ    77.5
```

As already mentioned in the book, the function PERCENTILE_CONT introduced in SQL Server 2012 is used to compute percentiles assuming a continuous distribution model. However, this function wasn't implemented as a grouped ordered set function; rather, it was implemented as a window function. This means that you can use it to return a percentile along with all detail rows, but to return it only once per group, you need to add some filtering logic. For example, you can compute a row number with the same window-partitioning specification as that of the PERCENTILE_CONT function and arbitrary ordering, and then filter only the rows where the row number is equal to 1. Here's the complete solution code computing the median score per test:

```
WITH C AS
(
  SELECT testid,
    ROW_NUMBER() OVER(PARTITION BY testid ORDER BY (SELECT NULL)) AS rownum,
    PERCENTILE_CONT(0.5) WITHIN GROUP(ORDER BY score) OVER(PARTITION BY testid) AS median
  FROM Stats.Scores
)
SELECT testid, median
FROM C
WHERE rownum = 1;
```

It's a little bit awkward, but it works.

Prior to SQL Server 2012, you had to be more creative, but you could still use window functions to achieve the task. One solution was to compute, for each row, a position within the test based on score ordering (call it *pos*) and the count of scores in the respective test (call it *cnt*). To compute *pos*, you use the ROW_NUMBER function, and to compute *cnt*, you use the COUNT window aggregate function. Then you filter only the rows that are supposed to participate in the median calculation—namely, the rows where *pos* is either equal to *(cnt + 1) / 2* or *(cnt + 2) / 2*. Note that the expressions use integer division, so any fraction is truncated. When there is an odd number of elements, both expressions return the same middle point. For example, when there are 9 elements in the group, both expressions return 5. When there is an even number of elements, the expressions return the two middle points. For example, when there are 10 elements in the group, the expressions return 5 and 6. After you filter the right rows, what's left is to group the rows by the test ID and return for each test the average score. Here's the complete solution query:

```
WITH C AS
(
  SELECT testid, score,
    ROW_NUMBER() OVER(PARTITION BY testid ORDER BY score) AS pos,
    COUNT(*) OVER(PARTITION BY testid) AS cnt
  FROM Stats.Scores
)
SELECT testid, AVG(1. * score) AS median
FROM C
WHERE pos IN( (cnt + 1) / 2, (cnt + 2) / 2 )
GROUP BY testid;
```

Another interesting solution available prior to SQL Server 2012 involves computing two row numbers—one in ascending *score, studentid* ordering (*studentid* added for determinism), and another in descending ordering. Here's the code to compute the two row numbers followed by its output:

```
SELECT testid, score,
  ROW_NUMBER() OVER(PARTITION BY testid ORDER BY score, studentid) AS rna,
  ROW_NUMBER() OVER(PARTITION BY testid ORDER BY score DESC, studentid DESC) AS rnd
FROM Stats.Scores;
```

```
testid      score rna  rnd
----------  ----- ---- ----
Test ABC    95    9    1
Test ABC    95    8    2
Test ABC    80    7    3
Test ABC    80    6    4
Test ABC    75    5    5
Test ABC    65    4    6
Test ABC    55    3    7
Test ABC    55    2    8
Test ABC    50    1    9
Test XYZ    95    10   1
Test XYZ    95    9    2
Test XYZ    95    8    3
Test XYZ    80    7    4
Test XYZ    80    6    5
Test XYZ    75    5    6
Test XYZ    65    4    7
Test XYZ    55    3    8
Test XYZ    55    2    9
Test XYZ    50    1    10
```

Can you generalize a rule that identifies the rows that need to participate in the median calculation?

Observe that when there's an odd number of elements, the median is where the two row numbers are the same. When there's an even number of elements, the median elements are where the absolute difference between the two row numbers is equal to 1. To merge the two rules, the median elements are in the rows where the absolute difference between the two row numbers is less than or equal to 1. Here's the complete solution code that relies on this rule:

```
WITH C AS
(
  SELECT testid, score,
    ROW_NUMBER() OVER(PARTITION BY testid ORDER BY score, studentid) AS rna,
    ROW_NUMBER() OVER(PARTITION BY testid ORDER BY score DESC, studentid DESC) AS rnd
  FROM Stats.Scores
)
SELECT testid, AVG(1. * score) AS median
FROM C
WHERE ABS(rna - rnd) <= 1
GROUP BY testid;
```

Conditional Aggregate

Our next task involves computing a running total that always returns a non-negative value. That is, if the running total is negative at a point, return zero instead. Then, when you move to the next item in the sequence, you proceed from 0. For sample data, use the following code, which creates and populates a table called T1:

```
USE TSQL2012;

IF OBJECT_ID('dbo.T1') IS NOT NULL DROP TABLE dbo.T1;
GO

CREATE TABLE dbo.T1
(
  ordcol  INT NOT NULL PRIMARY KEY,
  datacol INT NOT NULL
);

INSERT INTO dbo.T1 VALUES
  (1,   10),
  (4,  -15),
  (5,    5),
  (6,  -10),
  (8,  -15),
  (10,  20),
  (17,  10),
  (18, -10),
  (20, -30),
  (31,  20);
```

According to the description of the task, here's the desired output for the given sample data, computing a non-negative sum of *datacol* based on *ordcol* ordering:

ordcol	datacol	nonnegativesum
1	10	10
4	-15	0
5	5	5
6	-10	0
8	-15	0
10	20	20
17	10	30
18	-10	20
20	-30	0
31	20	20

I'll present an elegant solution devised by Gordon Linoff that uses window functions. Here's the complete solution code, followed by its output (adding the intermediate computations *partsum* and *adjust* to help explain the solution):

```
WITH C1 AS
(
  SELECT ordcol, datacol,
    SUM(datacol) OVER (ORDER BY ordcol
                       ROWS BETWEEN UNBOUNDED PRECEDING AND CURRENT ROW) AS partsum
  FROM dbo.T1
),
C2 AS
(
  SELECT *,
    MIN(partsum) OVER (ORDER BY ordcol
                       ROWS BETWEEN UNBOUNDED PRECEDING AND CURRENT ROW) as adjust
  FROM C1
)
SELECT *,
  partsum - CASE WHEN adjust < 0 THEN adjust ELSE 0 END
    AS nonnegativesum
FROM C2;
```

ordcol	datacol	partsum	adjust	nonnegativesum
1	10	10	10	10
4	-15	-5	-5	0
5	5	0	-5	5
6	-10	-10	-10	0
8	-15	-25	-25	0
10	20	-5	-25	20
17	10	5	-25	30
18	-10	-5	-25	20
20	-30	-35	-35	0
31	20	-15	-35	20

The code defining the CTE *C1* creates an attribute called *partsum* that computes a plain running total of *datacol* based on *ordcol* ordering and calls it. This *partsum* attribute can be negative because the values in *datacol* can be negative. Then the code defining the CTE *C2* queries *C1*, creating an attribute called *adjust* that computes the minimum *partsum* value up to the current point. Finally, the outer query checks whether *partsum* needs to be adjusted to compute the non-negative sum.

If *adjust* (the minimum *partsum* so far) isn't negative, there's nothing to adjust. If it is negative, *adjust* needs to be subtracted from *partsum*.

It can take a few rounds of going over this output to see that the logic works, but it does!

Sorting Hierarchies

Suppose that you need to present information from some hierarchy in a sorted fashion. You're supposed to present a parent before its child elements. Also, you need to be able to control the order among siblings. For sample data, use the following code, which creates and populates a table called dbo.Employees (not to be confused with the existing HR.Employees table that has different data):

```
USE TSQL2012;

IF OBJECT_ID('dbo.Employees') IS NOT NULL DROP TABLE dbo.Employees;
GO
CREATE TABLE dbo.Employees
(
  empid    INT         NOT NULL PRIMARY KEY,
  mgrid    INT         NULL       REFERENCES dbo.Employees,
  empname  VARCHAR(25) NOT NULL,
  salary   MONEY       NOT NULL,
  CHECK (empid <> mgrid)
);

INSERT INTO dbo.Employees(empid, mgrid, empname, salary) VALUES
  (1,  NULL, 'David'  , $10000.00),
  (2,  1,    'Eitan'  , $7000.00),
  (3,  1,    'Ina'    , $7500.00),
  (4,  2,    'Seraph' , $5000.00),
  (5,  2,    'Jiru'   , $5500.00),
  (6,  2,    'Steve'  , $4500.00),
  (7,  3,    'Aaron'  , $5000.00),
  (8,  5,    'Lilach' , $3500.00),
  (9,  7,    'Rita'   , $3000.00),
  (10, 5,    'Sean'   , $3000.00),
  (11, 7,    'Gabriel', $3000.00),
  (12, 9,    'Emilia' , $2000.00),
  (13, 9,    'Michael', $2000.00),
  (14, 9,    'Didi'   , $1500.00);

CREATE UNIQUE INDEX idx_unc_mgrid_empid ON dbo.Employees(mgrid, empid);
```

Suppose you need to present employees in hierarchical order—always presenting the manager before subordinates—and sort siblings by *empname*. To achieve this task, you can use two main tools: the ROW_NUMBER function and a recursive CTE. You define a regular CTE called *EmpsRN* first, where you compute an attribute called *n* representing a row number partitioned by *mgrid* and ordered by *empname, empid* (*empid* added for determinism if needed):

```
WITH EmpsRN AS
(
  SELECT *,
    ROW_NUMBER() OVER(PARTITION BY mgrid ORDER BY empname, empid) AS n
  FROM dbo.Employees
)
SELECT * FROM EmpsRN;
```

```
empid  mgrid  empname   salary      n
------ ------ --------- ---------  ---
1      NULL   David     10000.00    1
2      1      Eitan     7000.00     1
3      1      Ina       7500.00     2
5      2      Jiru      5500.00     1
4      2      Seraph    5000.00     2
6      2      Steve     4500.00     3
7      3      Aaron     5000.00     1
8      5      Lilach    3500.00     1
10     5      Sean      3000.00     2
11     7      Gabriel   3000.00     1
9      7      Rita      3000.00     2
14     9      Didi      1500.00     1
12     9      Emilia    2000.00     2
13     9      Michael   2000.00     3
```

Next, you define a recursive CTE called *EmpsPath*, where you iterate through the employees one level at a time, starting with the root (CEO), then to direct subordinates, then to subordinates of subordinates, and so on. You construct a binary path for each employee that starts as an empty path for the root, and in each level of subordinates, you concatenate the manager's path with the binary form of n (the row number). Note that to minimize the size of the path you need only enough bytes to cover the maximum number of direct subordinates a single manager can have. For example, for up to 255 direct subordinates, a single byte is sufficient; for up to 32,767 direct subordinates, two bytes are sufficient; and so on. Let's assume that we need two bytes in our case. You can also compute the level of the employee in the tree (the distance from the root) by assigning the level 0 to the root, and for a subordinate, you add 1 to the manager's level. Here's the code that computes both the sort path and the level:

```
WITH EmpsRN AS
(
  SELECT *,
    ROW_NUMBER() OVER(PARTITION BY mgrid ORDER BY empname, empid) AS n
  FROM dbo.Employees
),
EmpsPath
AS
(
  SELECT empid, empname, salary, 0 AS lvl,
    CAST(0x AS VARBINARY(MAX)) AS sortpath
  FROM dbo.Employees
  WHERE mgrid IS NULL

  UNION ALL
```

```
    SELECT C.empid, C.empname, C.salary, P.lvl + 1, P.sortpath + CAST(n AS BINARY(2))
    FROM EmpsPath AS P
      JOIN EmpsRN AS C
        ON C.mgrid = P.empid
)
SELECT *
FROM EmpsPath;
```

```
empid  empname   salary     lvl   sortpath
------ --------- ---------- ----  -------------------
1      David     10000.00   0     0x
2      Eitan     7000.00    1     0x0001
3      Ina       7500.00    1     0x0002
7      Aaron     5000.00    2     0x00020001
11     Gabriel   3000.00    3     0x000200010001
9      Rita      3000.00    3     0x000200010002
14     Didi      1500.00    4     0x0002000100020001
12     Emilia    2000.00    4     0x0002000100020002
13     Michael   2000.00    4     0x0002000100020003
5      Jiru      5500.00    2     0x00010001
4      Seraph    5000.00    2     0x00010002
6      Steve     4500.00    2     0x00010003
8      Lilach    3500.00    3     0x000100010001
10     Sean      3000.00    3     0x000100010002
```

What's left to do to guarantee that the employees are presented in the desired order is to order the rows by *sortpath*. You can also achieve indentation in the output based on the employee's level in the hierarchy by replicating a string *lvl* times. Here's the complete solution code:

```
WITH EmpsRN AS
(
  SELECT *,
    ROW_NUMBER() OVER(PARTITION BY mgrid ORDER BY empname, empid) AS n
  FROM dbo.Employees
),
EmpsPath
AS
(
  SELECT empid, empname, salary, 0 AS lvl,
    CAST(0x AS VARBINARY(MAX)) AS sortpath
  FROM dbo.Employees
  WHERE mgrid IS NULL

  UNION ALL

  SELECT C.empid, C.empname, C.salary, P.lvl + 1, P.sortpath + CAST(n AS BINARY(2))
  FROM EmpsPath AS P
    JOIN EmpsRN AS C
      ON C.mgrid = P.empid
)
SELECT empid, salary, REPLICATE(' | ', lvl) + empname AS empname
FROM EmpsPath
ORDER BY sortpath;
```

Observe in the output of this solution that a manager always appears before his subordinates and that siblings are sorted by *empname*:

```
empid        salary                  empname
-----------  ----------------------  --------------------
1            10000.00                David
2            7000.00                 | Eitan
5            5500.00                 | | Jiru
8            3500.00                 | | | Lilach
10           3000.00                 | | | Sean
4            5000.00                 | | Seraph
6            4500.00                 | | Steve
3            7500.00                 | Ina
7            5000.00                 | | Aaron
11           3000.00                 | | | Gabriel
9            3000.00                 | | | Rita
14           1500.00                 | | | | Didi
12           2000.00                 | | | | Emilia
13           2000.00                 | | | | Michael
```

If you need siblings to be sorted differently—say, by salary—simply change the ROW_NUMBER function's window ordering clause accordingly:

```
WITH EmpsRN AS
(
  SELECT *,
    ROW_NUMBER() OVER(PARTITION BY mgrid ORDER BY salary, empid) AS n
  FROM dbo.Employees
),
EmpsPath
AS
(
  SELECT empid, empname, salary, 0 AS lvl,
    CAST(0x AS VARBINARY(MAX)) AS sortpath
  FROM dbo.Employees
  WHERE mgrid IS NULL

  UNION ALL

  SELECT C.empid, C.empname, C.salary, P.lvl + 1, P.sortpath + CAST(n AS BINARY(2))
  FROM EmpsPath AS P
    JOIN EmpsRN AS C
      ON C.mgrid = P.empid
)
SELECT empid, salary, REPLICATE(' | ', lvl) + empname AS empname
FROM EmpsPath
ORDER BY sortpath;
```

Here's the output of this query:

```
empid        salary                 empname
-----------  ---------------------  ---------------------
1            10000.00               David
2            7000.00                | Eitan
6            4500.00                | | Steve
4            5000.00                | | Seraph
5            5500.00                | | Jiru
10           3000.00                | | | Sean
8            3500.00                | | | Lilach
3            7500.00                | Ina
7            5000.00                | | Aaron
9            3000.00                | | | Rita
14           1500.00                | | | | Didi
12           2000.00                | | | | Emilia
13           2000.00                | | | | Michael
11           3000.00                | | | Gabriel
```

Summary

I can't keep myself from admiring the beautiful design of window functions. They're engineered to overcome a number of shortcomings of more traditional SQL constructs, and they lend themselves to good optimization. You saw in this book that there are so many querying tasks that can be handled both elegantly and efficiently with window functions. I hope you will think of what you saw as just the start and find interesting and creative ways of your own to use them.

Standard SQL sees the great value in window functions and therefore keeps adding more and more functions and functionality. Microsoft made an important investment in adding some of the missing support for window functions in SQL Server 2012, and I think that for many implementations, this will make a big difference. I hope very much that Microsoft will follow the standard and keep adding more support with each new version of SQL Server.

Index

Symbols

A

B

C

About the Author

ITZIK BEN-GAN is a mentor with and co-founder of SolidQ. A SQL Server Microsoft MVP since 1999, Itzik has taught numerous training events around the world focused on T-SQL querying, query tuning, and programming. Itzik is the author of several books about T-SQL. He has written many articles for *SQL Server Pro* as well as articles and white papers for MSDN and *The SolidQ Journal*. Itzik's speaking engagements include Tech-Ed, SQL PASS, SQL Server Connections, presentations to various SQL Server user groups, and SolidQ events. Itzik is a subject-matter expert within SolidQ for its T-SQL related activities. He authored SolidQ's Advanced T-SQL and T-SQL Fundamentals courses and delivers them regularly worldwide.

What do you think of this book?

We want to hear from you!
To participate in a brief online survey, please visit:

microsoft.com/learning/booksurvey

Tell us how well this book meets your needs—what works effectively, and what we can do better. Your feedback will help us continually improve our books and learning resources for you.

Thank you in advance for your input!

CPSIA information can be obtained at www.ICGtesting.com
Printed in the USA
LVOW110229101112

306679LV00018B/26/P